Make Your
Tomorrow Better

Michael E. Cavanagh, Ph.D.

PAULIST PRESS
New York/Ramsey

To my wife, Marie,
and our children
Michele, Christine, Janelle and Michael

A portion of this book appeared in *What To Do When You're Feeling Guilty* and is reprinted with permission of Claretian Publications, 221 W. Madison, Chicago, Ill. 60606. Another portion is reprinted with permission of St. Anthony Messenger, 1615 Republic St., Cincinnati, Ohio 45210. The author gratefully acknowledges both permissions.

Library of Congress
Catalog Card Number: 80-80638

ISBN: 0-8091-2293-6

Published by Paulist Press
Editorial Office: 1865 Broadway, New York, N.Y. 10023
Business Office: 545 Island Road, Ramsey, N.J. 07446

Printed and bound in the
United States of America

CONTENTS

INTRODUCTION

Make Your Tomorrow Better means four things. "Make" means action. This is in contrast to the sentiment: "I hope things get better tomorrow." This passive stance rests perilously on the mercy of others, the unevenness of events, and the fallacy of "fate." If tomorrow is going to be better than today, there is but one way this will happen: I am going to have to *make* it better.

"Your" means two things. It means only *you* can make tomorrow better. Your job can't; your friends can't; your loved ones can't. There are people with great jobs, good friends, and devoted loved ones who have terrible tomorrows because they are not relating well with themselves or others. "Your" also means it is important to make *your* tomorrow better before you try to make someone else's tomorrow better. If you are tense, depressed, or unhappy, trying to help another will be similar to the blind leading the blind.

"Tomorrow" means literally tomorrow. It does not mean: "After I graduate ..." or "When I move away from home ..." or "After we're married [or divorced] ..." or "After the children are grown ..." or "When things slow down a little at work ..." or "When I retire...." It means that if I don't make plans today to change *tomorrow*, the future will be a carbon copy of the present, or worse.

"Better" means doing at least one thing more effectively. Tomorrow can be only one of three possibilities: It can be worse than today; it can be the same as today; or it can be better than today. We can't always have "better" tomorrows, but the more we decrease "same" and "worse" tomorrows, the more life will become something to look forward to, rather than something to endure or to dread.

1

The ideas and feelings within this book are based on the following axioms.

1. People who understand some of the general principles, as well as some of the intricacies and subtleties, of human behavior are in a better position to change tomorrow than those who lack this knowledge.

2. We sculpt each tomorrow—it is not already waiting for us. If things "go well" tomorrow, it is primarily because we *made* them go well. If things go poorly, we are mainly responsible for the situation.

3. Love is not going to make tomorrow better. Facing the reality of today unflinchingly and learning the psychological competencies to deal with it are the only behaviors that will make tomorrow better.

4. All of us are worse than we think in some ways, and better than we think in other ways. It is critically important to discover both the dark places and the bright spots, so that navigating will be easier and more satisfying tomorrow than it is today.

5. Most serious problems are caused by an accumulation of small mistakes, just as not taking proper care of the minor problems in an automobile can cause even the most expensive car to break down. If we can learn what needs a little "tightening" and what needs a little "loosening" in daily life, serious problems can be prevented.

6. We won't make tomorrow better:
By compulsively asserting ourselves, because there will be times when it will be more appropriate to accede or to sacrifice.
By talking ourselves into feeling that we are "O.K.," because there will always be parts of ourselves that are not "O.K." and that need work.
By learning the games people play, because the cynical, wary attitude that this engenders will place a distance between ourselves and others.
By intimidating people, because we shall find it diffi-

cult to live with ourselves, and others will find it impossible to live with us.

By having sex, if sex is meant only to anesthetize the pain of tomorrow.

By sweeping unpleasant feelings (fear, anger, guilt) under the rug, because they will merely pile up, and we will eventually trip over them.

By being more free, if freedom means ignoring the realistic needs of other people.

By chasing after wealth, power, or status if there is no deeper meaning in life that these achievements will serve.

7. As long as there is a tomorrow there is a realistic reason for hope. *Anyone* can make tomorrow better.

A fifteen-year-old can make tomorrow better and so can an eighty-five year old.

A poor person can make tomorrow a better day and so can a wealthy person.

An emotionally disturbed person can make tomorrow better and so can a mentally healthy person.

A physically handicapped person can make tomorrow better and so can a physically robust person.

A mentally slow person can make tomorrow better and so can a mentally gifted person.

A prison inmate can make tomorrow better and so can a free person.

Each chapter of this book is a personal invitation to make your tomorrow better.

1

BECOMING PSYCHOLOGICALLY STRONGER

Psychological strength is to the psyche what physical strength is to the body. The more psychological strength a person has, the more resistance there is to psychological stress; the more resilience there is to recuperate from psychological setbacks; and the more energy there is to make investments in life and to enjoy its dividends.

There are two main ingredients to psychological strength: psychological need fulfillment and the psychological competencies necessary to bring about the need fulfillment.

PSYCHOLOGICAL NEED FULFILLMENT

Human beings have two kinds of appetite: a physical appetite and a psychological appetite. Adequately satisfying both is important if we are to be fully alive. If our physical appetite is not sufficiently satiated, we experience hunger pains, then malnutrition, then starvation, and finally death. Exactly the same is true for our psychological appetite. We can suffer the symptoms of psychological malnutrition, psychological starvation, and psychological death, just as surely as their physical counterparts.

Symptoms of psychological malnutrition and starvation differ widely: alcoholism, child molesting, stealing, rape, phobias, anxiety attacks, delusions, withdrawal, disorientation, compulsions, euphoria, hallucinations, am-

5

nesia, depression, psychosomatic disorders; hysterical deafness, blindness, paralysis; paranoia; pyromania, and anti-social behavior.

But these psychological *symptoms* do not represent separate psychological *problems*. There is only one basic psychological problem—failing to get basic needs met adequately or getting them met in destructive ways. The more the individual is starving, the more severe the symptom.

We are very familiar with our physical appetite. We know when we are hungry; we know what kinds of food we desire; we know how and where to get food; and we know when we've eaten something that doesn't agree with us. Unfortunately, we are far less familiar with our psychological appetite, even though it is critically important for *both* our psychological *and* physical welfare.

Often a person who is careful to eat three nutritious meals each day may think nothing of not eating a decent psychological meal for weeks, months, or even years, wondering why he feels depressed, tense, frightened, or unhappy. We are often not in touch with our psychological needs or, if we are, we don't know how or where to get them met. Some people who make a fetish of eating nutritional foods, eat meal after meal of psychological junk food, weakening and damaging their systems without realizing it.

With regard to our psychological appetite, there are four specific needs: the need to feel safe; the need to feel accepted; the need to feel effective; and the need to be self-actualized. The first three are considered basic needs, and, when they are adequately met, the individual is ready for dessert, i.e., self-actualization.

THE BASIC NEEDS

The need to feel safe means freedom from the fear of being harmed by someone else, the fear of harming another, and the fear of harming oneself. In infancy, these fears involve physical dangers, but as the child matures, the fear of physical dangers is gradually replaced by the fear of psychological threats. The basic psychological fears are the fear that someone will damage our self-concept; that inadvertently or purposefully we shall hurt someone whom we care for or love; or that we will cause ourselves some harm by saying or doing something that is self-defeating.

The need to feel safe is our most basic need. To the extent that I feel reasonably safe with myself and the people around me, I can allow others to feel safe in my presence. People who behave in threatening or defensive ways don't feel safe, and, consequently, they can't allow others to feel safe.

Some people have their safety needs under control by the time they are five years old. Others are still distracted by safety needs at fifty years of age. As long as a person is still struggling to get safety needs met, it is difficult to give full attention to anything or anyone else. Like a soldier in the midst of combat, this person is concerned about little except keeping alive. Frequently trying to avoid psychological minefields and frisking people for weapons, this individual is prevented from feeling at ease with people. In a sense, this person doesn't care if he is liked, but is concerned almost solely with survival.

Once an individual feels relatively safe, he can move up to the next step: the need to feel accepted. Variations of feeling accepted are: feeling liked, needed, affirmed, important, and, at its deepest level, the need to feel loved. This need is active in early childhood and is manifested in very young children who ask: "Do you love me?" This is the initial step in the development of self-love. As early as nursery school, an astute observer can separate the child who feels liked and accepted from the one who feels unlikable and rejected. This need usually remains very active until eighteen or twenty years of age when the individual feels liked and accepted enough to be ready to move on to the next need.

If the child's and adolescent's needs for love and acceptance are not adequately met, he will continually seek acceptance, often at great cost. For the privilege of being accepted, this individual is often willing to be hurt and exploited.

As with the need for safety, the need to feel accepted and loved will continue to be inordinately powerful and interfere with one's overall functioning until it is adequately met. For some people, it means buying acceptance from others until the day they die.

When an individual feels sufficiently accepted, he is free to concentrate on a higher goal: to become an effective person. This means the need to feel capable, useful, strong, skilled, knowledgeable, and competent.

Feeling effective means feeling capable as a person, not merely as a carpenter, teacher, or surgeon. The effective person feels basically in control of his life: functions well with people, and fulfills adequately both professional and life roles. A man who feels effective as an attorney but not as a father, or who feels effective as an attorney and as a father, but not as a husband, will be less strong psychologically than if he felt effective in all three roles.

Being effective means being able to live most days reasonably well, to get a number of needs met, and to meet a reasonable number of needs in others. It means having the ability to remove the obstacles to one's growth and to make a positive difference in the lives of other people.

People in this stage strive to be effective for self-centered reasons. The focus is on performing, achieving, and being recognized as successful. This is a healthy and important stage in the growth process and is preparation for striving to be effective for the sake of others, which is part of being self-actualized.

However, some people never grow out of this basic need to be effective. As a result they are so distracted by the need to perform well that they often lose sight of the overall situation. As a college student on a date, this individual tries so hard to be the perfect date that he lacks the spontaneity and relaxation that makes a date enjoyable. As a business person, this individual is like a computer, performing well technically, but overlooking the human dimension. As a parent this person acts like a technician, seeing to it that the children behave correctly but giving little warmth or affection in the process.

The needs to feel safe, accepted, and effective are the meat, potatoes, and vegetables of our psychological appetites. In a sense, all human beings have needs to feel safe, accepted, and effective, all at the same time. For example, an eight-year-old does not have to wait until he is eighteen before needing to feel that he performs well. Nor does one have to be in the self-actualization stage to be altruistic. But each of us has a "home base"—a need area where we reside most of the time. People who are at the safety stage can need to be accepted and need to be effective and even need to be creative in the self-actualized sense. But the majority of this person's energy and behavior is spent in seeking safety. The same is true for the other need stages. A person who generally resides in the self-actualization area will at times spend energy refurbishing the needs to be safe, accepted, and effective. But these occasional side-trips do not typify this person's behavior.

In terms of satisfying these basic appetites, five situations can occur. The best situation occurs when a person can get these needs met with reasonable consistency and in a nutritious, healthy way. Ordinarily, it takes the first thirty years of life to feel sufficiently satiated so that one feels ready to move on—to graduate to self-actualization needs.

Sometimes an individual's needs are not met adequately. Just as in physical nourishment, if an appetite is not met for a short period of time, the individual will experience hunger pains. The psychological equivalent of "hunger pains" are mild psychological symptoms such as tension or depression that are distracting but not debilitating. If a person goes for a longer period of time-consuming, inadequate psychological meals, he will experience symptoms of psychological malnutrition which causes symptoms that are more distracting and discomforting. And, if a person is getting few psychological needs met over a greater length of time, starvation symptoms will be experienced: deep depressions; severe anxiety attacks; incapacitating fears or breaks with reality. These symptoms occur because the individual lacks sufficient psychological competencies to get needs met or is living with people who are psychologically anemic themselves and cannot afford to share psychological groceries.

An individual can satisfy one or all three needs, but in a non–nutritional or toxic way. For example, a person may be getting safety needs met as a result of a dependency relationship in which he feels very safe. But, because it is a security-blanket type of relationship, the individual's growth is actually being stunted or regression is taking place. The person is eating psychological junk food which tastes good but has little or no nutritional value. It is not rare that a person can be in such a relationship for twenty years and not grow in any significant way. Or an individual may get the need for acceptance met by prostituting deeper values in order to buy the acceptance. This represents the consumption of toxic emotional food that could eventuate in serious psychological symptoms.

Some people are overfed emotional groceries and become psychologically overweight: bloated, soft, and weak. This is more likely to occur in childhood and early adolescence when parents provide great psychological feasts free of charge. In other words, the child need do nothing more than exist to feel entirely safe, lovable, and capable. The problem is that by passively being fed, the child is deprived of learning the skills necessary to forage for food on his own. As adults, these individuals may marry someone who takes over the catering role of the parents which is comparable to using artificial means to keep someone clinically alive. The individual who does not find such a person will slide into deep depression because he never learned how to find his own food.

Some people do not possess the competencies to get emotional groceries in natural, healthy ways, so they steal them from others. The stealing may be dramatic, as in raping someone to get hostility and sexual needs met, or in robbing another to get hostility, financial, and prestige needs met. But most stealing is subtle. It is done by embezzling emotional groceries from others by means of manipulation, exploitation, conning, and lying.

There are some practical considerations regarding the concept of psychological needs.

The only way human beings can get their psychological appetites adequately satisfied is to relate with other human beings. One cannot make himself feel safe, accepted, or effective. Only other people can give us the emotional groceries we need. People who relate the most frequently, genuinely, and deeply with others will never go hungry. They will possess the strength to withstand stress and to give emotional groceries to others without counting the cost. People who live solitary lives or who relate destructively or superficially with others will have impoverished psychological diets.

Once a particular need is met, it is not met forever. It is important to keep maintenance dosages coming in. A starving person may eat a great meal and feel full, but this does not mean he need never eat again. It merely means that if the person continues to eat properly, he will no longer be distracted by the pain of hunger.

A person can give away emotional groceries only to the extent that he receives them. By the same token, a person who feels scared, unlovable, or incompetent is in no position to offer others a sense of security, love, or worth. This principle contradicts a popular axiom that it is only important to give to others. I've worked clinically with too many people who have dedicated their whole lives to giving and ask and receive little or nothing in return. They eventually become psychologically emaciated and resemble living corpses. They are confused because they did all the right things, yet are near psychological death at forty or fifty years of age. They are resentful and gradually realize they have wasted the better parts of their lives because they believed the maxim that giving is more important than receiving. The principle that a person cannot give what he does not have is no less true in mental health than it is in any other area.

There is a close relationship between one's need level and the quality of one's commitments. Since it normally takes approximately thirty years to meet these basic needs adequately, a large percentage of people get married and choose careers on the basis of the appetite that is active at the time. A person who at twenty-two years of age is still struggling to get safety needs under control will choose a lover whose specialty is meeting safety needs. The feeling of finally finding someone with whom one can feel perfectly safe is so exhilarating that it is christened "love." The same is true for a twenty-two-year-old still in the midst of getting acceptance needs met. The individual chooses someone who meets his needs to be accepted and loved, and this feels so good that it is called "love." The problem is that this person has not found someone *to love* but someone *to be loved by*—which is all the difference in the world.

The problem with choosing marriage partners and careers based on basic needs is that if and when the individual matures beyond the particular appetite, i.e., moves from safety to love, love to effectiveness, or effectiveness to self-actualization, the partner or career may no longer be of interest. Some people trade in spouses and careers each time they grow to a new need. It takes more patience, but it is easier in the long run to wait until one's basic needs are fairly well met before one considers making a life commitment.

There are a number of areas in which things can go wrong regarding psychological nutrition. If an infant and child has parents who are psychologically starved and therefore unable to give sufficient emotional groceries, the child either becomes weak and psychologically fades away, i.e., withdraws from life, or the child becomes a psychological scavenger, looking for emotional groceries everywhere and willing to pay any price for emotional crumbs.

A second area in which things can go wrong is when the parents give the child sufficient emotional groceries but never teach the child the psychological skills necessary to get food on one's own. As a result, the individual is incapable of leaving home; or, if he does leave home, the reserve of psychological groceries gradually becomes depleted, usually within three years. The result is that the young person lacks the psychological energy to meet the responsibilities of each day and experiences the resultant symptoms.

A third problematic situation occurs when a person is offered good psychological groceries from the significant others in his life, but the individual refuses to accept them. There is a medical equivalent to this called *anorexia nervosa* in which a person is offered plenty of food but refuses to eat. In other words, the person is starving himself. The cause of psychological self-starvation is complex. Briefly, it includes the presence of one or more of the following: Guilt may cause the individual to want to punish himself by not accepting necessary nourishment;

fear of people may lead the person to unconsciously choose to starve rather than be hurt by others; and anger may cause the person to incapacitate himself as a way of hurting people who depend on and love him.

SELF-ACTUALIZATION NEEDS

Once a person has satisfied his basic needs, he is ready for the highest level of need fulfillment, i.e., self-actualization needs. Self-actualization means that a person is no longer distracted by basic needs, but, like a hungry person who has just eaten, is free to explore the world outside. The focus is no longer "What can I do to feel safe, accepted, or effective?" but "What can I do to become the person I want to become? What can I do to make *you* feel safe, accepted, and effective? How can I best give my love to you?"

Although there are several self-actualization needs, the following four are common ones.

1. The need to give love. This is in contrast to the basic need *to be loved.* The difference in the verbs is all the difference in the world. One must first feel accepted, important, needed, and affirmed before he can give love. While one is in the midst of getting the basic need to be loved met, he cannot *give* love no matter how much he is convinced that this is possible. The person can *rent* love, i.e., enter into a subtle agreement that states: "I'll make you feel loved if you make me feel loved." The emotions that accompany this agreement are so pleasurable and so strong that it leads the partners to believe this *must* be love. The only person who can truly give love is one who feels reasonably safe, reasonably loved, and reasonably effective. The absence of any one of these strengths makes a person a pseudo-lover.

2. The need for self-direction. When a person is quite dependent on others for basic need fulfillment, he is often unduly influenced by what other people think and expect. The person wants to keep his psychological grocers happy so that they will continue to send groceries. But when a person has adequately satisfied his basic needs, he is then freed to be more fully the person he truly is. The person does what he feels is right and does not count the loss in emotional groceries.

This does not mean that the self-directing person is impervious to the needs or values of others. It also does not mean that the individual no longer needs others. It means that the person is not selling off important parts of the self for the purpose of feeling good.

3. *The need for creativity.* The self-actualized individual is free to become truly creative. He is no longer tied to conventionality for the sake of pleasing others. Self-actualized people can allow themselves to experiment, take risks, and fail without suffering any significant loss to their security, love, or self-esteem. They can even allow themselves to be ridiculed for their creativity without doing damage to themselves. Creativity here does not refer solely to artistic creativity, but pertains to political, philosophical, economic, scientific, religious, romantic, and social creativity as well.

4. *The need for a purpose in life.* The self-actualized person has an existential purpose in life. Non-actualized people can have a material purpose in life, e.g., to make a million dollars before age thirty. But the purposefulness of actualized people is non-material and non-selfish. Most existential purposes in life involve some variation on the theme of making life easier for others and making the world a healthier and happier place. This purposefulness may or may not involve a religious motif.

In reality, there is no such thing as a self-actualized person, because self-actualization is infinite. No one can become fully self-directing, loving, creative, and purposeful. These needs, unlike the basic psychological needs, never become satiated. Human beings can grow psychologically until the day they die; or they can stop growing at five years of age; or they can regress to infancy. What they do depends upon their psychological competencies and the opportunities that their environment affords them.

The growth from basic needs to self-actualization can be seen in the diagram below.

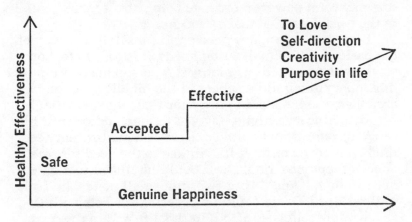

RELATED NEEDS

Basic and self-actualization needs have satellite needs which are an important part of what moves us to grow or to regress. This section will discuss secondary needs and how they can be growth-producing or destructive, and how needs compete with each other in a positive or negative way.

SECONDARY NEEDS

Secondary needs are satellite needs that spin off basic needs and self-actualization needs. Examples of some secondary needs are the need for: power, prestige, wealth, religion, privacy, sex, quiet, independence, fun, honesty, and altruism.

One cannot tell automatically which basic or self-actualization need a particular secondary need flows from. To make this judgment, one would have to know something about the person. For example, a need for power could be a satellite of the need for safety. For one person, the more power she has, the more she feels safe from threat. A second person may seek power because he thinks it makes him more attractive to people, thus meeting the need to be accepted. A third person may seek power so that she can better implement her ideas and plans, thus meeting her need to feel effective. And a fourth person may want power in order to bring about more justice in the world, a self-actualization need.

Because a secondary need can be a satellite of any of the basic or self-actualization needs, it is easy to fool ourselves with regard to our motives. A person may become a missionary and build a school in the middle of a desolate area. Because he is doing this "for God," he feels that he is functioning on a higher level of human endeavor. If his religious motivation is linked to a self-actualization need, then he is correct. But if it is linked to the need for safety or for acceptance, he isn't. It could be linked to a safety need in that, being a "big fish in a small pond," he feels unthreatened. Or he could be covering his bets with God as a way of feeling safe both in this life and in the next.

The person's religious motivation may be linked to the need for acceptance in that in his everyday life he feels like a nobody, but as the leader of a needy community, he is greatly loved and appreciated. While there may be nothing inherently wrong in doing good work for less mature motives, the individual will not be nearly as effective as he could be and may get himself into problems that would have been avoided if he had been functioning from more mature motivation.

On the other hand, a person may have a strong need to enjoy life. At first glance, this may appear selfish and childish. But under closer scrutiny, it may be that this person gives a great deal of himself in his work. He genuinely cares about people and is deeply committed to giving them his best efforts. He realizes that when he doesn't refuel his psyche, he becomes depleted and less helpful. Consequently, his play is as important to him as his work. In this example, the need for fun could be a satellite need that is linked to a self-actualization need.

DESTRUCTIVE NEEDS

When a person is starving, either because he lacks the competencies to obtain food for himself or because there is no food in his environment, he will eat garbage to keep alive. All he can think about is that eating the garbage fills a void in his stomach and some of it may even taste good. But he can't afford to consider the possible long-term consequences that the food may be tainted and that he may die from it. Or the starving person may spot another person whose arms are full of groceries. Because he is starving, he assaults the person and steals the food.

Exactly the same things happen when people are starving emotionally: they will get their needs met any way possible and, if they must damage another in the process, they will.

Destructive needs (sometimes called "neurotic needs"), like secondary needs, are satellite needs. They are primarily satellites of the needs for safety and acceptance. It is less likely that a destructive need would be a satellite of the need for effectiveness, and it is impossible for it to be linked with self-actualization needs. Most often destructive needs are directly linked with a secondary need and indirectly linked with a basic need. For example, a person may embezzle a quarter of a million dollars so that he will feel the prestige (a secondary need) that he has always wanted. The basic need that is met could be any of the three basic needs.

When a secondary need is met in ways that damage the individual or those around him, it is a destructive need. Examples of some of the more destructive needs are the need: to hurt or be hurt; to reject or be rejected; to fail or cause another to fail; to suffer or cause others to suffer; to confuse or be confused; to appear foolish or cause others to appear foolish; to ignore another or be ignored; to be depressed or cause others to be depressed; to enslave or be enslaved; to frighten or be frightened; to be weak or cause others to be weak; to demean or be demeaned; to seduce or be seduced; to kill or be killed. While it took only one paragraph to list twenty-eight destructive needs, 90 percent of the problems a person ever has, or the world ever has, generate from one or more of these destructive needs.

Destructive needs, like secondary needs, satisfy basic needs. But this concept is often difficult to understand. How in the world does being depressed or rejected, or hitting or killing someone meet the basic needs of feeling safe or feeling accepted? The following are some examples that demonstrate how destructive needs meet basic needs.

The need to cheat. John has a very powerful need to be seen as effective. Because his average intelligence only nets him average marks in college, he cheats on exams, boosting his grade point average significantly. His destructive need to be seen as effective is stronger than his need to be honest.

The need to be sexually promiscuous. Helen has strong needs to feel accepted and needed. But her poor self-concept convinces her that no one would want to get close to her. She discovers that when she offers her body to men, she is popular, receives attention, and feels needed. She decides it's better to be accepted for her body than to be rejected for her self.

The need to frighten people. Jim has an overriding need to feel safe from threat. He learns that if he can scare people with his acerbic wit, sarcastic tongue, and critical thinking, they will remain at a distance. As long as he keeps people off-balance and skittish, they can't hurt him, and he feels safe.

The need to criticize people. Sally has a strong need to feel effective. Since she is not effective, she finds that it reduces her anxiety when she criticizes and tears down people. If people are on a higher rung of the ladder than she is, knocking them off allows her to feel superior.

The need to fail. Tom has a strong need for acceptance. The problem is, the people in his life expect him to succeed and, when he does, no one pays much attention to him. If anything, they are jealous of him and don't like him. He has discovered that when he fails, he is given generous amounts of attention, support, sympathy, and comfort. He realizes that, for him, failure is infinitely less stressful and more rewarding than striving for success.

The need to be depressed. Mary has a strong need to feel safe. What threatens her safety most is her great fear of failure. When she is feeling good, she is expected to take ordinary risks in life which causes her to panic. Consequently, she learns that when she feels depressed she is incapable of taking risks and people no longer expect her to do so. She finds more security in defining herself as a depressed person than as a frightened person or a failure.

The need to manipulate others. Frank has a strong need to be effective. He feels that if he is "just himself," he will be ineffectual. To remedy this, he gets people to do what he wants by employing seduction at one time and intimidation at another. This two-pronged prod works well for him and gets him what he wants in life.

The need to be dishonest. Judy has a strong need to be accepted, liked, and to feel important. The problem is that when she is honest with people, they are less inclined to give her the great acceptance that she requires. She remedies the situation by not communicating who she really is, thus psychologically prostituting herself daily. If necessary, she lies to get even more attention.

The need to be unreliable. Ralph has a strong need to feel safe and secure. Unfortunately, he does not trust his abilities. Every time someone asks him to assume some responsibility, he feels threatened. He soon discovers that if he is unreliable (forgetful, capricious, careless), people ask him less and less to put his abilities on the line. He feels more secure being defined as "unreliable" than as "stupid."

Each of these examples portrays a person who is hungry for need fulfillment but who lacks the psychological competencies to get the need met in a constructive, growth-producing way. It is destructive needs that spoil friendships, scuttle marriages, mire politics, dehumanize religion, and make life three times as difficult as it has to be.

At one time or another all of us indulge in a destructive need. And each time we do it is a public admission that we lack the psychological competencies to get needs met in a constructive way. When we are aware of what destructive needs look like, we are in a better position to strengthen the relevant competencies in ourselves and others.

COMPETING NEEDS

Competing needs occur when equally strong needs are mutually exclusive. The tension created by competing needs is directly correlated with the strength of the needs. If I have a need to lose weight and a need to eat a chocolate eclair, I will experience some tension but not nearly as much as if I have a need for financial security and a need to change careers at midlife. The majority of stresses in life can be boiled down to competing needs; to the struggles we experience within ourselves that we often blame on others.

Competing Basic Needs. Our needs to feel safe, accepted, and effective compete when we are at a level of growth (or regression) that places us equidistant between two of them. For example, a college student may be wedged between safety needs and acceptance needs. She wants to remain on familiar ground (safety need) by holding onto her limited group of friends from high school. But her acceptance needs becken her to join a sorority and develop new friends. The closer she comes to deciding not to join, the more her acceptance needs cause anxiety; the closer she comes to deciding to join, the more her safety needs cause anxiety. She may spend dozens of hours trying to decide what to do.

Another college student may be between the needs to feel accepted and to feel effective. He wants to be accepted by his friends and to spend a great deal of time with them. On the other hand, his effectiveness needs are calling him to spend great amounts of time studying. When he is with his friends, he is distracted by the thought that he should be studying; when he is studying, he feels lonely and unimportant, and wishes he was with his friends.

Competing Secondary Needs. Secondary needs often compete among themselves. A person may have a strong need to help the poor and an equally strong need to receive a comfortable income.

Another person may have a need to be a virgin yet have an equally strong need to have premarital sex.

A parent may have strong achievement needs at work and have equally strong needs to have a close family life.

A business man may have equally strong needs to be honest and to have prestige. He knows that if he is honest at work, he will not be promoted; if he is promoted, it is because he was dishonest.

Sometimes healthy secondary needs compete with destructive needs. A person may have equally strong needs to succeed and to fail; to study hard and to cheat rather than study; to be honest and to lie; to help people and to hurt them; to enjoy life and to suffer through life; to be accepted and to be rejected; to build relationships and to destroy them; to care about life and to resign from life.

No one can offer another person a way of avoiding competing needs or the conflict caused by them. Healthy needs that compete with each other are a natural part of the complexity of human nature. But it can be helpful to understand the nature of competing needs and some relevant principles.

The longer the time spent vacillating between the needs, the more tension will arise because neither need is getting met. The danger here is that a person will almost haphazardly finally choose one competing need over another simply to reduce tension. The individual then erroneously interprets the relief and happiness attendant to having made the choice as a sign that the choice was a correct one. In reality, the peace may simply be the result of reducing the mounting tension whether or not the decision was a good one.

Another way to reduce or extinguish the tension caused by competing needs is to decide to meet neither need. A person faced with a decision to go to graduate school or to get married may finally decide to do neither and go to Europe for a year. This could be a good decision if the person is not ready for either choice. Or it could be a sign that the person lacks the psychological strengths to make important decisions.

A choice that will invariably create significant tension occurs when a person attempts to meet *both* competing needs, refusing to sacrifice one for the other. For example, a married person may have a strong need for a happy marriage and an equally strong need to experience an extramarital relationship. When this person does both, the likely result will be that the fulfillment of both needs will eventually be annihilated.

When a person is experiencing competing needs, his communication will be replete with double messages to the people involved in the needs. For example, the person may have equally strong needs to be intimate and to be independent. This individual sends messages that state: "I'd like to get closer to you." As the other person accepts the invitation, a second message is sent: "I'd like to keep a safe distance between the two of us." The receiver of the messages is torn between the two communications and feels that whatever he does, it will be the wrong thing.

As with all psychological tension, the tension between competing needs can be used poorly or well. It can be used poorly by prematurely choosing one need over another simply to reduce tension. Or the tension may be allowed to immobilize the person, thus saving him from having to make any decision. Or the person can attempt to meet both needs in a futile effort to "have one's cake and eat it too."

The tension can be used well when it helps hone the relationship between one's needs and one's values to a sharper perspective. A need tells us what we'd like to do right now in order to feel less anxious. A value tells us whether fulfilling the need will be to the overall advantage of ourselves and of the other people involved. This balance between needs and values is a key to mental health, and it causes negotiations that never cease. The person who is myopic and attends to only his needs will receive short-term satisfaction but long-term misery. The person who is equally short-sighted and focuses only on values and ignores needs, will live a righteous but unfulfilling life.

OBSTACLES TO NEED FULFILLMENT

When one or more of the psychological needs (safety, acceptance, effectiveness, self-actualization) is interfered with, an emotional reaction automatically occurs, i.e., an emotional spark is set off. Analogously, we have a psychological intravenous that carries life-sustaining and growth-producing psychological nutrients. When a person or situation arises that clamps the intravenous shut, either partially or totally, we experience a reflexive emotional reaction. Although there are scores of emotional reactions, they can be boiled down to four basic ones: fear, anger, guilt, and hurt.

Fear is the most common one and stems from the apprehension that one's survival or growth is being threatened. The person is forced to question, consciously or unconsciously: "Maybe I'm not as safe as I thought ... or as lovable as I thought ... or as effective as I thought." The intensity of the fear depends upon the situation and the importance of the people involved.

Anger stems from the reaction, conscious or unconscious: "How dare you shut off my supply of safety, love, or effectiveness?" Anger also often acts as a cover-up of fear, because it is easier to feel anger at another than to feel fearful regarding oneself.

Guilt is an emotional reaction which occurs when the person is responsible for not getting a personal need met. For example, a student may not study for an examination and receive a "D" grade. The student realizes it was his fault and feels guilty at letting down himself and his parents who are paying for the education.

Hurt occurs when a person feels that he has a right to expect that a particular need will get met, but it isn't. For example, a man gives his wife a watch for her birthday. Instead of reacting with surprise and joy, she frowns and says that she doesn't need a watch and, if she did, it wouldn't be the kind of watch that he bought.

Sometimes when a need is blocked, a person can feel

more than one of these emotional reactions, and in a traumatic situation a person may experience all of them, e.g., in the sudden death of a loved one.

The intensity of the emotional reaction depends upon the number of needs that are blocked and the extent to which they are blocked. An individual who receives a mild reprimand at work will feel a small crimp in his need to feel effective and will experience a mild emotional reaction of fear or anger. A second individual may learn that his wife and children have been killed in a vehicle accident. This event may almost completely tie off all three basic needs, causing very intense emotional reactions of fear, anger, hurt, and guilt.

The combination of a blocked need and the resultant emotional reaction is called "stress," or "anxiety," or "tension." When a person experiences great stress all at once, or less severe stress over a period of time, the psyche becomes weakened and symptoms begin to appear. The symptoms are warning signs that there is an overload of stress (anxiety, tension) and indicate that something must be done to meet the blocked need and reduce the emotional reactions. Typical symptoms are anxiety attacks, depression, phobia, obsessions, compulsions, antisocial behavior, addictions, sexual misbehavior, psychosomatic disorders, disorientation, hallucinations, and delusions.

A person who realizes that he is feeling tense can use this sensation to track down the cause and remedy it before tension builds to the point that symptoms develop.

If a person can say "I'm feeling tense [anxious, stressful]," he can often follow the tension to its cause by asking:

- Which of my needs is being interfered with?
- Who or what is interfering with it?
- What specific emotional reaction am I experiencing: fear, anger, hurt, guilt?
- What steps can I take to reduce the tension in a constructive way?

When a person becomes adroit at these "search and solve" missions, he will keep stress minimal by siphoning it off the psyche and using it to remove daily obstacles to growth and happiness.

When one or more of the four emotional reactions occur as a result of an obstacle to need fulfillment, the next question is: "What will happen to the feeling?" There are five things that can happen to the feeling as described and diagrammed below.

1. The person admits the feeling caused by the blockage (fear, anger, guilt, hurt) and uses the feeling to remove the obstacle to need fulfillment. This is the only option that will result in the successful resolution of the problem.

John admits to himself that he is angry at Mary: "She shouldn't have kidded me in front of her friends the way she did." He then uses the feeling in a constructive way and discusses it with her: "I'd like to talk to you about what happened last night because I've felt angry since then, and I'd like to clear the air."

The diagram below is a graphic representation of this situation. It indicates that an obstacle is blocking the flow of emotional groceries between John and Mary.

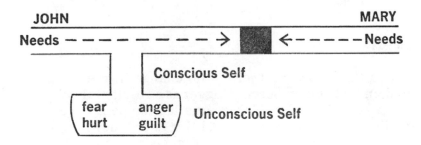

The following diagram shows the constructive resolution of the problem. John has used his anger to melt away the greater part of the obstacle so that emotional groceries can continue to flow between him and Mary. The small residue of the obstacle will gradually be swept away by the continuing flow of warm emotions.

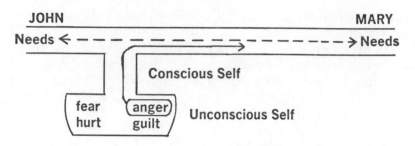

2. *The individual may admit the feeling (as in the above situation) and may attempt to use it to remove the obstacle. However, the other person refuses to discuss the issue in a helpful way; consequently, the obstacle remains.* This situation is shown graphically in the following diagram.

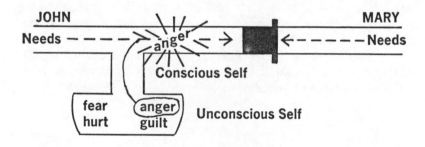

Needs

In this situation, there is no change in the obstacle and, in fact, it may become bigger as a result of the failed attempt to resolve it. If this situation happens once in a while, a person may wait until things cool down and try again, or leave it alone, hoping that good communication on other issues will indirectly melt the obstacle.

If this situation is somewhat typical in a relationship, the individual must decide what is more important— keeping the relationship despite starving in it and suffering the psychological symptoms that accompany starvation (depression, anxiety, sexual problems, phobias, psychosomatic disorders, addiction, etc.) or discontinuing the relationship because the psychological symptoms represent a price too dear to pay.

3. The individual admits the feeling but uses it destructively. Graphically, the situation appears as follows:

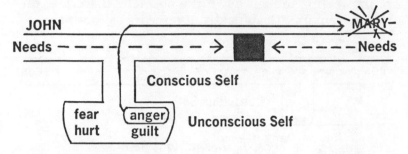

John says to Mary: "I never realized how stupid and cruel you could be until last night." In this example, John has attacked Mary instead of the issue which is causing the obstacle. In effect, John has shot his emotional grocer (Mary) so that the grocer will be disinclined to make any further deliveries for a while, or forever, depending upon the size of the wound.

4. The individual admits the feeling but does not use the feeling to remove the obstacle. This situation is shown in the following diagram:

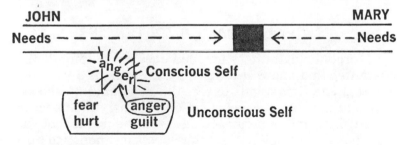

John says to himself or to a third party: "I'm furious at her, but I can't tell her because it will only make matters worse." The anger is not communicated to Mary but remains lodged in John's conscious self. If this happens with any degree of consistency with Mary or the other people in John's life, he will begin to choke and suffocate on his emotions and suffer the accompanying psychological symptoms.

5. *The individual does not admit the feeling ("I'm not angry")*. As a consequence, the individual is ineligible to use the feeling to melt down the obstacle; therefore, the obstacle remains. Graphically, it appears as follows:

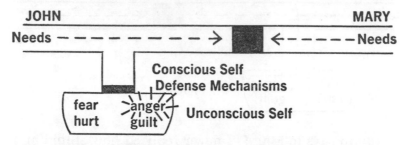

In this situation, the feeling is relegated to the unconscious level by defense mechanisms. If this happens with any degree of consistency, the repressed and denied feelings will incubate and fester, causing psychological symptoms.

To the extent that a person learns good competencies, he will have adequate need fulfillment. To the extent that he has adequate need fulfillment, the individual will possess good psychological strength. And to that extent will he live an effective and reasonably happy life.

PSYCHOLOGICAL COMPETENCIES

Merely being hungry for food does not automatically guarantee that one will receive food. Eating is a two-step process. The first step is to feel the need and the second step is to take the necessary action to satisfy the need. In other words, once a person decides that he wants food, he must possess the skills to get the necessary money to purchase it, to get the necessary transportation to get to the store, and to relate in ways at the store that will eventuate in getting the food. The same is true for psychological appetites. A person may feel: "I wish I felt more accepted," but this, in itself, will do little to stem hunger. He must now use the psychological skills—or develop the psychological skills necessary to bring about the sense of feeling acceptable.

A psychological competency is a learned ability that

helps a person relate with others in ways that bring about mutual need fulfillment. There are five kinds of psychological competencies: physical, intellectual, emotional, social, and moral. Analogously, competencies are like a string of bridges that allow the transporting of food (needs) from one place (person) to another. To the degree that the bridges are soundly built, there will be smooth interchanges. To the extent that the bridges are broken or missing, there will be damaged food (non-nutritional needs) or no food.

Although there are dozens of psychological competencies, the ten discussed here are some of the most basic ones.

1. Trust (vs.) ⟶ Naiveté ⟶ Distrust

The person who has learned to trust himself and others can allow others to come reasonably close. This permits an easier and more abundant sharing of psychological groceries.

The naive person lets people "in" indiscriminately and often gets hurt. After this happens for a while, he decides to withdraw and becomes distrusting, keeping everyone at a distance or "out" completely. Most cynics were once naive. The individuals on either end of this spectrum deprive themselves and others of adequate need fulfillment.

2. Assertive (vs.) ⟶ Aggressive ⟶ Passive

The person who has learned assertiveness is able to approach people and see to it that he gets his needs met. This individual stands up for himself and gets a fair share in life.

The aggressive person grabs his fair share and more. In the process he hurts and alienates others who then are disinclined to share their psychological groceries.

The passive person waits to be fed, and depends almost entirely on the benevolence of others. As a result, this individual is often neglected and left hungry.

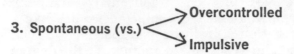

3. Spontaneous (vs.) → Overcontrolled / Impulsive

People who have learned spontaneity are relaxed with themselves and therefore put others at ease. They are "up front" people who can be trusted to be honest. Overcontrolled people are tense and make others nervous. This precludes much closeness or genuine interest in the relationship. Impulsive people are seen as potentially threatening and unpredictable; hence, people are not likely to come very close to them.

4. Interdependent (vs.) → Self-centered / Symbiotic

The person who has learned to be interdependent moves freely among people. This individual can allow himself enough dependence on others to be interested in and appreciative of them while maintaining autonomy.

The self-centered individual meets all of his own needs. He feels no real need for others and transmits this attitude to them. Hence, others leave him alone, depriving him of the rich variety of emotional groceries necessary for a full and vibrant life.

The symbiotic person depends on others for emotional life. As a result, this individual cannot be honest with others because he is afraid to lose them. This person must "sell" himself in order to obtain the fulfillment of psychological needs. Since this person has no "self" as a foundation, his needs are unquenchable. It's like water being poured into a cup with a hole in the bottom.

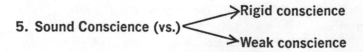

5. Sound Conscience (vs.) → Rigid conscience / Weak conscience

People who have developed sound consciences have a benchmark that allows them to make choices that permit them to maximize the good in life and to avoid the evil (destructive).

Individuals with rigid consciences are often judgmental, humorless, and subtly resentful of people who do not share a similarly constricted value system. This attitude tends to alienate people. Others with weak consciences often behave in ways that hurt others which also estranges them.

6. Healthy sensitivity (vs.) →Thin-skinned →Thick-skinned

People with healthy sensitivity are sensitive enough that they enjoy the nuances of emotional relationships. They feel warmth, goodness, joy, along with hurt and sadness. They are alive to the world about them.

People who are thin-skinned are easily hurt and often feel that others are purposely hurting them. This creates inordinate "bleeding" that causes the individual to become very distracted with himself and resentful of others.

Thick-skinned people often were thin-skinned at one time. Because they were hurt, they developed extra thick layers of defenses. These individuals close out many of the finer experiences of life and believe that they can subsist on few or no psychological groceries.

7. Comfortable sexuality (vs.) →Promiscuity →Asexuality, Confusion

People who are comfortable with their sexuality relate well with both sexes. They enjoy being the sex they are and are sexually attracted to others in a non-conflictual way. Their sexuality is an integral part of them and is not something apart or distracting.

Promiscuous people get physical needs met, but, because of the hit-and-run nature of their contacts, they get few if any other needs met. Hence, their restricted diet gradually takes its toll.

People who are asexual, i.e., those who are not psychologically atuned to their sexuality, are often depriving themselves of a very important area of need fulfillment. Their "neuter" orientation often makes them narrow in their interests and social relationships.

The individual with sexual conflicts is often tense and feels inadequate. Such individuals tend either to be withdrawn as a way of hiding the confusion and conflict, or to be aggressive in order to present a facade of bravado. In either case, mutual need fulfillment is severely reduced.

8. Transparency (vs.) ⟩Too open ⟩Too closed

Transparent people allow others to see them as they really are. They are not distracted by themselves. They lose little or no energy in giving a good impression or hiding weaknesses. This allows them to be attentive to others and to be perceived as trustworthy and genuine.

People who are "too open," i.e., "everything that is in their head comes out of their mouth," embarrass themselves and others and are usually avoided.

People who are "too closed" are often ignored or disliked. They are ignored because no one knows them and, thus, no one cares about them. They are disliked because "You never know what he is thinking," and usually the worst is assumed.

9. Positive self-regard (vs.) ⟩Grandiosity ⟩Self-deprecation

People with positive self-concepts are confident, reasonable, non-threatened, and non-threatening. People who are grandiose overplay their cards and end up losing a lot of personal encounters. People with negative self-concepts think so little of themselves that they attract either no one or people with equally negative self-concepts. In either case, the mutual need exchange will be minimal.

10. Sense of humor (vs.) ⟨ "Clown"
                          "Wet blanket"

People with a sense of humor can often defuse anxiety for themselves and others by seeing a lighter side to situations. People who are "clowns" use humor destructively to hide behind their "clown mask" so that no one will know who they really are. They may also use humor in a hostile way against others. This attitude puts other people at a disadvantage because they can't respond for fear of being the "spoil sport."

The "wet blanket" views any type of humor as childish and a waste of time. This individual carries the full burden of life, and his dourness keeps people at a distance.

To the extent that an individual possesses adequate amounts of each of these competencies, he will enjoy mutual need fulfillment. To the extent that a person lacks these competencies, he will have psychological "hunger pains" which will manifest themselves in one or more psychological symptoms.

It is important to realize that these are all *learned* abilities, and, as a general principle, one is never too old to learn them.

This chapter is actually an overview of the remainder of the book that will treat the nature of psychological needs and competencies in more detail: how we deal constructively and destructively with reality, thus enhancing or interfering with our need flow; how to understand our emotional reactions of fear and anger as well as love, sex, guilt; how to communicate these reactions in ways that will better meet our needs and, consequently, help us meet the needs of others in a more fulfilling way.

Reflection Questions

1. On the scale of needs (safety, acceptance, effectiveness, and self-actualization), where is my "home base"? Is this where I want to be?

2. When I feel "psychological hunger pains," what

specific need is usually not getting met? What can I do to get it met?

3. Do I tend to be good at sharing emotional groceries, or do I too frequently "eat and run"?

4. Of the emotional reactions of fear, hurt, anger, and guilt, which do I handle the best? Which do I handle the worst?

5. Of the ten psychological competencies described in this chapter, which two do I need to develop the most? What are some practical ways I can accomplish this?

Thoughts to Contemplate

1. Being effective means being able to live most days reasonably well, to get a number of needs met, and to meet a reasonable number of needs in others.

2. The only way human beings can get their psychological appetites adequately satisfied is to relate with other human beings.

3. There is a close relationship between one's need level and the quality of one's commitments.

4. The need *to give* love and the need *to be* loved. The difference in the verb is all the difference in the world.

5. When a person is starving, either because he lacks the competencies to obtain food for himself or because there is no food in his environment, he will eat garbage to keep alive.

2

KNOWING OURSELVES AND THE WORLD AROUND US

A person once told me: "If it weren't for reality, I would function fine." Most of us feel that way once in a while. The more psychological strength we possess, the more we can afford to perceive reality accurately because we are confident of our skills to handle it. The less psychological strength we possess, the more we avoid facing the difficult parts of reality because we do not have the competencies to deal constructively with it. No one has so much psychological strength that he never tampers with reality.

Difficult or unpleasant parts of reality are comprised of people or events that threaten one or more of our basic needs. It is someone or something that makes us feel less safe, less accepted or liked, or less effective. Since we are faced with such threats daily, we are continually afforded the opportunity to face reality squarely and deal with it, or to skirt reality, thus making us ineligible to deal with it constructively.

The accuracy of our perceptions is extremely important because this dictates our behavior. If a person looks at a chair and perceives a chair, he will sit calmly and continue what he is doing. If a person looks at a chair and sees a lion, he will likely shoot it or jump out a window. Some people are forever psychologically shooting people or jumping out of windows because they misperceive reality.

For the purposes of this discussion, reality will be described as two-dimensional as diagrammed below.

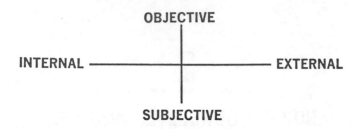

Internal reality is what exists within us. It is comprised of our thoughts, feelings, memories, hopes, and values. When I feel happy about receiving a promotion, my happiness is my internal reality.

External reality is what exists outside of us. When my boss tells me I've been promoted, this is external reality.

Objective reality is what actually exists. When my boss promotes me because I've earned the promotion, this is what exists.

Subjective reality is a person's perception of objective reality. When my boss promotes me because I've earned the promotion, but I perceive the reason as being that he is "kicking me upstairs," this is my subjective reality.

The closer subjective reality resembles objective reality—both internal and external—the better the chances are that appropriate and constructive behavior will result. The more that subjective reality differs from objective reality, the more inappropriate and destructive will be the resulting behavior.

The psychological dynamics of the perceptual process are diagrammed below.

Reality is both internal and external reality. It will be perceived in one of two ways: accurately or inaccurately. When it is perceived accurately, it is accepted in its original form. When it is perceived inaccurately, a process of perceptual tilting intercepts and bends reality to suit the perceiver. Defense mechanisms and defense activities are the instruments used in this process.

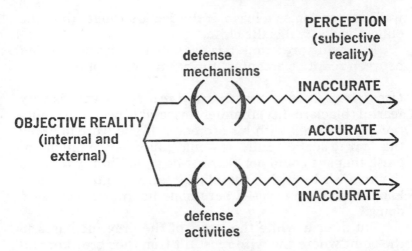

This chapter will discuss the process of perceptual tilting and the nature of defense mechanisms and defense activities.

PERCEPTUAL TILTING

We can divide objective reality into three colors: white represents reality that is pleasant; black represents reality that is unpleasant; and grey represents reality that is unclear or ambiguous.

Perceptual tilting means that we tilt the objective reality in the direction that makes us most comfortable or least anxious. So, black reality can be tilted to a grey or white perception; white reality can be tilted to a black or grey perception; and black or white reality can be tilted to a grey perception. When perceptual tilting occurs, subjective reality will not match objective reality and inappropriate or destructive behavior will follow.

There are two elements that cause perceptual tilting: overdriven feelings such as fear, anger, guilt, love, and hope; and overdriven needs such as the need to feel liked, effective, or rejected.

"Overdriven" means that the feelings and needs are stronger than the person's psychological strength to control them. Analogously, it is like a small child trying to walk a large dog on a leash. If the dog is stronger than the child, the dog walks the child.

Following are numerous examples of the interaction between reality, perceptual tilting, and perception.

Overdriven fears: tilting internal reality. A wife is very fearful (black reality) that her husband is becoming emotionally involved with his secretary. If she were to allow this fear to surface fully, it would cause her so much anguish that she could not bear it. She significantly reduces the anguish by tilting the black reality to grey; "I don't know what's going on—I sure hope he knows what he's doing."

But after a while the stress of the grey increases to the point where the wife must tilt from her grey perception to white: "He's just a good business man who realizes that the nicer he is to his secretary, the harder she will work for him." The tilting process allows the wife to skirt the anxiety connected with her real fear and precludes her having to deal directly with her husband on the issue. Whether or not the husband was having an affair is of no consequence in this situation. The entire process revolves around the wife's internal fear and what she does to try to relieve it.

The problem is that the fear doesn't disappear but causes her to start drinking during the day, something that she has never done. Her drinking provides a double service: It anesthetizes her against the deep fear, and it gives her something less threatening to hang the fear on. She is no longer fearful of losing her husband; she's frightened about having a drinking problem.

Overdriven fears: tilting external reality. A man is offered an important promotion at work (white reality). Deep down, he is fearful that he lacks the skills to handle successfully the responsibilities that the promotion will entail. To reduce this tension, he tilts the white reality to grey: "I wonder what they have up their sleeves, because they've never noticed me before." Soon he tilts the grey to black: "I know. They want me to do their dirty work for a few extra dollars in pay." On the basis of this perception, he refuses to take the promotion. His tilted perception al-

lows him to avoid facing his fears of inadequacy and res-
cues him from accepting the promotion and possibly
failing miserably. The problem is that if his fears are
well-founded, he cannot increase his skills because he
doesn't acknowledge the fear. If the fears are not well-
founded, he has deprived himself of the opportunity to
grow, to exercise some responsibility, and to increase his
income.

Overdriven anger: tilting internal reality. A married
man is told by his mother that she would like to move in
with him and his family because of her failing health.
The man's deepest reaction is fury (black reality) that she
would put him in this predicament. But he has been
taught that loving sons never have intense angry feelings
toward their parents. Since he wishes to feel that he is a
good person, he tilts the black reality to a grey perception:
"Gee, I have some ambivalent feelings about mother
placing me in this situation." But how can a good son
have *ambivalent* feelings about his mother? So, he subtly
tilts the grey to white: "Well, after all, she's lived her
whole life for me, and I would be very selfish to feel angry at her. Of course I'll take her into the family. I think it
will be good for all of us." His tilting helps him avoid the
guilt and self-castigation that would accompany the deep
resentment of his mother and precludes having to refuse
her request. The problem is that the resentment does not
disappear and will be redirected toward his mother in
subtle ways; or it will be displaced onto his wife and children; or it will remain lodged in his psyche, eroding his
body and/or personality.

Overdriven anger: tilting external reality. A college student is angry at a professor who gave him a "D" on a mid-
term examination and who wrote a note on it that said
"Your thinking is sloppy!" Since this student prides himself on being a clear and logical thinker, he reacts to the
mark and the note with intense anger. Shortly after, this
student asks the professor a question in class. The professor responds: "That was a good question. It shows that
your thinking is becoming more critical" (white reality).
But the student's anger causes him to tilt the white reality

to a black perception, namely, that the professor is being condescending and glib. The student replies sarcastically: "Well, I'm *so happy* you are pleased with my progress!" The problem is that the professor who is trying to be supportive and helpful feels the sting of the student's response and decides to take no further interest in the student's welfare.

Overdriven guilt: tilting internal reality. A married man is having an affair with a woman at work and feels deeply guilty (black reality). The more guilt he feels, the more he can't concentrate, sleep, or eat, and the more irritable he becomes. The more irritable and unreasonable he becomes, the more his wife reacts by becoming cold sexually, by spending more money on herself, and by nagging him. Gradually, he begins to feel that having an affair is a sensible thing. His wife will drive him crazy if he doesn't and that wouldn't do her or the children any good. As he views his affair in this new light, he not only does not feel he is doing anything wrong, but actually thinks he is providing a service for the family (white perception). Since he no longer feels conscious guilt, he can continue the affair. The problem is that his unfaithfulness creates an increasing distance between him and his family which causes psychological problems. He wishes he knew why his wife is increasingly depressed and his children are having such difficulties in school, because he feels he has given them everything.

Overdriven guilt: tilting external reality. A woman works at an exclusive department store. She likes her work and the people with whom she works (white reality). After working there for some time, she notices that distracted customers often give her a ten dollar bill thinking it is a five or one dollar bill. Since she feels that she needs the money more than the wealthy customers, she pockets the difference. After she has done this for a few months, her attitudes toward the job change. She used to like her boss, but recently he's been a "drip." The ladies that she worked with were so darling and helpful when she was new, but now they are "old busybodies." It used to be fun helping the customers select clothes, but now it's just a hassle. She feels that her fellow workers don't like her, and she doesn't like the customers. She finds that she can no longer tolerate the situation and quits. Unknown to her, guilt has caused her to tilt a white reality to a black perception, spoiling something that was once good. She never connects her job dissatisfaction with feeling guilty for cheating the customers. Because she fails to see the relationship, she will continue comparable behavior in the next job, causing herself repeated unhappiness.

Overdriven love: tilting internal reality. A young man loves a girl very much (white reality). He dreams of marrying her, having children with her, and living happily ever after. The girl likes him and would like to be his friend, but she has no romantic or sexual feelings toward him. As the man gradually realizes this, his hurt and despair begin to build. Before it reaches a painful level, he tilts his white reality to a black perception: He only *thought* he loved her, but now realizes it was an adolescent infatuation toward an immature, selfish girl. He now feels a combination of apathy and antipathy toward her. Although he feels better now that he "realizes" that he hasn't lost anything, in fact he has. He's lost someone who could have been a good friend, and he's lost a beautiful feeling that would have been good for him, whether or not the feeling was returned in equal amounts.

Overdriven love: tilting external reality. A woman loves a man very much. But the man has some serious problems (black reality). Because of her overdriven love for him, she continually tilts the black realities concerning him into white perceptions. He attended college for one semester, but rarely attended class. She knows that this happened because he didn't get proper advice from the faculty; consequently, he took boring courses which caused him to lose interest. He has held four jobs over the past year, but she realizes that this is because none of the jobs tapped his unique talents. He got thrown out of group therapy because he took a swing at the therapist who suggested his macho image was covering up some deep feelings of inadequacy. She was furious at the therapist for being so insensitive. He takes pills by the handful, but she knows this is only to calm his nerves. And he got arrested for a residential burglary, but he did it only to get bail money for a friend. In time, she will be shocked, confused, and depressed when she hears that he left town with a woman twice his age whom he met only a week earlier in a bar.

Overdriven hope: tilting internal reality. A girl ready to begin college has a strong hope (white reality) that her parents will allow her to go away to college. She sends out "feelers" such as: "I wonder what it will be like being away at college next year?" and her parents have always responded: "Well, I guess we'll just have to wait and see." Such reactions lead her to believe that she will be allowed to go away to school. But, late in the year, her parents tell her that, after lengthy consideration, they want her to attend the local college. She is crushed, but to avoid the deep disappointment and resentment that she is going to feel, she decides that leaving home would be a mistake (black reality). She hopes to stay home, at least for the first year, where she'll have the support of her family and friends and won't have to work to pay for her room and board. She quickly erases her original hope and wonders whatever possessed her to want to leave home. She has tilted her hopes 180°. The problem is that the deep disappointment and feelings of injustice which she can't feel or articulate because of her tilting will cause her to do poorly in college and result in "the most miserable year of my life."

Overdriven hope: tilting external reality. A young man's fondest hope is to get accepted into graduate school. He applies to the school of his choice and receives a letter stating that his qualifications are impressive and that his application is being given serious consideration along with other applications (grey reality). He interprets this letter as telling him that he is as good as accepted, and the rest is mere formality. He tilts from a grey reality to a white perception. As a result he does not bother to apply to any other schools. Two months later he receives a letter stating that although his qualifications were impressive, the school received hundreds of impressive applications and so he would not be accepted this year. He is furious that the school led him to believe that it was going to accept him. And he is panic-stricken at the thought that he has no other options.

Three needs that often cause tilting are the needs to feel liked, to feel effective, and to be rejected. Needs do not lend themselves to internal tilting, so the examples will be of tilting external reality.

Overdriven need to be accepted: tilting external reality. A man has a strong need to be liked by everyone. In fact, however, people generally dislike him (black reality) because he tries too hard to *make* people like him. His strong need to be accepted and liked causes him to continually tilt negative realities to white perceptions. He notices that his fellow workers never invite him when they go for a drink, but the reason is that they realize he likes to go right home. He knows he has been passed over for promotions twice, but this is because they gave the promotions to married people who had to support families. People are always asking him to do favors for them, and certainly they wouldn't ask him if they didn't like him. He has many friends who love to have him tag along, and they really like his sense of humor because they always laugh at his jokes. People are always playing practical jokes on him because they know he's a good sport who can take it. The problem is that his inaccurate perceptions give him no reason to evaluate his behavior and make some helpful changes. He will continue to act in inappropriate and abrasive ways, depriving himself of many of the good things in life.

Overdriven need to be effective: tilting external reality. A woman is faced with some black reality. She is called to the police station to pick up her seventeen-year-old son who was arrested for speeding, having a baggie of marijuana in his vehicle, and being under the influence of alcohol. To allow the black reality to stand, she would have to question the very positive image she has of herself as a mother, and psychologically she can't afford to do that.

After she talks with the officer, she drives her son home and finds that the policeman's story does not jell with her son's. This allows her to tilt the perception into the grey area: "I'm so confused by all this." After she hears her son's story for the third time and she gets a good night's sleep, she awakens with "a much better perspective on the situation." She has managed to tilt the grey to white.

Now she understands the situation. Her son was speeding to get his friends home so their parents wouldn't worry. The baggie of marijuana, of course, wasn't his, but belonged to that no good Jimmy Smith who is always getting her son into trouble. Her son *wasn't* under the influence of alcohol—he had two cans of beer which just proves he's a normal seventeen-year-old boy on his way to manhood. The problem is that this mother's tilting deprives her of being a help to her son. It also causes the son to respect his mother less because it is clear to him that she needs to see herself as a good mother more than she needs to be one.

Overdriven need to be rejected: tilting external reality. A man unconsciously has a destructive need to be rejected. His experiences have taught him that sooner or later he will be rejected, so he'd better reject others first and avoid the deeper hurt. He is dating a woman at work and is beginning to like her a great deal. He also realizes that she is becoming equally fond of him (white reality). The more emotionally involved they become, the more his anxiety increases. To reduce his anxiety, he begins tilting white reality to black perceptions. He notices that recently she has been spending less time with him, that she hasn't answered her phone the last few times that he called, and that when they are together she seems distant and disinterested. He decides that these are clear signs that the woman is beginning to reject him (black perception). Before she has the opportunity, he writes her a letter terminating the relationship. He has tilted from white to black to avoid the ultimate agony of being rejected. The problem is that he has deprived himself of a good relationship and has deeply hurt and confused the woman.

The next section will deal with defense mechanisms, one of the two instruments used to tilt our perceptions of reality.

DEFENSE MECHANISMS

A defense mechanism is unconscious or sub-conscious behavior designed to help a person perceive something that he strongly needs to perceive—even though it is *not* present in reality. Defense mechanisms also allow a person *not* to perceive something that he doesn't want to perceive—even though it is present in reality.

Since defense mechanisms are sub-conscious or unconscious, a person is unaware when he is employing them. A person may protest: "I'm not rationalizing—I really mean it," and yet be rationalizing very heavily. This is a frustrating concept for most people because we don't like to think that we do things without realizing exactly what we are doing. We are convinced that we are well aware of our needs, fears, motives, angers, jealousy, pride, and guilt.

Defense mechanisms are learned; they are not inherited, nor do they just happen. Most learning comes from one's parents or whomever one's caretakers were. A specific defense mechanism—or mechanisms—can be "passed down" from generation to generation. Some families have denial as a favorite defense mechanism. No matter what terrible things are happening, they deny their presence or deny that the events are terrible. Other families use projection. When something bad happens, it is always someone else's fault. Other people somaticize. Whenever a fearful event is anticipated, they become ill.

These tendencies toward specific defenses can be traced back for generations. As our society becomes more sophisticated, however, changes in "favorite" mechanisms occur, and more sophisticated defense mechanisms may be used. For example, a college graduate may drop his family's defense of denial, because he is too in-telligent to fool himself in such an obvious way. He then may develop the defense of intellectualization which still protects him from unpleasant reality, but in a "classier" way.

Defense mechanisms are habitual and click on and click off as unnoticeably as an eye-blink. They also can shift dramatically. In thirty seconds a person can shift from projection: "It's all my husband's fault" to self-dero-gation: "It's all my fault." The individual can be deeply convinced that both sentiments are true, even though they are separated by less than a minute in time. It is not unusual for a therapist to see a patient who is moderately depressed in the first half of the session (caused by re-pressing anger) become euphoric in the last half of the session (caused by reaction formation to depression). The naive therapist would feel that the therapy session was a very good one, because the person came in so depressed and left so "happy."

Defense mechanisms can be normal or abnormal, al-though they are never mentally healthy (the ideal). Anal-ogously, it is normal not to have perfect eyesight, but it is always better to have perfect eyesight.

Defense mechanisms are normal and can be helpful when they temporarily hold off reality, allowing the per-son to recoup and reconnoiter his options so that reality eventually can be attacked in a more effective manner. A less helpful use of defense mechanisms, but still "nor-mal," is to hide small segments of reality so that one can at least get through the day. Ideally, however, it would be better if one didn't need psychological crutches—even small ones.

Defense mechanisms become abnormal when they are numerous and interfere with reality to the extent that one's behavior is frequently inappropriate. This sets up a self-perpetuating dynamic: We misperceive reality and thus react inappropriately. This, in turn, causes others to react negatively to us. Denying this negative reaction causes us to tilt the perceptual process even more, creat-ing a vicious circle with a downward spiral. We will now list and explain various defense mechanisms.

1. Repression. The primary defense mechanism underlying all others is repression. The person erects barriers so that the threatening *internal* reality never reaches consciousness. Internal reality includes inner feelings, ideas, desires, impulses, wishes, and memories that would cause a person a good deal of fear or guilt if he came to awareness: ideas such as: "I'm not as competent as I think I am"; feelings such as: "I resent my mother"; wishes such as "I wish my husband were dead, and I was free again"; memories of sex play with a sibling, etc. The idea *and* the feeling can be repressed ("I *never* cheated in college"), or the idea may be allowed to reach awareness but not the feeling, e.g., "I cheated throughout college, but I don't feel guilty about it."

Unfortunately, repressed feelings do not evaporate but often return in disguised forms. A man may repress his very strong sexual attraction toward his secretary. As his feelings increase in intensity, he awakens one morning unable to go to work. He experiences a strong fear (phobia) of approaching his place of employment. As far as he knows, he has no sexual feelings toward his secretary, only an overpowering sense of panic when he thinks about going to work. In a sense, he has made a deal with his psyche. He will agree to be phobic if his psyche forbids him to return to work where he may begin to realize his real feelings toward his secretary.

2. Denial. The inability to acknowledge threatening aspects of *external* reality is known as denial. For example, even though five doctors have told a mother that her child is retarded, she refuses to believe it. A more pathologic example would be the refusal of a man to accept the fact that his wife has died. Situations that are frequently denied are: conflicts in marriage; maladjustive behavior in one's children; terminal illness in oneself or in a loved one; the "handwriting on the wall" that one is: failing in school, or losing one's job, or that one's children are headed for trouble, or that one's drinking is getting out of hand. There can be partial denial ("We fight, sure, but it doesn't mean anything") or total denial ("We never fight—you can't call those silly disagreements 'fights' ").

Denial differs from repression in that outside information and data that are observable to others are denied, e.g., a doctor's report. In repression internal ideas and feelings are kept out of awareness—things not directly observable to others.

3. Rationalization. This defense mechanism protects us from conscious stress in two ways.

First, it presents logical and socially approved reasons to justify selfish or socially unacceptable behavior. A person using this defense can present good reasons for: hitting his wife; unfaithfulness to a spouse; cheating on his taxes; not spending enough time with his children; and even for stealing and killing. Such behavior can not only be justified, but sometimes can be made virtuous, e.g., the Spanish Inquisition, the slaughter of millions of Jews, and "Robin Hood" type of activities such as "ripping off" the rich to give to the poor ("It's a big corporation; they won't miss it").

Secondly, rationalization softens disappointments or failures. "Sour grapes" says: "I didn't want the promotion anyhow"; and "sweet lemon" says: "I'm really glad I got fired because now I have a lot of free time to do what I want."

4. Intellectualization. One can use this defense mechanism to interfere with or cut off normal emotional responses of anger, hurt, fear, or guilt. This defense acts on the principle: "As a mature individual I should have this emotional reaction; therefore, this is the emotional reaction I have." A religious person experiences the death of a loved one, and, on the deepest levels, feels a profound sense of loss, fear of the future, and anger at God. But his "head" tells him he should feel "happy" because the loved one is now with God. Consequently, the person employs his intellect to control his deepest emotions to fit what he should feel. He now reassures himself: "I'm just happy she is with God," leaving his feelings of loneliness, fear and anger to smoulder and reappear in other forms.

Other variations of this defense mechanism are attitudes such as: "No sense crying over spilt milk"; "There's no use getting upset; there's nothing I can do about it anyway"; "How can I get upset when I'm just getting what I deserve?"; or "I don't blame my husband at all for walking out on me."

The common factor in all these attitudes is that deeper emotions are being squashed by logic. Feelings should be felt and not selected for consciousness on the basis of whether they are logical or illogical; justified or unjustified; mature or immature; moral or immoral. Feelings don't make a person good or bad. Destructive behavior is much more likely to occur when "bad" emotions are "intellectualized" away than if they are felt and given full consideration.

Separating incompatible attitudes by logic-tight compartments is another type of intellectualization. For example, a physician may give lectures on drug abuse and sell stimulants illegally to high school students; a marriage counselor may preach faithfulness but be unfaithful in his own marriage; a person may believe strongly in democracy but also be racially prejudiced. A very idiosyncratic logic allows these individuals to carry off inimical types of behavior without much, if any, *conscious* conflict.

Self-derogation is also a type of intellectualization. This is a very subtle defense because of all defenses, it doesn't look like a defense. This individual admits: "I'm a terrible husband"; "I'm a very ineffectual boss"; "I'm an awful mother"; etc. The defense aspect becomes obvious when despite profound self-castigation, no positive changes are forthcoming. It is as if the individual is saying two things: "If I admit I'm no good first, there is no way *you* can hurt me," and "Now that I've admitted it, that's all I have to do." This is one of the most difficult defenses to work with because the individual is *intellectually* accepting his faults but is unable *emotionally* to rectify them.

Rationalization and intellectualization have something in common (and can be used together) in that they both misuse cognition to reduce anxiety. They differ, however, in that rationalization offers reasons (albeit false ones) to soften the anxiety connected with failure or unacceptable behavior, whereas intellectualization severs the link between behavior and its normal affect.

5. *Projection.* Projection has two parts. First, it transfers the blame for our own shortcomings, mistakes, and misdeeds onto others. For example, a student may blame a professor for an "unfair" exam; the professor may blame his students for being "uninterested"; the unfaithful husband blames his wife's "coldness"; parents may blame their children for problems in the marriage. Fate and bad luck are overworked objects of projection as are inanimate objects, e.g., blaming one's car for getting into an accident.

Secondly, projection allows us to attribute our own unacceptable impulses, thoughts, and desires to others. When some people experience thoughts and/or feelings which are threatening or repulsive to them, they do away with them by pinning them onto someone else. This "shift of ownership" not only allows the individual to feel cleansed, but permits him to feel superior to the other person who now possesses these negative attitudes. The most common ideas and feelings that are projected are:

"I dislike you" projected to "You dislike me."

"I'd like to have sex with you" projected to "You'd like to have sex with me."

"I'd like to get you fired" projected to "You'd like to get me fired."

"I'd like to reject you" projected to "You'd like to reject me."

"I'd like to control you" projected to "You'd like to control me."

"I'm frightened of you" projected to "You're frightened of me."

"I don't want to get close to you" projected to "You don't want to get close to me."

"I don't care about me" projected to "You don't care about me."

The person who projects sculpts a reality into his likeness and then throws stones at it to prove to himself and to others that he is not that kind of person.

6. *Displacement.* This means discharging pent-up feelings, usually hostility, on persons or objects less dangerous than those which initially aroused the emotions. For example, I'm very angry at my boss but can't admit it to

myself. I meet my wife after work and become furious *at her* because she is five minutes late. My wife is a safer target for my anger because she can't fire me, whereas my boss can. Or I may be furious at my wife (but can't admit it to myself), but hit my punching bag so hard I knock it off its hinges. The punching bag can't hurt back, but my wife can.

Repressed fears of murdering a hated husband may be displaced to fear all sorts of dangerous weapons such as guns, knives, or poisons. Scapegoating is a part of displacement in which an individual may get out all his fears and anger at a minority group, or at his adolescent son, or at his church. Displacement allows the individual to discharge dangerous feelings without even knowing to whom such feelings were originally directed, hence avoiding the risk of loss of love, guilt, and possible retaliation. Often displacement is combined with projection, but they are not identical for two reasons: Projection says: "I don't have anger within me, *you do*," whereas displacement says: "I'm not angry at my wife; I'm angry at my *children*." Projection places *blame* on another, whereas displacement thrusts strong *feelings* on another.

7. Regression. Regression occurs when a person is unable to get his needs met by mature behavior, and therefore reverts to an earlier type of behavior that "used to work" to get love, attention, sympathy, etc. A child may revert to bed-wetting when a new sibling is born in order to win back some of the attention which has been lost to the new brother or sister.

An adolescent may revert to a temper tantrum to release his anger because he feels incapable of verbally communicating it. A middle-aged man may return to the promiscuous sexual behavior of his college days because he is unable to obtain sexual gratification or self-assurance with more appropriate sexual behavior. A woman may feel that the strain of being a wife and mother is too much and return to her mother.

8. Fantasy. This defense mechanism allows the individual to get needs met and feelings expressed in make-believe reveries, play, and daydreams. Fantasies also serve a healthy purpose and are a defense only when a person achieves so much in fantasy that he doesn't feel the need to do much in reality; when he is expressing love or anger in fantasy that *should* be expressed to real persons; when he spends so much time in fantasy that it interferes with the living of life. Two basic types of fantasy are the "conquering hero" ("I'll make everyone respect me") and the "suffering hero" ("I'll make everyone wish they had been nice to me").

9. *Reaction formation.* This defense mechanism enables an individual to express an unacceptable impulse by transforming it into its opposite. For example, an individual may have very strong sexual needs and curiosity, but cannot tolerate these in himself. So, he becomes a leader against pornography, and part of his responsibility is to read many pornographic books in order to censor them. Or the individual who has some deep hostility within himself becomes a leader in peace movements and vents his hostility for a good cause. This explains, in part, the violence seen in some "peace" demonstrations—this is the "waging war against war" syndrome.

Another example is the mother who deeply resents her child but overprotects or over-loves him, damaging him severely but under an acceptable emotion. In everyday behavior, reaction formation may take the form of developing an "I don't care" attitude to conceal feelings of rejection and a craving for affection; or assuming an air of bravado when we are fearful; or being excessively polite to someone we don't like—so much so that we make him feel uncomfortable. The two-fold service that this defense provides is that it allows the individual to partially satisfy repressed desires and at the same time deny their presence.

10. *Acting-out.* In this defense mechanism the basic impulses of anger and/or sex are "acted out" rather than "worked through." The healthy way of working-through anger, for example, is to admit its existence; discover the cause of the anger; identify the people involved in the

cause; and constructively communicate one's anger regarding the situation.

An example of acting-out behavior can be seen in a student who properly identifies his teacher as the source of his anger, but lacks the psychological competencies to communicate his anger in a constructive way. Instead, he chooses to slash the tires on the teacher's car. This behavior is a "defense" because the student vents his anger without the possibility of rejection.

In other cases, the anger may be so repressed that the person is not aware of it. This is seen in the youth who vandalizes a school or savagely assaults someone. When asked why he did it, he responds: "I don't know." And that's the truth; he *doesn't* know. Other forms of acting-out behavior are: arson, stealing, rape, alcohol and drug abuse. Most delinquent behavior is acting out an anger that is misdirected from parents to other segments of society.

11. Somatization (adjustment by ailment). This defense mechanism is the non-insightful use of illness, either real or imaginary, as a way of handling stress. For example, a person develops a severe headache before a threatening task so that he must excuse himself from facing the task or so that he has a built-in excuse if he does poorly. Another defense characteristic of somatization is that it is often a very effective distraction from one's emotional problems. A man "fears absolutely nothing in life"—he "just has ulcers." A woman has no conflicts about her sexuality; she just has dysmenorrhea (inordinately painful menstrual periods). A man has "no anger toward anyone"; he "just has high blood pressure." A woman says she feels no guilt at all; she is "just thirty pounds overweight."

In each of these examples, the people allow themselves to be so distracted by their body that they are saved from looking at their psyche.

Some typical physical symptoms that often have an emotional basis are: migraine headaches, ulcers, menstrual problems, overweight, low back pain, allergies, eczema, rheumatoid arthritis, bronchial asthma, frigidity, and impotence.

The final section of this chapter will deal with the second instrument used in the tilting process, namely, defense activities.

DEFENSE ACTIVITIES

Almost any behavior can be misused as a defense against facing some part of reality that we wish to avoid. In addition to the defense mechanisms mentioned above, there are other behaviors which deserve special mention despite the fact that they include some overlapping with the defense mechanisms. Most of the behaviors listed below are not inherently defensive. It is not the behavior itself, but the way it is used that makes it a defense. These behaviors are often subtle when they are used as defenses because many of them can be viewed as virtuous.

1. "Disequalizing." In this defense activity, we don't allow people to be equal to us because when we are face-to-face with someone, we are much more vulnerable than if they are a few feet above us or a few feet below us. There are two kinds of "disequalizing": "pedestaling" and "subordinating."

"Pedestaling" entails boosting other people onto pedestals, making them near-perfect and untouchable. When we place people on pedestals, we don't have to get angry with them because *we* are the ones at fault. We never argue with them, doubt them, or feel disappointed in them. We bask in their rays and are just thankful to be around them.

"Subordinating" means lowering another person into a position beneath us. This is done by assessing another person's "qualifications" and deciding that we are more qualified. The other person is only a high school graduate, and we have had two years of college; the other person is divorced and we are not; the other person makes less money than we do, or is less attractive, or belongs to a different ethnic group. Once we have subordinated the other person, he no longer poses a threat to us.

2. Work. Work can have both constructive and destructive components. It is a defense activity when it is used partly, or totally, as a distraction from unpleasant reality or as an anesthetic to kill the pain of reality. It can also be a defense against feelings of inferiority in other important areas. For example, as long as a man feels that he is a successful businessman, he allows himself to feel he is an overall success, even though he may be failing miserably as a husband or father. Work can be a defense if it is used as a wedge between the worker and the significant others in his life. The person who works fifty or sixty hours a week is separated from his loved ones during this time. When he is finally with them, he is usually "too tired" to get emotionally involved. Work can be a defense against the criticism of fellow workers or one's bosses. If the person works ten or twelve hours a day, work can subtly manipulate others away from criticizing him, because he is so "dedicated" and may quit the extra work if he feels unappreciated. Unfortunately, overwork is often so rewarded socially that it is a difficult defense to drop.

3. Humor. Humor has many sides, some of them healthy and some unhealthy. One of the unhealthy sides occurs when humor is employed as a defense activity. This can be done in a number of ways. When humor is hostile, it can be a three-pronged weapon. First the sharp edge of the humor hurts the other person. This is defensive behavior because the individual employing the humor uses the hostile humor to camouflage the real cause of the hurt or frustration. The recipient of the hostile humor is also under pressure not to retaliate lest he be seen as a poor sport who can't "take a joke." In effect, this is analogous to hitting somebody who can't hit back. Finally, when a person uses hostile humor, the individual often does not have to face his own real anger because the laughter reinforces the idea that he is "just kidding." This person perceives himself as having a "great sense of humor" rather than a "deep sense of anger."

Humor can be a defense against feeling tension that should be felt. It is well known that humor can break the tension in a situation. However, if the tension is appropriate and should be used as energy to resolve a problem or to look at reality more clearly, then valuable energy is being dissipated by humor. Some people have a sense of humor which increases with the degree of tension that they feel.

Humor also can be used to maintain a distance between the humorist and those that should be closest to him. The clown's mask keeps everyone laughing and everybody distant. No one gets beyond the mask to discover who the person really is. The notion that clowns are privately sad people may not be too far from the truth.

4. Pacifiers. The four main behaviors that can be used as pacifiers are eating, drinking, smoking, and sleeping.

Eating and drinking (both alcoholic and non-alcoholic beverages) are common pacifiers and, when overdone, can be destructive psychologically (as well as physically). When a person feels anxious about work, instead of getting in touch with the anxiety and connecting it to some event, he stuffs himself with food and/or drink, and then feels "good." Consequently, the person no longer feels so upset about work, but is deprived of the opportunity to at least consider changing something about the work situation—a change that could be a very helpful thing to do.

Pacifier elements are perhaps most clearly seen in smoking. As the smoker feels the slightest bit of tension building, he fumbles for cigarettes, matches, etc. Between the ritual of lighting up and the drug-induced calm the first few puffs create, the person has successfully excluded both the tension and the cause of the tension from ever coming close to awareness.

Sleeping, either periodically during the day or for a prolonged time during the night, totally removes a person from conscious reality. If a person had no defense other than the four pacifiers, he could remain out of touch with inner feelings for a life-time.

5. Talking. As long as a person is talking, he is not listening, either to the other person or to himself (his inner needs and feelings). Some individuals employ "word walls" to keep people at a distance. In therapy, the continual talker may leave "feeling better" primarily because the therapist was kept at a distance and, therefore, safe, rather than because any real personality growth took place in the session.

A part of talking that is a very common defense is eluding direct questions. A wife may ask her husband: "Do you love me as much as you did when we were first married?" The husband replies: "Oh, don't be so silly, I think you're going through the menopause." While the husband may or may not have a valid point, he has not answered the question—a question that obviously needs answering. Although the husband himself is probably unaware of it, he has swiftly and subtly shifted the focus to his wife. If she "bites," she will have to spend the next ten minutes defending herself for having such "silly" thoughts. During all this time, the husband does not have to examine all the possibly threatening ramifications of her question.

Talking can also be a defense activity when it is confused with relating. Speech can be superficial, i.e., for all practical purposes, nothing of meaning is being communicated. Speech can be cognitive, i.e., ideas are being transmitted. Speech can also be affective, i.e., a person's feelings are being shared. "Relating" means very little superficial speech and a good deal of cognitive AND affective communication are occurring. Some people's speech is solely superficial, while that of others is purely cognitive. Some marriages are actually built on a combination of superficial and cognitive communication with little or no affective sharing. Such individuals feel that the more noise that emanates from their mouth, the more they are relating. In fact, few emotional needs are met in such transactions.

6. *Searching.* It is somewhat of an avocation for some people today to "search"—search for "the truth," search for "themselves," search for a good religion, therapist, lover, etc. Obviously, each one of these could be a healthy pursuit. But professional searching can also be a defense activity in and of itself. As long as a person is searching, especially when the search is outer-directed, he never has to look within the self. The person who spends years "looking for the right person" could better spend that

time "becoming the right person." Also, as long as a person is searching, he doesn't have to settle down and doesn't have to stake out a claim on some psychological space and live with it for a while.

These people go from one search weekend to another; one search workshop to another; one search guru to another. They are so busy looking, talking search jargon, finding guides and being a guide, reading search books, and searching for places to search next, a larger part of life is going right by them. This is a very subtle defense because searching looks good. The searcher is "getting into himself" and "getting intimate" with others—but, for the professional searcher, it's a project—it's not living.

7. *Laziness.* Laziness is almost always, if not always, a defense activity. However, it is important to distinguish between "lazy time" and "leisure time." Leisure time can be very important to a person's mental health. Leisure is *doing* something enjoyable and has beneficial side-effects. The person who takes off an afternoon to play golf is not necessarily lazy. He is *doing* something, and the side-effect may be that he is rejuvenated to approach the rest of his work week with renewed vigor. On the other hand, the lazy person wastes time, and what he does while wasting time has no beneficial side-effects.

The lazy person is a frightened person. He is afraid of failure and/or involvement, but the fear is hidden under the label of "lazy." The lazy student and the lazy athlete are afraid they will fail. So, even if they perform poorly in the classroom or on the athletic field, they can console and reassure themselves that they could have succeeded if they simply had wished to exert more effort. This allows them to maintain the self-concept of being capable without having to risk really trying and failing.

The same principle is true with people who are "too lazy" to date or to be good spouses or parents. As long as these individuals exert limited energy in their roles, they can have the satisfaction of knowing they could get close to someone while, at the same time, precluding the possibility.

The lazy person can also be an angry person. Laziness

can be a passive, indirect way of demonstrating anger—of getting back at the person toward whom the anger is directed. This is almost never conscious. It is as if the lazy student is saying to his parents: "You want me to do well in school so that you'll feel proud of yourself. Well, I'm not going to—I'm not interested in school." This translates: "I'm not interested in making you happy." The lazy husband is often saying: "I'm unable to demonstrate my anger at you directly, so the best I can do is not work so that you have to work—or not work as hard, so you can't have the luxuries you desire." The lazy clergyman may be saying by his laziness: "The authorities don't do what I want; why should I do what they want?"

A great deal is lost in dealing with others if we buy the idea that they are "just plain lazy." In fact, they are "just plain scared" or "just plain angry"—or both. Laziness hides these feelings from the person as well as from those around him. The more a lazy person is pushed to get going, without dealing with the underlying causes of the laziness, the more "lazy" he is likely to become, because the coercion is merely feeding into this fear and/or anger.

8. *Being "upset."* Some people are genuinely upset and have good reason to be. Others use being upset as a defense without even realizing it. There are three ways in which being upset can be a defense activity. When a person is very "upset," reality is effectively screened out. The focus is then placed on the upset rather than on the cause of the upset. Analogously, as long as one is distracted by the smoke caused by a fire, he doesn't have to examine the fire.

A woman may be so upset by the feeling that her husband is going to leave her that she cannot examine the accuracy of her perception; she cannot discuss the reasons why her husband would want to leave her; she cannot make a decision as to what steps she should take to bring the issue out in the open. Attempts by friends to reduce the woman's upset are met with hostile resistance because all she really wants to do is to be upset so as to block out everything else.

Being upset can be used to keep others at a distance. Some people can relate to others only when they are upset because they lack the competencies to relate in other ways. After a while, they wear down even their most benevolent friends and relatives who then tend to "be busy" when the upset person calls. This gives the upset person even more reason to be upset, because he now has proof that people don't *really* care. These individuals go around drowning people with their upset and then feel lonely because there is no one left to care about them. This is a defense in that the individual can hold onto the feeling that he really wants to solve his problems and get close to people, yet not have to take the risks involved in doing so.

Becoming upset can be used as emotional blackmail. The message here is "Don't do anything or tell me anything that will upset me, because, if I get upset, you'll pay for it." The price is that one will be drenched in a rain of wrath and feel guilty that he was the cause of such anguish in the other person. Being upset has been an effective defense when people whisper: "I don't dare tell him because he will get so upset, and it isn't worth it." In effect, the upset person has blackmailed others from presenting unpleasant reality. Consequently, "upset" people feel no need to change anything about their behavior.

9. *Sex.* Sex can be a defense activity in a number of ways. Sexual behavior can be an inappropriate outlet for tension. If a person reduces tension from another life situation through sexual activity, he has "ripped off" his psyche. Psychological energy that is meant for one area has been taken and embezzled into another. The problem with this is two-fold: The source of the tension is not changed and therefore will continue to create stress; and the individual is really using the sexual partner as a tranquilizer, which will be confusing and possibly hurtful to both parties.

Sexual activity can be used as a safe substitute for emotional involvement and intimacy. Unfortunately, sexual intercourse is often referred to as being "intimate" with another person. But, in reality, this is intimacy in only one area: sexuality. It does not necessarily include being intimate intellectually, emotionally, socially, or morally. As someone has said, "Some people merely remove the fig-leaf from their genitals and cover their souls with it."

10. Boredom. Boredom is a self-imposed emotional limbo. The bored person is a frightened person—frightened of failure and of getting hurt. When an individual anesthesizes himself with boredom, he can no longer be hurt or fail. Moreover, the person does not have to face intense fears because boredom successfully hides them and others can be blamed for the boredom. Consequently, this individual is two steps removed from being in touch with his own deeper fears. Boredom, in this case, is better than love, because one gets hurt in love; better than trying, because you can fail if you try; and better than anger, because anger can get you in trouble.

Boredom often starts a self-perpetuating mechanism in that people find bored people boring and, hence, stay away from them. Thus, the more the bored person is left alone, the more bored he becomes. If we can see that boredom in ourselves and others is actually a cover-up for fear, this will be the first step to becoming "unbored."

11. Religion. Religion can be a constructive or destructive force in one's life. As a defense activity, religion can be used to hide important parts of the psyche both from oneself and from others. When a religion teaches that certain feelings are evil (anger, sex), that normal, human needs are to be eschewed, or that natural imperfections are "sins," there is great pressure to deny the presence of these realities in oneself. The individual is forced either to choose the "evil" within the self or to choose God. This leads to the burial and abscessing of important parts of oneself— much of which may be healthy or at least normal, so that the individual can qualify as a "religious person." The result is a pseudo-angelic personality pasted over a growing abscess. If the abscess metastasizes a great deal, it will eventually eat through the angelic personality and cause real problems. If the abscess remains somewhat contained, the person may never suffer psychological problems, but will live forever in an unreal world that deprives him of the opportunity to grow emotionally and spiritually past childhood.

Religious dogma can be used as a defense against having to make decisions and to accept the responsibility for the results. If dogma dictates one's behavior, it protects the individual from having to look at who he really is and what his 'needs are, and from having to build up psychological muscles by struggling through a decision-making process and accepting the consequences of a decision. The more a religion stresses individual freedom of conscience, the less it will open itself to be used as a defense in this particular way.

A very subtle use of religion as a defense is that employed by the person who predicates his life on the syllogism: I am a very religious person, and religious people do only good things. Therefore, whatever I do must be a good thing. While the error in this logic is clear, a great deal of destruction has been perpetuated through the ages by this very same logic. Some people wake up each morning, reassure themselves with this thinking, and are free to do exactly what they wish without a second's pause. Unfortunately, some of what they do may be quite destructive to themselves and to those nearest them. But they remain assured that they must be "O.K.," never having to delve into their deeper motives.

Religion can also be used as a defense activity when it stresses ritual over reality, thus attempting to use religion as a short-cut to growth. If one attends services regularly, lives by the doctrine, and prays enough, things should turn out all right, without further effort on the individual's part. But merely praying, for example, that one's marriage will get better is unlikely to effectuate much change in the marriage. When used constructively, rather than as a defense activity, prayer can give a person the strength to define the marital problem clearly and communicate with one's spouse about it, and to take the risks involved in solving the problem.

12. *"Love."* True love is not likely to be a good medium for defense activity. But for every person in a true love relationship, there is at least one person in a pseudo-love

(dependency) relationship. This pseudo-love can protect a person from the reality within himself, the reality of the loved one, and the reality of life.

The adage "Love is blind" is a good characterization of pseudo-love. Whereas true love gives one the strength to view reality even more sharply, pseudo-love as a defense activity places blinders on the lovers, protecting them from the threatening parts of reality. Major imperfections in a lover gradually diminish into mere idiosyncracies through the "magic of love." Lovers typically "smell blossoms when the trees are bare," which is a rather harmless hallucination in itself, but when carried over to other parts of life, it can be disastrous. Pseudo-lovers dare not entertain their own doubts about themselves or the lover. They dare not ask the questions that need to be asked; nor share the imperfections that need to be shared; nor deal with themselves or the other honestly. For to do so would threaten the relationship and, to these people, the relationship is more important than reality— more important than life itself.

This pseudo-love acts as an unhelpful buffer against "the outside world." The "lovers" feel a false sense of security, and their attitude toward life is: "Everything will be all right now that we have our love to protect us." They no longer have to risk facing reality, which precludes any further growth.

Love in this situation is used as a narcotic to dull the pain involved in relating with reality: the world of work; the world of friends; the world of family; the parts of the world that are imperfect, hurtful, unjust, and competitive. In all the ways that true love promotes growth, pseudo-love reaps destruction.

The problem with defense mechanisms and defense activities is that they protect us from the very information we need to plot an effective life. The person who habitually uses defense mechanisms and/or defense activities when faced with stress is like the driver who closes his eyes when approaching sharp curves. He successfully blocks out the threat but is likely to drive over a cliff.

Every day we are required to pay "psychological dues" for the privilege of being a human being. These dues are experiencing and dealing with the pain of fear, anger, hurt, and guilt that occur each day to varying degrees. If we refuse to pay our dues on a daily basis, tilting reality for months or years by using defense mechanisms and defense activities, one of two things will happen.

First, we may put so much distance between ourselves and reality that we will gradually begin "living in another world," and our reactions will be inappropriate to the real world. For example, an employer may be so threatened by the stresses of his business that he daily uses defense mechanisms and defense activities to allow him to get through the day. He thinks he is keeping on top of the business and his employees, but more and more he is viewing the course of his business the way he *wants* to rather than the way it *is*. He continues his outdated business practices and the same demogogic way of relating to his employees that worked for his father. The time comes when his colleagues, competitors, and employees view him as being "out-of-it." His most talented employees leave him, and the ones that remain ridicule him. Here is a good man who got beaten by reality—something that never has to happen.

Secondly, an individual may be required to pay "psychological dues" in one lump sum, which sometimes can cause emotional bankruptcy. An example of this is "graduation neurosis," which is seen in the college student who glides easily through college, majoring in good times. He gives little serious consideration to who he is or what he wishes to give life. While classmates are struggling with normal identity conflicts, sexual conflicts, emancipating from parents, dating different people, making career decisions, working after school, and spending arduous hours studying, this student is "having a ball" and is bewildered as to how his peers can get so "up tight" about things. Soon after graduation—maybe in a matter of a few months or a year—he develops "graduation neurosis." He is hit gradually or suddenly with the realization that he is woefully ill-prepared to meet life. He experiences anxiety attacks that paralyze him. He now must pay his delinquent dues, and it is excruciatingly painful. It may take two or three years to catch up to where he should have been had he not sustained such a safe time during college.

In essence, we have two choices. We can suffer the momentary discomfort of facing each bit of unpleasant reality as it presents itself. Then we can deal with it as effectively as possible and move on with life. Or we can take the tongue-in-cheek advice of Satchel Paige: "Don't look back, something may be gaining on you."

Reflection Questions

1. In absolute honesty, what is one area in my life that I must admit I'm tinting white, when the reality is not white; I'm tinting black, when the reality is not black; I'm tinting grey, when the reality is either black or white?

2. Of the eleven defense mechanisms, which is my favorite one even though I hate to admit it?

3. We all use the defense of denial at least once in a while. Of all my weaknesses, which is the one I'm most likely to deny exists?

4. Of the twelve defense activities, which is my favorite? Why do I use it?

5. We all must pay "psychological dues" to earn the satisfaction that comes from growing. What psychological dues am I currently paying for my growth?

Thoughts to Contemplate

1. Some people are forever psychologically shooting people or jumping out of windows because they misperceive reality.

2. A specific defense mechanism can be "passed down" from generation to generation.

3. Feelings should be felt and not selected for consciousness on the basis of whether they are logical or illogical, justified or unjustified, mature or immature, moral or immoral. Feelings don't make a person good or bad.

4. Boredom is a self-imposed emotional limbo.

5. Every day we are required to pay "psychological dues" for the privilege of being a human being.

3

FEAR: THE BASIC EMOTION

Fear is man's basic emotion and one that is most shared with the lower primates. Although we are seldom frightened by the *same* dangers as animals are, we are frightened by *more* dangers because the psyche is a wider flank to defend than is the body.

Fear is the feeling of anxiety caused by the presence or pending presence of danger. The danger can be physical, but the vast majority of the threats we experience are psychological. Interestingly, some people who are virtually fearless in the face of physical harm are quite skittish when they meet a psychological threat.

Psychological threat attacks the self-concept. This is why what is a threat to one person is appropriately laughed off by another. If part of my self-concept is: "I'm an empathetic individual," and one of my students says to me: "I'm surprised at what you said in class today; I would have thought you to be more understanding than that," my psyche would perceive this as a threat, and I would react with fear.

If another student said: "Your diagram on the blackboard was atrocious; you certainly are not an artist," I would not find it a threat or feel any accompanying fear because part of my self-concept does not include "I'm a good artist."

Some dimensions of our self-concept that produce fear when threatened are the concepts that we are intelligent, important, creative, well-meaning, mature, reasonable, honest, sensitive, moral, and generous.

Fear is a pervasive emotion and affects us daily. Its value is primarily positive because fears can act as a warning signal of impending danger. Unfortunately, most of us define fear as "unpleasant" instead of correctly viewing it as helpful. It is when our fears are denied, exaggerated, or misplaced that they pose problems. Most of us underestimate how pervasive fear is for three reasons.

First, like other "unpleasant" emotions, we instantly shunt it out of awareness by defense mechanisms and defense activities. Some of the common defenses against fear are:

Repression: "I know I should be scared about losing my job, but I sure don't feel scared."

Denial: "I refused to go out with that boy because I just don't like him; it's not because he's sexually aggressive."

Projection: "Why are you frightened of me?"

Reaction formation: "I *volunteered* to lead my platoon into battle, so how could I be frightened of getting injured or killed?"

Displacement: "I'm not afraid of leaving my wife during the day; I'm just afraid of going to work."

Somatization: "I wasn't fearful of giving my speech; it's just that I got a terrible headache and had to cancel it."

Intellectualization: "I'm a little scared about starting psychotherapy, but I think it's a good thing to be scared so it doesn't bother me."

None of these seven people has the slightest inkling that each is too frightened to allow the fear to be experienced.

Secondly, we are unaware of fear because it is often hidden beneath the secondary emotions it generates. The most common emotion generated by fear is anger. This is a primordial, survival response often seen in animals. Frequently, when an animal is frightened, it instinctively attacks the source of the threat or anyone or anything that happens to be close by. Although we like to think we are far removed from such primitive behavior, a quick glimpse at our everyday behavior proves that we are not.

Anger hides our fear so quickly that we can hardly believe that fear is at the heart of the anger. We say with conviction:

"I wasn't *frightened* when I got fired; I was *angry.*"

"I wasn't *scared* when I discovered my girlfriend was dating another boy; I was *furious.*"

"I wasn't *afraid* when the teacher put me 'on the spot,' but I *resented* it."

In each case, however, it is likely that fear was the basic emotional response. Fear is a very natural reaction to being fired: "What am I going to do now?" Fear is an automatic reaction to learning that a loved one is dating another: "What's wrong with me that she needs someone else?" And fear is an obvious reaction to "losing face": "People will think I'm stupid."

Most angry feelings rebound off feelings of fright. Most "hostile" people are frightened people; most "arrogant" people are frightened; most "snobbish" people are frightened. When we can understand this, it opens up a new dimension of relating to ourselves and to others. If when I'm angry, I can ask myself "Underneath my anger, what part of me is *frightened* by what just happened?" and "What just occurred that threatened my self-concept?" I will have more data with which to understand myself and to communicate this fear to the source of the threat. We will also relate differently with another if we view the person as frightened rather than as hostile. If we view a person as hostile, we often react with hostility, reinforcing the fears and generating more hostility. If people are relating on the anger level when the problem lies on the fear level, a successful resolution of the conflict is unlikely. This is not to say that all anger can be traced to fear, but a good deal of it can.

Thirdly, we are unaware of the amount of fear in our lives and the lives of the people around us because fear is often called by another name—a more personally acceptable label. A classic example of this is when I asked a man: "Are you afraid that you are falling out of love with your wife?" He replied: "No, I'm not *afraid*—but I'm *frightened.*"

Words that are frequently synonyms for fear are: tense, agitated, anxious, apprehensive, apathetic, bored, discouraged, disturbed, frustrated, helpless, hesitant, impatient, insecure, keyed-up, miserable, nervous, reluctant, restless, perplexed, suspicious, and worried. The chances are great that when we use any of these words to describe how we feel, we are actually saying "I'm scared."

WHAT ARE THE FOUR WAYS TO DEAL WITH FEAR?

1. Utilize the fear as a tool for growth. The first step in utilization is to acknowledge: "I'm afraid." The next step is to isolate the exact cause of the fear: "I'm frightened that my boss is losing respect for me." One uses the fear in one or both of two ways. The individual reflects whether there is good reason to be frightened and works to rectify the situation if there is. For example, I may admit that my boss probably is losing some respect for me because I've been leaving work early a couple of times a week. If having his respect is more important than leaving work early, I shall make it a point not to leave early again. I successfully perceived the "caution light" my boss was flashing to me and rectified the situation before it became a problem.

In some instances, after one acknowledges the presence of fear, it is helpful to share the fear with the person who represents the source of fear in order to bring about a constructive resolution. For example, I may share my fear with my wife that we are spending too much time on our projects and not enough time together. She may agree and be thankful that I shared the fear with her, and we both can work to remedy the situation.

"Constructive" resolution does not necessarily mean a "happy" one; it means "healthy." For example, a boy may share his fears that his girlfriend is taking advantage of him, and that this makes him feel used. His girlfriend, upon hearing this, decides that she no longer wishes to be in a relationship with him. While this decision may not make either person "happy," it may be a healthy resolution for both parties.

2. Withdraw from the fear. In withdrawal the frightened person removes himself psychologically from the source of the threat. This can be done in one of two ways: A person can use his "psychological radar" to avoid being "hit" by a threat before it occurs. For example, a man may avoid a "sore point" with his wife even though he knows it is an issue that should be discussed.

Another type of psychological withdrawal is to use a defense mechanism or defense activity and "erase" the fear before it reaches consciousness (see page 00 for examples).

In the normal course of events, withdrawal is not a constructive way of handling fear because psychological growth necessitates facing and utilizing fears. However, in extreme cases where the source of the threat is pathological, withdrawal can be constructive behavior. For example, if a woman is married to a man who continually abuses her physically and psychologically, it would be constructive for her to withdraw from that relationship.

3. Control the source of the fear. By exercising control over the person who is representing the source of the threat, an individual can hold the threat in abeyance. This consists of "psychologically handcuffing" the source of the threat to render the person harmless. For example, a husband may be threatened by his wife's desire to have sexual intercourse more frequently. He half-consciously controls her in a way that makes it impossible for her to broach the topic with him. He "handcuffs" her by: appearing terribly tired all the time; complaining about his sore back; working late so that she is asleep before he goes to bed; looking at her with disgust when she musters up enough courage to make advances; and making cynical comments whenever sex is brought up in any context. He has imprisoned his wife because she represents a threat to him. Meanwhile, he complains to his "drinking buddies" that his sex life is rotten, as a way of denying to himself his own deep fear of sex.

Another method of control is "psychological pickpocketing." This consists of stealing emotional groceries from another without the risks entailed in earning them honestly. For example, a student with a strong fear of failure manipulates a teacher into feeling sorry for him, thus excusing him from taking an important test.

Control is ordinarily a destructive way of handling

fear. The only exception would be when the threat is pathologically harmful and the lesser of evils is holding the threat at a safe distance as a temporary measure before evacuating the scene.

4. Attack the source of the threat. This occurs when we meet the source of threat with aggression as an attempt to annihilate it. For example, a professor tells a student: "I'm concerned that you are doing poorly in my course." The student replies: "The only reason that I'm doing poorly is that you are *teaching* and *grading* poorly." If the student can "blast" the professor, then on an irrational level he feels that there is nothing left to fear.

Attacking, either physically or psychologically, is the least effective and most destructive way of handling fear. It is predicated on the myth that one's fears will disappear if one can destroy the person who is activating the fear. Attacking automatically saturates the situation with anger which further disguises the real issue: fear. Even in pathological situations, attack is never an appropriate response because pathology is only increased by hostility.

WHAT ARE SOME COMMON FEARS AND HOW DO WE HANDLE THEM?

The fear of intimacy. Emotional intimacy means that two people allow themselves to touch each other deeply. It requires complete honesty, transparency, and trust. It also requires the ultimate in vulnerability because to the extent that we render ourselves open and defenseless, to that extent we are naked to hurt. Because most of us have equally strong needs to be intimate and to avoid hurt, intimacy can be a conflictual area.

We can *utilize* the fear of intimacy by acknowledging that we are afraid to be completely vulnerable to another person, regardless of how much we love and trust him. Our head says: "This person loves you; he would not hurt you," but our heart says: "I've been hurt by people who loved me as much, if not more, than this person does."

Once the fear of intimacy is acknowledged, we can make it work *for* us. We can share this fear with the other person so that the natural ambivalences in the relationship will be understood as fear and not as disappointment, dislike, or rejection. It's better to say: "I'm getting scared; let's talk about it," than "I'm not scared; I just need some distance from you."

The fear of intimacy can also act as a calibrator for the "closeness-distance" dimension of a relationship, insuring that the individuals do not get "too close, too fast" and needlessly spoil the relationship.

We can *withdraw* from the fear of intimacy by concocting reasons why the relationship will "never work." We assure ourselves that the *other* person is "afraid of intimacy"; the other person is "too demanding," "too shallow," or "too immature." Other reasons can be manufactured as well: "I'm not ready to settle down; I want to give myself totally to my profession until I get established," or "I have too many personal problems to foist myself on somebody at this time," or "I want to be free to date others, and I'd feel guilty doing it and being that close to this person."

While any one of these reasons could be valid, they can as easily be fabricated so that the "only sensible thing to do" is to terminate the relationship. This individual continues the search for "the right person," failing to realize that the fear of intimacy will transform any "right person" into the "wrong person."

We can *control* the other person so that he cannot get close enough to activate fully our fear of intimacy. We do this by behaving in any way that will place a "safe distance" between us. This behavior may be "playing it cool"; it may be acting unpredictably so the other person can never quite get a "handle" on us. We may intellectualize our relationship so that our brains are touching but our hearts are not. We may "disappear" for periods of time after an emotionally close encounter. We may use "shyness" as a way of hiding who we are. We may continually focus the attention on the other person, thus keeping it off ourselves. We may keep a few semi-intimate relationships going concurrently, so we don't have to get "too close" to any one person. Married people can use "the kids" to create the distance and, when they have opportunities to get away by themselves, they invite another couple to fill in the gap left by the absence of the children. In each of these situations, the individual gets just enough needs met to remain in the relationship, but not enough needs met to feel loved.

We can *attack* the other person because, when wounded, the other person won't pose much of an emotional threat. Some stratagems of attack are: ridiculing, picking fights, manipulating, exploiting, emasculating, and setting up "no-win" situations in which the other person is "damned if he does and damned if he doesn't."

This person assures himself: "How could I be frightened of getting close to this person; half the time I can't even stand him." A childhood example of this is the well-known fact that little boys throw the most rocks at the little girls they love the most. This gets the girls' attention, which is rewarding in itself, without having to endure the panic that would be created by a more tender kind of discourse.

The fear of rejection. This is the fear that we will be unacceptable to someone (or to an organization) that we like, admire, respect, or love. The intensity of this fear corresponds greatly to how well one accepts oneself. For people who are self-accepting, this fear is less intense. But for others to whom acceptability depends largely on which or how many people accept them, this fear can be powerful.

We can *utilize* this fear of rejection constructively by acknowledging it and understanding that it is a normal fear. No one likes to be rejected by someone he admires or respects. We may ask ourselves: "How much does being accepted by him mean to me?"

If it means a great deal, what gap is there within me that needs filling, and will any one other than I be able to fill it?

If it doesn't mean a great deal, what is there to be nervous about?

What will happen to my existence if I am not accepted by him? One month from now, how will I be essentially different?

Am I willing to "sell off" some of myself to gain acceptance? If the answer is no, then I can rest peacefully in that security. If the answer is yes, exactly what is it that is more important than myself?

We can *withdraw* from the fear of rejection by feigning disinterest so that "it doesn't matter one way or another if they accept me." Unfortunately, this "disinterest" will be communicated and create a reason to be rejected when none existed previously. We can assiduously avoid situations in which rejection is possible. If I don't try out for the debating team, they can't reject me. If I don't ask a girl out for a date, she can't say "no." If I don't apply to graduate school, I can't get refused.

Also, through the "magic" of defense mechanisms, we can transform a rejection into an "acceptance." If the girl I ask out on a date declines my invitation, I can interpret this as an indication that she views me as too much of a threat sexually. Thus, rather than feeling rejected, I feel more virile.

If I receive a failing grade in my oral comprehensives, I feel "great" because the three "most creative" students in the class also were failed in their comps.

We can *control* the situation by being a subservient pleaser, thus "buying" acceptance. However, sooner or later, we must realize that we have not been accepted for who we are, but for what we are willing to do.

We can also subtly force people into situations in which they are indebted to us; therefore, they *have* to accept us. If I'm willing to lend you my perfect physics notes, you have to invite me out with your friends for a beer. If I give you the down payment for your house, you have to have me over to your home every Sunday. If I invite you to my cottage for the summer, you have to let me room with you in the fall.

Another way of guaranteeing acceptance is to play on a person's sympathy. If I bemoan that I'm going to be all by myself during the Christmas vacation, you *can't* refuse to invite me home with you. If I feel ugly, unlovable, stupid, and deprived, and I share these feelings with you because "you're the only person that would understand," then you've *got* to accept me. Obviously, the "acceptance" I am garnering for myself is not genuine, but for many people synthetic acceptance is better than nothing.

We can *attack* the source of the fear of rejection. We may operate on the axiom: "The best way to prevent rejection is to reject first." This individual creates a pseudo-issue, then reacts: "Well, if that's the kind of person you are, I don't want to have anything to do with you." By a person's obliterating the relationship, the possibility of rejection is precluded.

These individuals completely reverse the true dynamics of the situation and view themselves as the ones looking for someone worthy of their friendship and lamenting that no one seems to qualify. But, in truth, their fear of rejection makes it impossible for them to maintain any kind of meaningful relationship.

The fear of failure. This is the fear that we will try something, perhaps even invest our utmost into it, and not experience success. The objects of failure can be anything we try. We can fail an examination; fail on the athletic field; fail at work; fail at sex; fail in marriage. We can "fail" others and "fail" ourselves.

We can *utilize* the fear of failure constructively by allowing ourselves to feel the fear, and then by using the fear as an impetus to prepare for the fear-producing situation. If I can acknowledge that I am afraid of doing poorly in an approaching examination, I will want to reduce this fear by studying for the test. If I am fearful that my marriage is falling apart, I can convert that fear into seeking some marital counseling.

We can psychologically *withdraw* from the fear of failure by declining to participate in competitive situations. Or we may compete, but when the slightest indication presents itself that we may not be doing well, we quit under any guise that is acceptable to us. This behavior is based on the principle: "If you don't try something, you can't fail it."

Or, we can reduce our emotional investment in the task, falsely assuming the attitude: "Whether I get what I want or not doesn't really matter—either way will be O.K. with me." This attitude will be reflected in one's efforts and tip the odds in favor of failing.

We can psychologically *control* the fear by denying it, thus neutralizing the fear that should have been employed to prepare adequately for the task. Sometimes we wonder after someone fails a task: "Why didn't he *prepare* for it; he had two weeks to do it!" The naive observer answers: "He was too casual, too overconfident." A more accurate answer is: "He was too frightened to think about it, so he blocked it out of his mind until it was too late to devote adequate time to it."

The opposite can also occur. We can control the fear of failure by *overpreparing* for the event. Our compulsive preparation has three built-in problems. One is that we cram so much into our heads, or we try so hard to say and do the correct things, that we develop "tunnel vision." We get so distracted by certain parts of the situation that we miss the overall purpose, the connecting theme to the situation. Secondly, we are so exhausted by the time the task is at hand, or during the task, that we are behaving more on "instinct" than on reason which causes us to falter. Thirdly, we can't face the task until we feel that our preparation has been perfect and, since it is "never" perfect, we fail the task by default. We soothe ourselves by saying: "If only I had one more day to prepare, I would have been successful."

We can *attack* the fear of failure. We may do this by ridiculing the situation, thus detoxifying it. If oral comprehensive exams "don't test anything," then even if I fail them, I really have failed nothing. If a job interview is "just a charade because the job has already been filled," then if I don't get the job, I don't fail anything. If marriage is just a "neurosis of the middle class," then getting a divorce would not be viewed as a failure, but as a sign of success.

The consequences of attacking the fear of failure are unfortunate. If I am successful at the task that I belittled as "unimportant," I can't really enjoy my success without contradicting myself. If I fail the task, I will learn nothing from my failure, thus repeating the same mistake at a later date.

The fear of change. This fear deals with trying something new or different or becoming something different. The fear is that change will bring forth a state worse than the present one. An individual may be in a relatively good situation, but be fearful of changing because he may not find something better. When the fear of change is very strong, people may choose to remain in an unnecessarily difficult or destructive situation rather than take the risk of getting into a worse situation.

Examples of situations that may need changing are: one's way of reacting to a specific problem or to life in general; one's relationship with one's parents; a romantic relationship; a marriage relationship; or a situation at work. "Change" can mean remaining in the situation but altering one's way of handling it, or in some cases it may mean leaving the situation.

We can *utilize* the fear of change by acknowledging that it exists and attempting to pin-point its exact source. We can ask ourselves:

What *specifically* could get worse if I changed the situation?

Could it get worse, or am I creating a false fear so that I won't have to act?

If one or two things *could* get worse, how many things are likely to get better that would cancel out what could go wrong?

Do I realize that, while some things could get worse, in the overall perspective *I* could get better?

Do I value myself so little that I don't think I'm worth more than what I've got?

Do I feel so guilty about things that I don't feel that I *deserve* to be any happier than I am now?

We can *withdraw* from the fear of change by using different ploys to avoid facing the need for change. We can build up defense mechanisms and defense activities that camouflage the deathly sameness or the patent destructiveness of a situation. As one person put it: "I've gotten so used to the stink, I don't even notice it anymore."

We can finagle so many rewards for suffering that we would be "foolish" to give up a "psychological gold mine."

We can earn enough "credits" to qualify as a "professional sufferer," taking pride in how well we are able to handle a loathsome situation.

We can adopt a "philosophy of martyrdom" ("Life

will be better in the next world, so I'll wait for that"), and a "gallows humor" that helps us become tolerant or even comfortable with an unnecessarily difficult situation.

We can "supernaturalize" a destructive situation by "offering up one's pain to God," thus assuring oneself a "higher place in heaven." A poor decision is transformed into a spiritual virtue.

We can develop the mentality: "A good captain goes down with the ship." The result is that *both* a good captain *and* the ship are lost, a ship that was probably irreparable anyway.

We can *control* the fear of change. We do this by acknowledging to ourselves and to others that we really should make a change, either in our behavior or in a situation. We allow ourselves to catch a glimpse of a problem and even admit the value in changing it. But our resolution to change insiduously evaporates into one or more of the following placebos:

"I'll wait until the end of the year, and if things aren't better by then, I'll have to do something."

"I'll speak to my husband [mother, boss] about it and see what he [she] says."

"As soon as things calm down a little, I'm going to leave."

"I think if I don't worry so much about it, things should get better."

"From now on, I'm just going to develop a more positive attitude toward the situation."

"If I'm not feeling better by Easter, I'm going to seek some professional help."

We can *attack* the fear of change by frenetically rushing about "changing" everything without much thought, reason, or plan. The idea is to fool ourselves and others into thinking we are making some important changes. But, when all the dust has cleared, nothing of any significance has really changed, or what *was* changed was never related to the problem from the start.

For example, some people feel unhappy so they launch a series of changes. They change friends, jobs, residences, religions, and therapists in their pursuit of happiness. But these changes are superficial and often inappropriate. If a person needs to increase his sense of responsibility in order to be happier, moving from one town to another or from one job to another will be futile because the one change that should be made is successfully eluded.

The fear of freedom. This is the fear of being bound by significantly less restraints or by no restraints. It is a very subtle fear because most people realize that they fear the imposition of restraints and "naturally" assume that they would welcome its opposite, namely, freedom. But this assumption is invalid for many people. The more freedom we have, the more free rein our impulses have; the more we have to set our own limits; the more we must carve out our own existence; the more we have to assume responsibility for our own behavior; and the more we are left alone by others.

We can *utilize* this fear of freedom by acknowledging it and focusing on exactly which elements of freedom frighten us. Are we afraid that we'd give in to our impulses if we had fewer restraints; that we'd quit work and do nothing all day; that we'd get involved in a marathon of sexual experiences; or that we'd go around telling off all the people who ever hurt us? Are we afraid that we would panic and not know what to do with freedom once we got it? Are we afraid that, being free, we'd feel guilty because all our friends were still "in prison"? Are we afraid we'd fail and have no one to blame it on but ourselves? Are we afraid we'd be lonely "out there" all by ourselves with no one to patrol us?

We can ask ourselves which of these fears are the more imposing and what can we do to reduce or extinguish them.

We can *withdraw* from the fear of freedom. We can convince ourselves that we are as "free as I want to be right where I am." Such individuals often protest: "My goodness, what would I want with any more freedom than I have right now?" Certainly, some or many people do not need any more freedom than they have. But there are easily as many people who are psychologically suffocating in an over-restrictive environment and don't realize it. They are like sick pets who are "put to sleep" by removing oxygen from the room. The animals have no idea what is happening; at best they feel "peaceful" and at worst they feel drowsy. But what they are doing is dying.

We can *control* the fear of freedom. We can do this by placing shackles on ourselves and blaming others for it.

Examples of self-shackling are:

"If it weren't for not wanting to hurt my parents, I'd move out and live in the dorms at the university."

"If it weren't that I've already invested two years in college, I'd quit and do something I'd really enjoy doing."

"If only I had a car, I'd ask the girl in the next apartment for a date."

"If it weren't for the children, I'd get a divorce and start a new life for myself."

"If it weren't for the people I'd hurt, I'd break off this engagement and date a whole bunch of new people."

"If it weren't for me being so loyal to my boss, I'd take the promotion that was offered by another department."

The identical theme runs through all these self-shackles: "If it weren't for somebody else [or something else], I could be free."

We can *attack* the fear of freedom by ambushing "liberators." "Liberators" are people or opportunities that come into our lives, offering an increase in freedom. A benefactor tells a promising employee: "I will give you a year off with pay if you return to school and finish your last year of college so that you can have more choices in life." The "ambusher" replies: "I really appreciate that, but I like work here in the factory and besides, I wouldn't want to leave the friendships I've developed here in town."

A man inherits a decent amount of money. His wife is overjoyed because now he can quit his second job and have more freedom to do what he wants with his time. He immediately puts the money into a trust fund for his children because "they'll need it more than we do."

One friend tells another: "Be sure and be completely open and honest with me. If ever I do anything that bugs you, please let me know." The ambusher assures his friend that he will. However, he privately tells himself that the friend was just being nice but didn't really mean it. So, the ambusher declines an invitation to freedom.

In all of these examples the individual declines an invitation to more freedom because of the fear it presents.

HOW CAN FEARS RUN YOUR LIFE?

When fears are relatively strong, they can significantly influence and sometimes control the major portions of one's life. It is important to distinguish between "present fears" and "historical fears." Present fears are relatively disconnected from the past and are an appropriate reaction to a fear-producing event.

For example, a young wife, in the midst of an argument with her husband, hears him say: "Sometimes I wonder if I wouldn't be happier single." She reacts internally with a twinge of fear which she instantly coats with anger, and she replies: "Maybe it would be better *for me,* too, if you were single again." Perhaps the real issue eventually surfaces and is dealt with, dissipating the fear and the anger. In any event, the wife was devoid of historical fears and reacted solely to the present fear.

Historical fears are more complex. The immediate fear is merely the "tip of the iceberg" of a larger mass of fear that has accumulated for years. This mass of fear stems from one or two traumas in a particular area whose reverberations continue to ripple throughout the psyche. Or the mass of fear is the result of a series of lesser hurts in a particular area that have left a tender spot on the psyche.

For example, a young wife had a father who walked out on the family when she was nine years old (a trauma); or she has experienced a series of lesser hurts: Every time she got very close to a friend, either she or the friend moved.

In either case, this woman hears her husband say: "Sometimes I wonder if I wouldn't be happier single." Her psyche automatically flashes: "HE'S GOING TO LEAVE ME LIKE THE OTHERS DID." She panics and frantically shifts gears into "Withdraw": She leaves the house and returns to her mother's home where she feels temporarily safe and protected.

She may "attack" instead of withdrawing. She physically attacks her husband as if to annihilate him as a threat, or she viciously attacks him psychologically to entrench a defensive position for herself: "Now I don't care if he leaves me or not."

To the casual observer, this woman's behavior in any of these cases is "inappropriate." But if we understand that her fear is not a present one but a *historical* one, her reactions are understandable. Unfortunately, she may not even understand the historical context of her fear because it has been covered over with years of defenses. When she "cools down," she apologizes and wonders how she ever lost control of herself that way. It is at this point that the wife and husband can sit down and discuss how she may be still burdened with antique fears.

Historical fears influence the present in another important way. They can cause the "Bottom-line Phenomenon." This means that our conscious, unfearful self writes the "top line" of a situation, but the less conscious, fearful self writes the "bottom line." And it's the bottom line toward which all the other lines insiduously dovetail. The following are some examples of the "Bottom-line Phenomenon."

The Top Line: A man says "I want that promotion so badly I can taste it."

The Bottom Line is: "If you got the promotion, you'd be so frightened you wouldn't know what to do with it."

The "middle lines" consist of all the man's diluted attempts to win the promotion, which are finally undercut by his failure to get his application in on time, thus sabotaging the opportunity. This man's basic fear of responsibility "won," and he doesn't even know it.

The Top Line: "The most important thing in my relationship with my husband is honesty."

The Bottom Line: "I'm terrified of unpleasant reality and married to a man who keeps things to himself so he'll protect me from the bad news in life."

The middle lines consist of the wife's begging for honesty from her husband, but making it clear that these are not legitimate invitations. She lives through her marriage bemoaning the fact that her husband keeps so many things from her. She knows they would have a much "fuller" relationship if only he felt free enough to be completely open with her. But, deep down, her psyche is very happy with the way things are.

The Top Line: A man in his late twenties says: "Boy, I sure hope I find the right girl soon; I'm getting awfully tired of being a bachelor."

The Bottom Line: "There's no way I want to find the 'right girl' because, if I do, I'll have to marry her and face my intense fear of commitment."

The middle lines consist of almost nightly pilgrimages to the "swinging bars," two or three broken engagements, and frequent complaints that "all the nice girls have already been taken." The young man's scared self whispers: "And thank God."

The Top Line: A woman says: "I would do anything to help my poor husband with his problem with sexual impotence."

The Bottom Line: "I hope his impotence lasts forever; otherwise, I will be faced directly with my deep fears of sexuality."

The middle lines consist of the wife's trying anything that might help, including accompanying her husband to his therapy appointments. But her attempts are perfunctory; her concern, motherly. When things seem to be getting better, somehow that's when she is least interested in having sex. At times she sympathizes, "my poor Jim." At other times she laments: "If only he didn't have his little problem, we would be the happiest couple in the world." But her frightened self is mopping its brow in relief.

When we find ourselves exclaiming: "I don't know why it is, but the most important things I try never seem to work out," it is likely we are being "bottom-lined." Our fears are sabotaging the processes instrumental to our receiving what we want most in life. The cure isn't trying new processes (middle lines) but in discovering what the bottom line is and dealing with that.

Whatever its basis, fear can be an extremely debilitating emotion if it is mishandled. It often seems "easier" to withdraw from a fear, or to attempt to control or attack the source of fear. Yet, all these ways of handling fear only complicate the situation and usually lead to further problems. Getting to the "bottom line" of our fears and acknowledging them is the first and often the hardest step in utilizing fear as a tool for growth.

Reflection Questions

1. Of the four ways to handle fear (utilize it; withdraw from it; control the source; and attack the source), which one am I most likely to use when I'm the most frightened? Why?

2. Of the five basic fears (fear of intimacy, rejection, failure, change, and freedom), which frightens me the most and which the least? How do I handle these fears?

3. What past fear in my life was so great that it might still be affecting me today, even though I don't realize it? How could it be affecting me?

4. What specific part of my self-image is the most vulnerable to threat (I am intelligent, sensitive, mature, sensible, strong, trustworthy, virtuous, insightful, likable, talented, honest, caring, etc.)?

5. What makes me most angry? What fear is hiding beneath that anger?

Thoughts to Contemplate

1. The most common emotion generated by fear is anger. Anger hides our fear so quickly that we can hardly believe that fear is at the heart of the anger.

2. "Constructive" resolution to a problem does not necessarily mean a "happy" resolution. It means "healthy."

3. Attacking, either physically or psychologically, is the least effective and most destructive way of handling fear. It is predicated on the myth that one's fears will disappear if we can destroy the person who is activating the fear.

4. We can supernaturalize a destructive situation by offering it up to God, thus assuring ourselves a higher

place in heaven. A poor decision is transformed into a spiritual virtue.

5. Many people fear freedom. The more freedom we have, the more free rein our impulses have; the more we have to set our own limits; the more we must carve out our own existence; the more we have to assume responsibility for our own behavior; and the more we are left alone by others.

4

ANGER AS A VIRTUE

The emotion of anger is extremely important for our mental health. It is a two-edged sword that cuts both constructively and destructively. Unfortunately, anger has an undeservedly bad reputation which ignores the fact that anger has brought about as much good in society as it has evil. Anger may have produced more good in society than love. For example, it seems that anger toward injustice has led to more positive social changes than has a love for justice.

Anger occurs when one of our psychological needs becomes threatened or blocked. For example, if my sense of safety, acceptance, or effectiveness is threatened or blocked, one of my emotional responses will be anger. When used properly, anger acts as an emotional solvent that dissolves and removes obstacles to need fulfillment. This is seen clearly in the experience of feeling "closer than ever" to a person after we have constructively communicated our anger. The statements often used to describe communicating anger: "clearing the air," "getting something off my chest"—describe the therapeutic effects of anger.

Unfortunately, many people have a real problem with anger. Some people report that they never feel anger. Others cannot connect the word "anger" with any feeling that they experience. They use words such as "upset," "frustrated," "disappointed," "confused," "annoyed," and "hurt," but deny that any of these emotions are connected with anger. Still others, while in the midst of a rage, deny that they are angry. Some of the angriest letters I have received as a columnist were from people protesting my statement that anger can be good.

This chapter will deal with how we avoid expressing anger constructively; where anger goes when it is not expressed constructively; and how to express anger in positive, effective ways.

HOW WE AVOID EXPRESSING ANGER CONSTRUCTIVELY

Some of the more typical rationalizations used to avoid expressing anger constructively include the following:

1. *"It's not nice ["Christian," "mature"] to hurt another person."* This rationalization is grounded in a misunderstanding both of religion and of mental health. God frequently demonstrated anger in the Old Testament as did Christ in the New Testament. I've never read anything in the mental health literature which states that anger, in itself, is "immature." In fact, one of the typical traits of a mature person is the ability to express anger in a wholesome way.

I suspect that the concern expressed in this rationalization is not as altruistic as it would appear. What most people are *really* saying is: "It's not nice to hurt people— because, if you do, you're liable to get hurt back." Probably many people would feel freer to express anger if they were promised immunity from reciprocated anger.

It is true that anger hurts people. If anger is expressed, it can hurt the recipient of the anger. If the anger is not expressed, it can hurt the person who is holding it in. But the concept of "hurt" needs to be better understood.

There is a difference between *feeling hurt* and *being damaged.* When my physician gives me a shot, I feel hurt, but I am not damaged; in fact, I will be stronger and healthier as a result of the shot. In our daily lives, it is necessary to receive and give "psychological shots" if we and the people we care about are to survive and grow.

It is extremely unfortunate that, because we have been taught that hurting another is wrong, there is a dearth of "emotional surgeons" in our lives. The result is that both we and our loved ones endure unnecessary emotional pain. Or, when "emotional surgery" is attempted, it is done so ineptly that the results "prove" how "devastating anger is." A mentally healthy person is willing to risk hurting another and getting hurt in return as the means of bringing about a more life-giving relationship.

2. *"There are some people toward whom we should not feel anger and toward whom we should not express it."* These "untouchables" include: people who love us very much; people who have been kind and generous to us; delicate people who "wouldn't understand and would be terribly hurt"; people in authority, especially if they are in a position to fire us; people with certain status: teacher, doctor, clergyman, therapist; people who are already under a good deal of stress; people who are old or infirm; and people who are deceased.

Unfortunately, this list includes about 80 percent of all the people that we care about enough to feel angry with them. They are the very people with whom we need most to express our anger. I have never heard of a person dying or "falling to pieces" when constructive anger has been shared with him. I *have* seen people die (both physically and emotionally) and "break down" because no one seemed to feel free enough to clear out the obstacles in the relationship.

3. *"If I expressed the anger I feel, it would hurt or demolish our relationship."* The question we should ask ourselves here is: "What kind of relationship is it that it could not tolerate my genuine feeling of anger?" The answer would have to be that it is a dishonest relationship built not on trust and concern but on keeping each other superficially happy. I have never seen a marriage harmed by constructive anger. I have seen some marriages destroyed by destructive anger. But the vast majority of marriages are destroyed because of the partners' inability to express constructive anger. These

marriages didn't "blow up"; they merely "died out." Both partners died of emotional starvation caused by continual and unrelieved blocking of mutual need fulfillment.

Expressing constructive anger will separate our real friends from our "fair weather" friends. If a person is willing to sacrifice the expression of his true feelings to retain a fair weather friend, he has many more problems than an inability to express anger.

4. *"It wouldn't do any good anyhow—it won't change anything."* This individual fails to realize that there is a twofold purpose to expressing anger. One is that sharing anger and its causes will hopefully give the other person information that will move him to rectify something in the relationship that is causing an obstacle. But the secondary purpose is to rid the angry person's mind and body of the "toxins" that build up when anger is held in (these toxins will be discussed in detail in the next section, "Where Does Anger Go?"). It is psychologically important for us to get rid of at least the "hot" parts of our anger. Whether the other person wishes to acknowledge them and deal with them is not a necessary requirement for unburdening ourselves.

The person using this rationale also confuses responsibilities. A good doctor does not say: "I should prescribe antibiotics for this person, but I know he won't bother to take them, so I'll just skip it." A good doctor says: "It's my ethical responsibility to prescribe the medication I think will help this person. It is *his* responsibility whether he accepts it or not." The exact same principle holds in the expression of anger. It is my responsibility to do all I can to help myself and the other person grow. If the other person is incapable or unwilling to share in this communication, it in no way relieves me of my responsibility to him or to myself.

5. *"Maybe I'm wrong"* or *"Maybe my anger is irrational."* Rational and irrational anger do the same amount of damage to the individual and to the relationship when they are unexpressed. When someone shares anger, he is not necessarily proclaiming that he is correct. He is sim-

ply declaring that he is angry. The only way to discover if anger is rational or irrational is to expose it to the light of open communication. Simply say: "I don't know if I'm off base here or not but. . . . " This can give an accurate reflection of the situation from the angry person's point of view.

Often the unstated fear in this rationalization is: "They'll think I'm really immature or crazy if I tell them why I'm angry." Often, such fears are unfounded, especially if the angry person can express the nature of the anger in a clear manner. When the fear of being wrong proves to be well-founded, it can still be a learning experience. The discomfort of this situation is minimal compared to that which results from holding in the anger.

6. *"You can't get angry at someone you love."* This individual has made love and anger mutually exclusive emotions whereas, in fact, they are mutually inclusive. The closer people get emotionally, the more vulnerable they are to hurt. And the more they get hurt, the more anger they will feel. If someone says: "We are very much in love and never hurt each other," I would doubt the genuineness of their love. They are "loving at a distance" and don't even know it. If someone says: "Oh sure, he/she hurts me sometimes, but I never feel angry," then I doubt this individual's ability to be in touch with his or her true feelings. Defense mechanisms such as repression, denial, or intellectualization are distorting the accuracy of the person's perceptions.

Mentally healthy people love and hate—sometimes in sequence and sometimes simultaneously. Many people have been taught that one either loves or hates—and if you hate (have strong negative feelings toward a person), then, automatically, it means you don't love the person. Consequently, mental gymnastics have to be called upon which allow the person to always feel "love" and never to feel anger. The anger goes "underground" and causes many other problems—the price one is obliged to pay for being an "anger-free" lover. Often these problems ultimately cause so much damage to the person and the relationship that the love that is present dwindles and sometimes dies. Throughout this process the people in-

volved don't understand why it happened because no one
had ever said an angry word to each other.

WHERE DOES ANGER GO?

There is no such thing as "unexpressed anger." Anger
is *always* expressed. The question is whether anger is expressed constructively or destructively. When anger is not
expressed constructively, it does not disappear or evaporate. It "goes" to one of five places.

1. *It goes into an "anger collection."* Just as someone col-
lects trading stamps and eventually cashes them in for
"free" gifts, people save up anger feelings and sooner or
later cash them in for "guilt-free angers." A few books of
"anger stamps" may be cashed in on a temper-tantrum;
not showing up to work for a day; getting drunk. Several
books may be cashed in for more destructive things: going
on a "bender"; having an affair; quitting a job; threatening physical harm; publically embarrassing the person
who is the target of the anger. And books that are collect-
ed for many years may be cashed in at "great value": run-
ning away from home; an assault; a divorce; a murder or
a suicide. All of these "cashing-in" behaviors are relatively guilt-free because the collector feels he has earned and
deserves his destructive behavior. People who murder a
spouse frequently declare: "He [She] had it coming for a
long time. Who wouldn't have done the same thing? What
would *you* do under the same circumstances?"

Cashing in anger stamps is quite destructive for two
reasons. One is that since it is only the "last straw" that is
reacted to, the person who is the object of the anger has
no way of knowing exactly what previous behaviors may
have been reacted to with concealed anger. Therefore,
the individual is in no position to alter any of the problematic behavior. Second, the "cashing-in" reaction is so
intense and inappropriate to the specific event that the
only results are confusion and destructive hurt. When anger stamps are cashed in one stamp at a time, it precludes
the building-up of anger and therefore significantly increases the chances of expressing the anger in positive,
constructive ways.

2. Passive-aggressive behavior. Many people who repress or deny their anger allow it to "leak out" in indirect, unconscious ways. Passive-aggressive behavior has three elements: First, it is motivated by anger, anger that is directed toward the person who is the cause of the anger or anger that is freefloating and which is splattered on anyone who happens to be nearby. Secondly, it is anger that is expressed indirectly; i.e., instead of confronting a person directly with the anger and dealing with the anxiety that this generates, the person launches a "sneak attack" which allows him to get rid of the anger without having to admit the anger and without having to accept responsibility for it. Finally, passive-aggressive behavior interferes with another's life in some way, either by causing the other person embarrassment, loss of self-esteem, frustration, or inconvenience. Passive-aggressive behavior is often a trait; i.e., it is the habitual way that a person expresses anger. Passive-aggressive people seldom have insight into the causes and effects of their behavior and resist considering the possibility that their behavior is motivated by anger.

The following are some typical kinds of passive-aggressive behavior.

Forgetting. There are two kinds of forgetting, natural forgetting and motivated forgetting. Natural forgetting is caused by an overloading of items to remember so that some items will be lost in the squeeze. Motivated forgetting is caused when we consciously or unconsciously don't want to remember something. Most forgetting is motivated forgetting; i.e., we tend very much to remember what we want to and forget what we want to forget.

When motivated forgetting unduly inconveniences or interferes with another's life, it is a manifestation of passive-aggressive anger. There are few things more frustrating than to count on someone to do something important for you and have them respond: "Oh, I forgot." It is interesting that some people almost never forget and others almost always forget. The difference is not the quality of memories, but the quantity of anger.

For example, a wife phones her husband at work and asks him to pick her up at the hairdresser at 5:00 P.M. Her husband had planned to join some fellow workers for a drink after work. Although he feels that his wife could just as easily drive herself to and from the hairdresser, he dutifully agrees to pick her up, failing to express his anger at her. But during the day he is "deluged with work" and "up to his ears in problems" and has a half-dozen meetings, all of which distract him so much that he drives straight home, forgetting to pick up his wife. As it turns out, she had to take a bus home. In essence, the husband accomplished "inadvertently" what he wanted to do; i.e., he punished his wife for being inconsiderate of him and spoiling his good time after work.

In short, people "forget" to do things when they lack the strength to say "no."

It is not a coincidence that "absent-minded" people who continually disrupt other people's lives by their forgetfulness are also the "nicest people." They are "nice" because they chronically repress their anger which spills out on others through their forgetfulness. And they are rarely faced with the consequences of their anger because people can't get angry with someone who is so "good-hearted" all the time.

Being late. People who are habitually late are passive-aggressive. They keep other people waiting, causing them to waste time and experience helpless frustration. These people can, with a mere "Oh, I'm sorry I'm late," slide out from being faced with the negative consequences of their destructively expressed anger.

I once taught a college student who came to every class five minutes late, distracting me and disrupting the class as he finally got settled in his seat. His excuse was that he had to travel across the whole campus from the previous class. The next semester I had the same student, and he came five minutes late to each class, even though his preceding class was in the same building as mine. His excuse was that the other teacher always kept him late. I pointed out to him that other students in the same class arrived on time and suggested that there must be another reason. He finally admitted that he resented being in the two courses because they made him examine his own behavior, and he didn't like what he saw. As a result, he disliked me for "causing" him this discomfort. His way of unconsciously "getting back" at me was to come to class late each day because he knew it made me angry. After he talked about it and got his anger out, he realized what he had been doing. From that day, he was never late again.

Hostile statements. These statements come in two varieties. One is the sincere statement—often presented as a compliment—but which has a "hook" in it. The following are some examples:

"Gee, you were always the dumbest kid in the class, and now you're a success—you must have gotten into your field at the right time."

"You look so nice I didn't recognize you."

"We got a good crowd for the lecture you're giving tonight. Of course, it's an interesting topic."

"You've gained a lot of weight, and you're losing some of your hair, but it makes you look very successful and mature."

A second type of hostile statement is couched in the comment: "I'm just kidding—you can take a joke, can't you?" Some examples are:

"I've often said that a psychologist is a person who makes money off of other people's problems, ha, ha. Just kidding—you people do wonderful work."

"Gee, sweetheart, your new hair style looks great—just like a bowling ball, ha, ha. All kidding aside—it's awfully short, but I love it."

"It must be great being a cop because you guys can take out all your hostility on other people all day long, ha, ha. I know you do more than just arrest people."

"I don't know how you manage to look so fresh and nice all the time—you must ignore your children and spend all day in front of a mirror, ha, ha. I'm just kidding; I know you're an excellent mother."

Both varieties of hostile statements are very effective as an outlet for hostility because the recipients are "damned if they do, and damned if they don't." They have two choices: They can swallow the hurt or anger and feel badly, or they can communicate their reaction and place themselves in the position of being viewed as "too sensitive" or "paranoid."

Some people "drop" one or two statements like these each day and wonder why people don't seem to be particularly happy to see them. After all, they're "just kidding" and certainly people couldn't be *that* sensitive as to take offense at their statements.

Because passive-aggressive behavior is mostly unconscious, these individuals are always the last to know how hostile they appear to others. Unfortunately, the people that have to live and work with these individuals are always the first to know.

3. Depression. It is well recognized that a major cause of depression is anger that is not being expressed outwardly. The anger is "kept in" and causes the person to "bloat up" with it. Instead of being directed toward its original object, e.g., a spouse, a parent, a child, a boss, the anger is directed at life or at oneself. The depressed person proclaims: "Life is absurd" instead of saying: "My husband is absurd," or "I'm a terrible person" instead of "My wife is a terrible person."

Symptoms of depression include feeling "blue," morose, helpless, alone, despairing, guilty, cynical, apathetic, disinterested, and tired. Other secondary symptoms of depression are problems with sleep (too much or too little), eating (too much or too little), or sex (too much or too little). There is a syndrome called "smiling depression" in which a person uses the defense mechanism of reaction formation to appear "too happy." It is as if the person were saying: "If I don't laugh, I'll cry." People can feel depressed for a day or for a life-time.

The depressed person has been taught that it is not all right to feel anger toward a loved one, but it is all right to feel anger toward life or toward oneself. When we examine the effects of depression we can clearly see the anger. The husband who protests that he is not angry at his wife, that he is just depressed and can't work, is indirectly forcing his wife to go to work. One depressed husband told me: "I hate to see her have to go back to work, but she'll have to support the family for a change." The "for a change" came out of his mouth before he had a chance to censor it and was a tell-tale sign of his resentment of having to assume the heavy responsibility of supporting the family while his wife frequented the country club and shopping centers.

A depressed wife may say: "I just hate to see Bill have to come home from a hard day at the office and have to cook, do the housework, and take care of the kids because I'm so depressed that I can't do it." Deep down, the wife may be angry at Bill because he seems to enjoy his work and his golf much more than he enjoys being with her. She can't admit to the anger this feeling creates, so she bottles it up and gets her anger out through her symptoms of depression.

The ultimate symptom of depression—suicide—is also the ultimate hostile act. It is hostile toward the person who commits suicide, and it is hostile toward the loved ones left behind because it floods them with guilt and remorse.

On a practical level, it can be very helpful to say "I feel angry today" instead of "I feel depressed today." With any degree of insight, a person could well discover some situations that made him angry within the past twenty-four hours even though the person did not realize it at the time. This places the person in a position to go back and handle the anger more constructively.

4. Psychosomatic disorders. These are physical symptoms that are caused by the individual failing to handle stress constructively. The main ingredients in stress are fear, anger, and guilt. Consequently, anger is one of the three major contributors to psychosomatic disorders. Some psychosomatic disorders commonly associated with repressed anger are "tension headaches," "stiff necks," high blood pressure, overweight, low back pain, impotence and frigidity, ulcerative colitis, chronic itching (pruritus), and rheumatoid arthritis.

As a psychotherapist it is interesting for me to watch these symptoms come and go during the span of a therapy session. A person will come in with a pounding headache, and, after twenty minutes of venting anger, the headache "magically" disappears. Or a person will come to a session feeling fine, but with the introduction of a topic that stimulates anger the person's back becomes so painful that he must get up and walk around or switch to a different chair.

People who have recurring psychosomatic symptoms generally are people with an overloading of anger. The symptoms, indirectly, can cause a good deal of anguish to those people toward whom the person feels angry. A husband looks forward for a year to a week's vacation alone with his wife. The morning they are to leave on vacation, the woman's hands are so crippled with arthritis that the trip must be cancelled. The husband will spend his week's vacation driving her to and from the doctor's office. A wife works hard trying to relax sexually so that she can get more pleasure out of intercourse with her husband. Just as she reaches a time when she begins feeling relaxed and satisfied sexually, her husband becomes impotent.

Because psychosomatic symptoms are such an effective distraction away from the underlying cause, namely anger, neither the wife in the first example nor the husband in the second will see any connection between the symptoms and their deeper feelings of anger toward their spouse. It may take several years of therapy for either person to see the connection between the physical symptoms and the angry feelings.

As with depression, instead of saying "I have a headache," it is more helpful to say "I'm angry at something"; or instead of saying "My arthritis is acting up again," it is more helpful to say "My anger is acting up again." In so doing, a person has a better chance of discovering the source of the anger and the physical symptoms should then diminish.

5. *Looking for trouble.* This is a behavior whereby a person, mostly unconsciously, creates a situation that will result in the person being presented with a "good excuse" to vent his wrath that should be directed toward someone else. "Looking for trouble" can be done in countless ways, but the following are a few common ones.

A driver in the fast lane sees a driver in the next lane anxiously wishing to get in the fast lane. Driver One slows down just enough to give Driver Two a chance to squeeze in front of him. Driver One purposely makes the distance very short so that he will have to brake suddenly to let Driver Two into the lane. Now Driver One has a good reason to be furious because "that idiot" in the car in front of him "almost killed all of us." This gives Driver One good cause to scream and swear for the next five miles. He thinks he is angry only with the other driver, but he actually vented three days worth of anger that should have been communicated to five other people.

A father comes home from work exhausted. He is also very angry at his boss who manipulated him into some extra work and at his wife who sits home all day "doing nothing." He hears his children playing with a ball in the next room and, on some level of awareness, knows that something is going to get broken. But, instead of immediately stopping the play, he lets it go until the noise reaches a crescendo, and finally he hears a lamp get knocked over. Now he has a "perfect right" to barge into the room and yell at the children about how insensitive they are and how much they don't care about him. He vents all his anger that should have been communicated to his boss and his wife.

A wife knows that money is a very touchy subject between her husband and his parents. In the middle of a family dinner the wife brings up the topic of finances, which immediately starts an argument between her husband and his parents that "completely ruins" the meal which she had prepared for two days. Now she can become furious at her husband who acted "like a child" and at her in-laws who didn't seem to realize that they were guests in her house. All the anger that has built up in her for the past week or two can come pouring out and give her a sense of righteous relief. The fact is, however, that she is angry with her husband about other matters and angry at her in-laws about still other issues. She's also angry with her best friend, and she is angry with herself. All of these angers should have been acknowledged and dealt with separately rather than lumped into one trumped-up situation.

In summary, we have two options. We can deny our anger or keep it to ourselves, which will cause us to violate ourselves and others in subtle and destructive ways. Or we can express our anger directly and constructively, which will, at best, create a mutual growth experience and, at worst, will create one-tenth of the stress caused by its denial or repression.

HANDLING ANGER CONSTRUCTIVELY

There are six steps in the process of communicating anger constructively.

1. Recognize that we are angry. As has been pointed out in this chapter, anger has many disguises. It is important to recognize these decoys as manifestations of camouflaged anger.

The obstacles to recognizing anger are many. We may have been taught that "appreciative" children don't feel anger toward their parents; that "good" marriages are not "tainted" with anger; that the feeling of anger means somebody is "wrong," and we don't like to view ourselves or our loved ones as "wrong." Maybe we were reared in a home with a good deal of *destructive* anger and erroneously equate all anger with destructive anger; maybe we know that if we recognize a feeling as anger we will have to do something about it, so it's easier to deny the anger, relieving us of any further action.

Mentally healthy people are not people without anger; they are people who express their anger constructively. Emotionally disturbed people are not people with "too much" anger, but people who are expressing whatever anger they have in a destructive manner. The difference between mental health and emotional disturbance is not how much anger a person has, but what he does with it.

So, the first step in communicating anger constructively is to admit: "I'm angry."

2. Identify the object of our anger. Recognizing that one is angry does not automatically guarantee that the object of the anger will immediately become known. This is so because some people are "easier" to feel anger toward than others. When a person is difficult to feel angry at, either because he is "lovable" or "mean," the anger can be shunted off onto someone or something else. I may be angry at my wife, but feel it toward my children. I may be angry at my mother, but feel it toward my wife. I may be angry with myself and feel it toward my wife.

It is important to be able to trace both the anger or the symptoms of anger to the correct starting point. I may *think* that I'm angry with my students, but realize that I felt angry before I walked into the classroom. I then realize that I was angry with the campus police officer who wouldn't let me park my car, but then I realize that I was angry driving to work this morning. I don't remember waking up angry, so whatever is causing the anger happened between the time I woke up and the time I left home. Since the children had already left for school, it looks as if my wife is the target. Now, what happened between me and my wife that I reacted to with anger?

3. Purify our motives. We must ask ourselves if our main purpose for communicating anger is to be helpful or hurtful. If we are interested in "getting back" at the other person rather than in removing an obstacle to mutual need fulfillment, the only result will be a negative one. If our attitude is: "I'm going to hurt you as much as you hurt me," no good will come of this.

Anger is a feeling to share, not a weapon with which to slay people. If we have to admit that our immediate impulse is to hurt the other person, it would be better to ventilate these "hot" feelings with a trusted third party as a way of taking some of the destructive edge off the anger. This does not mean that one must be dispassionate before one is ready to communicate anger. It merely means that fury can be dissipated, leaving a "workable" anger to communicate. Generally, when anger is "kept current," i.e., when it is communicated each time it arises, it is unlikely that anger will reach the "fury" or "rage" point. A constructive attitude is: "I'm very angry with you, and I'd like to talk about it now so that we can resolve this issue to our mutual satisfaction."

4. Focus on the current issue. The only issue that should be discussed is the immediate issue that caused the anger. This is in contrast to "sandbagging," which means resurrecting stale angers that go back six months and that were never aired. Sandbagging is often prefaced with: "I'm glad we're talking like this because there are a few things I've been meaning to tell you for a long time," or "As long as we're on the subject, two weeks ago you...."

Often when people get angry enough to express it, it is the "straw that broke the camel's back" that triggered off the anger. Consequently, *all* the "straws" are thrown into the discussion. Under ordinary circumstances, if we failed to deal with anger issues in the past, we lose our right to bring them up as part of our present anger.

The more we throw unrelated and past angers at the other person, the less he will be able to sort out his own ideas and feelings. Where there is one issue and it is current, then both people have a good chance of dealing with it in a reasonable, clear, and non-frantic way.

5. *Discuss the real issue.* Often there are two issues in the communication of anger. One is the *real* issue, and the other is the *pseudo-issue.* The real issue is what we are actually angry about. The pseudo-issue is a decoy because we are ashamed to admit to ourselves and/or to the other person what the real source of our anger is. For example, a man comes home from work three hours late because he attended an office party. His wife expresses anger at him because it is obvious that he has been drinking, and he could have gotten himself killed driving home. At first glance, the wife's anger appears to stem from her concern about her husband's safety. But the real issue, the "hidden agenda," is that she is angry because: (a) he expects her to cook dinner after she is finished cooking for the family—she feels *she* has to pay for *him* having a good time: (b) he was having fun while she was home cooking and washing dishes for the children; (c) he probably was flirting with the women who were at the party. But, because the wife does not want to appear "petty," "selfish," "jealous," or "overprotective," she denies possibly to herself and certainly to her husband that she has any of these feelings. The issue will not be successfully resolved because these two people are not attending to the real issue. The argument will go on for hours about how much

he had or didn't have to drink and what a capable driver he is or is not. The wife's fears, hurts, and angers will remain and sabotage communication between them for several days. If she had communicated the real issue, there would have been no more "heat," and a better understanding and feeling would have been the result.

6. *Express the anger constructively.* A person can be furious at another and still communicate the anger constructively. A constructive framework is: "I care far too much about our relationship not to share with you what I'm feeling." There are three common destructive stratagems in expressing anger. One is "psychological name-calling." Epithets such as: "You're so stupid ... insensitive ... immature ... selfish ... arrogant ... neurotic ... hostile ... defensive ..." are unlikely to set a comfortable atmosphere to discuss the issue at hand. The issue will become secondary to the argument over the derogatory labels.

A second destructive stratagem is to accuse the other person of having negative motives. For example: "You kept me waiting on purpose!" "You're just trying to make me jealous!" "You wanted to appear more intelligent than me." "You're just using me." It is legitimate to try to discover why a person acted in the way he did, but it is far better to *explore* the motives with the person rather than to prematurely *diagnose* them.

A third destructive stratagem is "going for the high ground." This means seeking some unfair leverage over the other person in order to win the argument rather than to resolve the problem. Some examples of "high ground" statements are:

"All our friends feel the same negative way as I do about you."

"Your problem is that you were an only child."

"If you understood more about human behavior, you wouldn't...."

"Of course, you're a man [woman]; you wouldn't understand."

"Wait until you get out in the real world, you'll see things differently."

None of these responses has a thing to do with any issue being discussed. If I'm angry at you, that's all that matters. Any of the sentiments expressed above are extraneous and irrelevant.

Constructive communication of anger means that honest discussion and even fighting can occur without one or the other person attempting to damage the other. The underlying principle is "We're both good people; let's resolve this in a positive way."

The actual difficulty involved in putting these principles into practice lies halfway between how simple it looks on paper and how impossible it looks in the midst of intense anger. But, like anything, it takes practice. After a time, one progresses from "doing it by the numbers" to a fluid, spontaneous expression without even being consciously aware of the traps that have been successfully avoided. When one reaches this point, anger no longer is frightening, but becomes a familiar tool for growth.

Reflection Questions

1. What is my favorite rationalization for not expressing anger. Why do I use it?

2. What one person in my life can make me the most angry? Why? How can I handle the situation better?

3. When I collect "anger stamps," what is the prize I usually cash them in for?

4. Who is the one person in my life to whom I could never say "I'm angry with you"? Why?

5. Of the three destructive stratagems (name calling; accusing of negative motives; going for high ground), which one am I likely to use? What steps can I take to change it?

Thoughts to Contemplate

1. Anger may have produced more good in society than love.

2. I have never heard of a person dying or falling to pieces when constructive anger has been shared with him.

3. The vast majority of marriages are destroyed because of the partners' inability to express constructive an-

ger. These marriages didn't blow up; they merely died out.

4. Many people have been taught that one either loves or hates—and if you hate, automatically it means you don't love the person.

5. The depressed person has been taught that it is not all right to feel anger toward a loved one, but it is all right to feel anger toward life or toward oneself.

5

UNDERSTANDING GUILT

Guilt is an often overlooked emotion, but, when used destructively, it can do as much damage as fear and anger when they are handled poorly. The more we can understand the dynamics of guilt, the more free we shall become both personally and interpersonally. This chapter will discuss three dimensions of guilt: personal guilt, guilt in marriage and parenthood, and controlling others with guilt.

PERSONAL GUILT

Guilt is the feeling of discomfort or shame that we experience when we have done something that we consider wrong, bad, or immoral. Guilt can be a help or a hindrance to growth.

Guilt is a help when it is healthy, i.e., when it is appropriate and when it initiates atonement. For example, if I have purposely placed another in a negative light, it is appropriate that I feel guilty. If this guilt motivates me to undo the harm that I have done and make the changes in my behavior that insure that I will not repeat this harm, the guilt is healthy and has acted as a catalyst to healing.

Healthy guilt is to the psyche (soul) what pain is to the body: an indication that something is wrong. When properly acknowledged and used, guilt is an important instrument in our growth.

Guilt is a hindrance when it is unhealthy, i.e., when it is inappropriate or when it fails to initiate atonement. If I feel guilty about my plans to marry a woman because my parents disapprove of her, I have two choices. I can break off the relationship to reduce my guilt, or I can marry her and feel a continuing guilt. In either case, my inappropriate guilt is damaging to myself and to others.

Guilt, both appropriate and inappropriate, is also a hindrance if it does not initiate atonement. For example, we can merely wallow in guilt—feel guilty but do nothing about it. Or we can push guilt out of awareness, which often causes behavioral symptoms.

The discussion that follows will explain some principles of personal guilt. By understanding them, we can make guilt work for us instead of against us.

The Dimensions of Guilt

We often view guilt as having only one dimension. This oversimplification creates a good deal of confusion and misunderstanding about the nature of guilt. In fact, there are three different dimensions to guilt: social guilt, theological guilt, and psychological guilt. The distinction between these dimensions is not merely of theoretical importance. The particular type of guilt determines the particular type of atonement necessary for growth and guilt reduction.

Social Guilt. Social guilt stems from behaving in a way that is injurious to another person. Its basis is the social dimension of our conscience that tells us that there are certain ways we *should* behave to help our fellowman, and there are certain things we *should not do* because they are harmful to others. For example, most people have learned that they should offer assistance to someone in distress and that they should not harm another's reputation unjustly. When we violate our social conscience, we experience a social guilt.

Theological Guilt. Theological guilt is experienced by religious people. It occurs when one behaves in a manner that places a distance between oneself and God. For example, an individual may feel that he should pray daily and, when he chooses not to do so, theological guilt results. A person who chooses to leave the religious life may feel a theological guilt. Or a person may sin and feel that this behavior has placed a distance between himself and God, causing him to experience a theological guilt.

Theological guilt occurs when we behave in a way that violates the religious dimension of our conscience. Non-religious people do not have a theological dimension and thus would not be subject to theological guilt.

Psychological guilt. Psychological guilt occurs when we violate our self-concept. Unlike social guilt, which is based on interpersonal relationships, psychological guilt is intrapersonal, i.e., it deals with one's relationship with oneself. For example, if part of my self-concept is that I am intelligent, the guilt I will feel when I do poorly on an examination will be psychological guilt. If I perceive myself as a good athlete and drop what could have been a touchdown pass, I will feel guilty. I may not recognize these feelings as guilt, but I can recognize the results of the guilt. On receiving a poor grade, I may force myself to study all weekend to punish myself. On dropping the potential touchdown pass, I slam my fist into the turf, causing myself pain.

The same situation can also occur when a person has a *negative* self-concept. If I perceive myself as stupid and get a good grade on a test, I feel psychological guilt because I violated my self-concept. To reduce the guilt, I exclaim: "I didn't deserve it—I just lucked out" or "The teacher felt sorry for me and wanted to motivate me." Paradoxically, the more successful this person is, the more guilt he experiences. Sometimes this individual unconsciously sets up failure in order to avoid the guilt produced by success.

These three kinds of guilt may be mutually inclusive or mutually exclusive. I may unjustly punish my son and hurt him deeply. As a result I could experience all three kinds of guilt stemming from this one act. A particular person could quit a job, feeling social guilt that he let down the boss, but experience neither theological nor psychological guilt. Another person could question God's existence and experience theological guilt, but feel no social or psychological guilt. A third person could fail an examination and experience psychological guilt, but not social or theological guilt.

The more we can recognize the differences in the three dimensions of guilt, the more we can use guilt as a tool for growth rather than merely as an uncomfortable feeling which should be quickly eliminated.

Each of the three types of guilt can be *conscious* or *unconscious.* Conscious guilt is that of which we are aware. I cheated on an examination, and I know I feel "badly," "ashamed," "not proud of myself." Being conscious of guilt is the necessary first step in using it to grow.

When guilt is intercepted and hidden before it reaches awareness, it cannot be used as an instrument for growth because for all practical purposes it doesn't exist.

It is also important to realize that a person can experience guilt, sometimes great guilt, as a result of having thoughts or feelings that the individual views as bad. In other words, one need not perform an action to feel guilty.

Guilt may be so great that the person represses the thought, feeling, *and* the accompanying guilt. When this causes behavioral symptoms of guilt, the person can honestly say: "I haven't done a thing I should feel guilty about, nor have I thoughts or feelings that would cause guilt." Everything has been pushed "underground." The challenge in this situation is to delve into the possibility that a person does feel anger or sexual feelings of which he is unaware, since most guilt can be traced to those two areas.

For people who are conscious of the thoughts and feelings that are causing guilt, it is helpful to discover what these thoughts and feelings mean. When the cause is found, the person can work on it, thus reducing or eliminating the source of guilt.

It is necessary to understand that often we should not feel guilt about our thoughts and feelings. Negative thoughts and feelings are safety valves that allow the "steam of stress" to escape harmlessly before it gets turned into actual behavior. As human beings, we will always have thoughts or feelings that we would not wish published in a newspaper. To feel guilty about them turns something into a problem when it is merely a part of human nature.

The following are ten signs that indicate the possibility of the presence of unconscious guilt. It is not necessarily true that unconscious guilt is the *sole* cause for many of these behaviors, but, when it is not the sole cause, it is a significant cause or the main cause.

1. The conviction that there is something wrong with oneself. Despite repeated reassurances to the contrary, a person may feel there is something physically or emotionally wrong with him. Physically, he may feel that a terminal ailment is present, or a venereal disease, or an unpleasant odor. Emotionally, the person may feel that he is losing his mind, is perverted or deviant in some way, unlovable, inferior, ugly, or worthless. Although there may be no basis in reality for any of these perceptions, the individual clings to them and tortures himself with them as a way of atoning for something that has been thought, felt, committed, or contemplated.

2. Addictions. Alcoholism, drug addiction, gambling, food addiction, and work addiction all have one thing in common: they deprive the individual of joy (love, warmth, affection). It is as if the individual's conscience is saying: "You don't deserve to enjoy life because of the evil things you have done or the immoral person that you are."

3. Indecisiveness. As long as a person allows himself to remain on the "horns of a dilemma," two things are happening. First, the person experiences a good deal of tension, and, secondly, he remains in an "emotional limbo" with regard to getting needs met in the particular situation. For example, the more I struggle with the decision to either marry or attend graduate school, the longer I am doing neither. This is self-depriving behavior common in guilty people who don't realize that they are guilty. These individuals think the problem is that they can't make decisions, and they often fool "helpers" into aiding them in the decision-making process when it is often a symptom of a guilt problem.

4. Creating disappointment. This is the "Is that all there
is?" syndrome. These individuals are always looking forward to some happiness and, when they reach it, they are
disappointed. The grass is always greener someplace else:
college will be great, but it is not; graduate school will be
better, but it's worse; marriage will be "super," but it's a
"drag"; retirement will be fun, but it's a bore.

5. Psychosomatic or hypochondriacal symptoms. Psychosomatic symptoms are real, physical symptoms that are
caused more by psychological factors than by physical
ones. Hypochondriacal symptoms are physical complaints that are imagined or are real but magnified.
When such symptoms are caused by unconscious guilt,
pain is very frequently part of the symptomology. Migraine headaches, rheumatoid arthritis, low back pain,
neck pain, inordinate menstrual pain (dysmenorrhea) often have unresolved guilt as a significant dynamic. Some
psychosomatic symptoms not only cause physical pain
but *psychological* pain as well; e.g., sexual impotence or
frigidity, some types of colitis and gastritis, and skin
rashes can be sources of embarrassment.

It is interesting to note that these symptoms often get
worse just prior to some event that a person is looking forward to enjoying.

6. Overdriven needs: To be perfect. The perfectionist sets
unattainable goals for himself and others. Consequently,
he is continually disappointed. No matter how hard he
tries, and how well he does, he is often left with the feeling "But I should have done better." This taints his feelings of success. For the same reason, others frequently
"disappoint" the person when they turn out to be more
real than ideal. On the deepest level, this individual's real
goal is not to be perfect; it is to feel disappointed.

To assume inordinate obligations. This person manages to assume obligations of a type or variety that effectively prevent enjoyment of life. Under the rationalization of being "responsible" or "Christian," this individual
ties himself into responsibilities that are, in reality, either not necessary to assume or are required only in part.
Throughout life, this person laments: "If only I didn't

have to stay with my parents, I could have a family of my own"; or "If only I didn't have to support my sister, we'd have enough money to do something we'd really enjoy."

To worry. This person moves from one crisis to another. The solution of each problem only opens the way for two more. This individual creates worry when none is appropriate. The more a situation should be cause for enjoyment, the more the person worries right through it. As one person put it: "I've worried right through the 'happiest' days of my life." The problem these individuals face isn't that they "worry too much"—it's that they don't feel they deserve to enjoy life.

7. *Habitually joining losing causes.* This behavior occurs in friendships, marriage, business ventures, political causes, etc. It is the "signing up for failure" syndrome. Examples of this include: the man who buys a restaurant which has failed under the last four managements; the woman who marries an alcoholic with the expectation of curing him with her love; the student who goes to a non-accredited law school, "knowing" that it will become accredited before he graduates; the man who marries a twice-divorced woman with three children even though he has known her for only six months. Each failure is met with surprise, even though close friends and relatives saw the "handwriting on the wall" from the start.

8. *Snatching defeat from the jaws of victory.* This type of individual does well until the very end and then manages to self-destruct. Examples of this behavior can be seen in many areas of life: the student who has an "A" going into the final examination and doesn't show up for the test; the person who, a week before he is to be promoted at work, suddenly decides to be "honest" and let his bosses know all his negative feelings toward them; the job applicant who is doing well in the interview and, as it is terminating, makes a smart-aleck remark that undoes the previous fifty minutes of good impressions.

9. *"Unthinking" behavior.* This is saying to someone you have no particular reason to trust—or every reason to *distrust:* "Please don't tell another soul but...." Uncon-

sciously, you *know* this person is going to broadcast the situation to the world to your serious disadvantage.

This is a girl who, though she knows better, allows herself to get pregnant before marriage.

This is the politician who publicly makes a self-defeating statement, even though he "knows better."

It is the student who forgets to hand in an important paper on the date it is due.

It is the person who is "accident" prone because he is so "distracted" by other things.

10. Religiosity. This is an unhealthy type of religious sentiment that has several characteristics. The relevant characteristic here is that religion is used in a way that creates unhappiness, bitterness, and resentment within the person. There is a legitimate place in healthy religion for suffering, self-denial, and choosing to live in difficult situations. When these are healthy behaviors, the person feels good within himself and good, or at least neutral, toward others. But some people use religion as an excuse to suffer and to be unhappy. This is motivated not by a positive attitude toward God but by a negative, guilt-ridden attitude toward oneself. This mentality is seen in the statement: "I'm not on earth to be happy, and if I'm not happy, you'd better not be happy either." So, when suffering leads to resentment rather than to love, it is a symptom of religiosity and unresolved guilt.

The common theme that runs through these guilt indicators is that the individual with unconscious, unatoned guilt spoils things for himself. If there is a good deal of such guilt, the person will behave in self-defeating ways, and large amounts of guilt will lead the individual to behave in self-destructive ways. It is as if the psyche is saying to the person "You can't get away with your misbehavior. If someone else doesn't punish you, then I will see to it that you will punish yourself."

In summary, it is important to understand each dimension of guilt, so that we can atone for it effectively. When we are aware that we are guilty and what we are guilty about, atonement will be easier. When we force the guilt "underground," it will surface in one or more of the ten indicators of guilt that were mentioned. We can use these indicators as a sign that we are feeling guilty about *something* and begin the process of attempting to discover the source of guilt.

Dealing Constructively with Guilt

Two basic principles underlie the process of constructively dealing with guilt. The first is that whenever we violate our social, theological, or psychological values we will experience guilt. This is true whether our values are reasonable or unreasonable and whether the guilt is conscious or unconscious.

The second principle is that when we do experience guilt, one of three things is going to happen to the guilt: The guilt will be used as an instrument of growth; the guilt will lodge itself in our psyche causing agitation; or the guilt will be pushed out of awareness so that consciously little discomfort is felt but the smouldering guilt will cause behavior symptoms (guilt-indicators).

From these two principles we can evolve a process of handling guilt in a constructive way. The process includes three steps:

1. Acknowledge the guilt feeling. This entails a person admitting: "I feel guilty." This is sometimes difficult for two reasons. One is that guilt sometimes hides beneath other emotions. A person may say: "I don't feel guilty—I feel depressed" or "I don't feel guilty—I feel ashamed," or "I don't feel guilty—I feel stupid." But once we are aware that guilt can camouflage itself with other emotions, we are in a better position to ferret it out.

Secondly, getting in touch with guilt is difficult at times because defense mechanisms have buried it. If the guilt is deeply buried, it will require professional help to unearth it. But if it is not deeply buried, it can be discovered with some introspection or by using guilt indicators as clues and "working backward." For example, a person may discover a cause-effect relationship between becoming disenchanted with work (a possible guilt indicator) and having unjustly won a promotion. So, even though this person had not connected the promotion with the guilt, it now appears that there is a real relationship.

2. Discern whether the guilt is appropriate or inappropriate. Guilt can be inappropriate in two ways. First, inappropriate guilt can stem from unreasonable values. Unreasonable values are those that are so broad that they are either unrealistic or unhealthy. Some common unrealistic moral values are:

"It is wrong to express anger." This value is inappropriate because there are times when it is not only morally correct to express anger, but it would be morally wrong *not* to express it.

"It is right to be obedient." The rightness of obedience depends upon the motives for being obedient and the moral growth or moral decline that accrues from the obedience.

"It is uncharitable to hurt another." It is uncharitable to be destructive to another, but hurting is charitable when it is a constructive and necessary part of the growing and healing process.

"Sex is sinful." Sex at times can be sinful, but just as often sex can be a good, beautiful, and spiritual experience.

"Breaking a promise is immoral." The morality of keeping a promise depends upon the motives underlying the promise, the spirit of the promise, and the moral good or harm that follows from the promise.

"Getting needs met is selfish." Meeting one's needs by damaging another person is selfish and wrong. Meeting one's needs in a healthy spirit of give-and-take is essential for mutual growth.

The second way that guilt can be inappropriate is when it is displaced or inordinately intense. An example of displaced guilt is a woman who feels she should invite her aging mother to live with her family but does not do so because of all the problems it will cause. Her "head" tells her that the decision is wise, but her heart suffers a deep and abiding guilt. The real cause of her guilt, however, is not the decision regarding her mother. The true source of guilt is that deep down, the woman feels she has not been a good wife. She feels that she has let her husband down as a source of attention, warmth, pleasure, and support, and this is her deepest guilt. But she finds it easier to displace the guilt from not being a good wife to that of not being a gracious daughter. This woman must separate her true guilt from her displaced, inappropriate guilt. She must then atone for the true guilt, and this will help her let go of the inappropriate guilt.

An example of inordinately intense guilt is a college student who cheats on an exam and feels great and prolonged guilt, totally out of proportion to the situation. In reality, the student has an added source of guilt—a deeper, hidden guilt because he has treated his girlfriend in abusive ways. Rather than face this source of guilt, he feels inappropriately intense in his guilt regarding the cheating. This man must separate the two true guilts— the one stemming from his treatment of his girlfriend and that stemming from cheating on the exam. He must then atone for each separately.

3. Atone for true guilt. Once true, appropriate guilt is isolated, it must be atoned for or it will continue to cause unconscious self-atonement, which is always destructive not only to the guilty person but often to innocent bystanders.

The purpose of guilt is to create a state of discomfort that will motivate a person to change the guilt-producing behavior. When a person misbehaves, he separates himself from the person damaged by the misbehavior, and he separates himself from himself. The latter is done by tainting a part of his self-concept so that it clashes with the loving parts of his self. Atonement means literally "at-one-ment," i.e., making oneself "one" with the person who was damaged and making the person "one" with himself.

Psychological atonement includes three behaviors. First, the individual must do whatever possible to rectify the damage to the other person. How this is done depends upon the kind of damage. If another person's reputation has been damaged, the situation must be righted. If the person cheated another out of some monies or goods, they must be returned. If the person damaged another's self-concept or virtue, attempts must be made to heal the wounds.

Second, the individual must discover *why* he behaved in a damaging way and take steps to prevent the repetition of such behavior. Merely apologizing for the misbehavior does nothing to prevent its future occurrence. For example, if a college student cheats on an examination, he must not only report this to the professor in fairness to the other students who would be negatively affected by the cheating, but he must discover what fears and needs caused him to cheat. Then, he can take the appropriate steps to deal with those fears and needs so that they will not cause similar behavior in the future.

Third, the atonement must be directly related to the misbehavior. For example, if a boss cheats his employees out of a total of $5,000 over the year, he must return the money in one form or another to the employees. Donating $1,000 to charity or a church at Christmas time is not appropriate atonement because he didn't take the money from charity or the church, and he still is making $4,000 on the deal.

These three elements of atonement are not important because they meet some external prescription for atonement. The point is that while we can fool our conscious self, we cannot fool our deeper self. And, until the deeper self has good reason to feel "at one," we will punish ourselves in ways that are damaging to ourselves and possibly to others.

At times, direct atonement may be damaging or impossible. For example, if a man has been unfaithful to his wife, it may do permanent damage to their relationship if he shares this information with her. In this case, atonement can be done indirectly. Instead of discussing the situation directly with his wife, the man can discover what the offending behavior means. Is there something lacking in his marriage emotionally or sexually? Was his behavior an attempt to reaffirm his own attractiveness or prowess and, if so, what does he feel he lacks? Was his behavior an indirect way of expressing anger at his wife? If so, what is the source of the anger, and how can it be used to help rather than to hinder the marriage?

Sometimes direct atonement is impossible, for example, when the person damaged is deceased. In this case, the atonement can be directed at others who are in need of help as a way of bettering the human condition.

In summary, two points should be remembered. One is that the purpose of atonement is not to relieve guilt to make the guilty person feel better. This is pseudo-atonement done for selfish reasons. The purpose of atonement is to heal the person who was damaged and to free the love within the guilty person that has been tamped down by the guilt.

Secondly, guilt, like any difficult emotion, does not disappear merely because it is dealt with constructively. Therefore, it is more correct to speak in terms of *reducing* guilt rather than *erasing* it. But, hopefully, the guilt can be reduced to tolerable limits so that it does not significantly interfere with one's life.

Of course, the best approach to guilt is to refrain from behaving in ways that will produce guilt. But, being human, we will violate our values, and, when we do, we can turn the event into an enriching experience, thus becoming stronger than we ever were.

GUILT IN MARRIAGE AND PARENTHOOD

A certain number of guilts seem to be indigenous to every state in life, because we often fail to distinguish between what is ideal and what is normal. When we fall short of the ideal in our particular state in life, we often feel guilty.

Learning to accept normal imperfections without discarding our ideals will reduce our inappropriate guilt. What appropriate guilt remains can be used to grow closer to the ideals of our particular state in life.

The Guilts of Marriage

The following sentiments often produce conscious or unconscious guilt in married people.

1. "Sometimes I wish I were still single." By its nature marriage contains constraints that are not present in the single life. No matter how much we love our spouse there are times when it would be nice to come and go as we please; to receive romantic affirmation from more than one person; to have more financial freedom; and to work half as hard as a married person must. This feeling is perfectly normal (unless it is frequent) and need not be met with alarm or guilt. It's part of being a normal human being.

2. *"Sometimes I feel closer to my children than to my spouse."* This is very common and understandable. Children are ordinarily much more "lovable" than adults. Children are cute, adore their parents, are entirely reliant on their parents, and do not possess an adult capacity to hurt. Children are safer than adults.

It is not uncommon that when tensions build between spouses, one or the other gravitates toward a child to get some love and reassurance. This does not mean that one loves his or her children more than one's spouse. It simply means that sometimes children are "easier" to love than adults, and it should not be a source of guilt.

3. *"Sometimes I feel that I could be a better sexual partner."* With the emphasis placed on sexual performance in our society, there are few people who don't feel they are disappointing a spouse sexually at one time or another. When a person is tired, upset, distracted, worried, or ill, sexual behavior will often be unsatisfying to both partners.

Feeling guilt about it will only add to the upset and worry and continue to create unfulfilling sex. It is more realistic to accept the fact that sexual behavior is like any other kind of behavior. Sometimes things go very well; sometimes they go very poorly; and most of the time they fall someplace in the middle.

The Guilts of Parenthood

Our society has created even more myths about parenthood than it has about marriage. As one parent put it only half-facetiously: "When I'm with my children I ask myself, 'Is what we're doing now something that Norman Rockwell would want to paint?' If the answer is 'no,' then I change it." The ideals of being a "good parent" are so unrealistic that many parents continuously feel guilty about their relationships with their children.

The following are some common sources of guilt in parenthood that are often magnified out of proportion.

1. "I don't spend enough time with my children." In one sense, *no* parents spend enough time with their children. On the other hand, if we spent as much time as we feel we "should," we would raise very overprotected and dependent children.

Often it is not the quantity of time that we spend with our child, but the *quality* of the time that is important. Sometimes it is very difficult to spend time with children. No matter how much we love our children, and no matter how beautiful they are, they are still human beings. And human beings can be boring, demanding, insensitive, irritable, selfish, and tedious. When one has had to deal with human beings all day, especially under difficult circumstances, sometimes the last thing one can tolerate is being with small human beings. This is perfectly normal and understandable, just as there are times when children don't want to be near their parents.

Human beings also have a limited amount of energy, and adults seem to have about half as much as children do. So, when massive amounts of energy have been expended on the necessary transactions of daily existence, sometimes there is no more energy left for the children. It is better to relax and become rejuvenated than to force oneself to spend "duty time" with children so as not to feel guilty.

2. "Sometimes I wish we hadn't had children." This is a difficult feeling because it goes against everything that is good and holy. Nevertheless, if parents are honest with themselves, they will admit there are times when they fantasize how nice it would be just to have each other and some precious time for quiet and relaxation.

This fantasy is more likely to occur when the children are causing a lot of tension; when they are self-centered; or when their orthodontist's bill cancels a vacation. This does not negate the beauty of children. But children are a stress, and the more children there are and the more conscientious the parents are, the more stress is present.

It is human to want to rid oneself of stress. It is more appropriate to allow oneself these occasional feelings, to understand them, and even to see some humor in them. To feel guilty and ashamed of this feeling only devalues one's self-concept, and this, in turn, makes the person a less effective parent.

3. *"Sometimes I really disappoint my children."* Every parent is, at one time or another, in one way or another, going to disappoint his or her children. This is true for two reasons. One cause is that children, because they are children, have *unrealistic* expectations of their parents. Parents are supposed to be "better than perfect." They are supposed to know everything; to be able to do anything; never to be confused; and never to make a mistake. Some parents get caught in this bind and try to balance on the pedestal. When they fall, they feel badly that they were not the god their children expected them to be.

Secondly, children also have *realistic* expectations of their parents. Yet, there are times when even the best of parents will not be able to meet a realistic expectation. This is because it is normal for human beings to fail at times to live up to both their own realistic expectations and those of others.

If parents never disappointed their children, what an unrealistic preparation this would be for meeting the real world. Children must learn at an early age how to handle disappointment. When they discover that their parents aren't perfect, then the children are freed from having to be perfect. Later, when the children discover that their parents are not only human but *very* human, they are freed to accept the weaker parts of their own humanity. And, when they discover that even people whom they love very much can disappoint them, then they are freed to genuinely love.

So, when we sometimes disappoint our children, we can recognize that it is a healthy preparation for life, and we need not feel guilty for that.

The more we can appreciate the limitations of our humanity, the more realistic our expectations of ourselves will be. We will frequently experience the tension between the ideal that we feel we "should" be and the reality that we are. If we allow the tension to remain in its original form, we can use it to diminish the gap between the ideal and the real. But, if we convert the tension into guilt, it will only lengthen the gap in the long run.

CONTROLLING OTHERS WITH GUILT

One of the more effective ways to control others—to get them to do what we want—is to foster guilt in them. Guilt can be used as an "electric prod" to keep others behaving as we wish. But outside of the purely pragmatic benefit of temporarily forcing another to do what we want, fostered guilt has no psychological value. In fact, it evokes so much fear, resentment, and loss of self-esteem that the person will regress rather than grow as a result of the guilt-evoking experience.

This principle is true even when we manipulate another away from a wrong decision and into a correct one. There is no virtue in using immoral means (usurping free will) to coerce another into behaving "morally." People do not learn through coercion but through inculcating a self-concept that will cause them to select behaviors that are good for themselves and those around them.

The question to ask ourselves is not: "Do I control others by fostering guilt?" because the answer to that question is "yes." Guilt induction is so pervasive in our society that it is a part of all of us, whether we realize it or not. The question is: "How can I recognize when I am fostering guilt in another so that I can stop it and communicate my needs in a more open and helpful way?"

An understanding of the following "guilt-grabbers" can help us gain some insight into our own behavior and that of others.

Guilt-grabbers: Parents Grab Children

1. "After all we've done for you. . . . " The idea here is that since the parents "slaved for their children" the least the children can do is to dedicate the rest of their lives meeting the parents' needs. But children are not "investments," and their purpose in life is not to be a "dividend." The only healthy reason for parents to work hard is so that *both* the parents *and* the children will have more material, emotional, and moral choices in life. Good parents work to allow their children freedom to live their own lives.

2. "Your brothers and sisters know how to show appreciation." The "grabber" here is couched in statements such as: "Your sister gave up her weekend to stay with me and take me shopping, and your brother spent four nights last week putting in cabinets for me. I certainly missed *you*—have you been all right?" The message here is "How did you turn out so different from your loving brothers and sisters?" To be viewed as "loving and equal" and, therefore, avoid guilt, this son or daughter will have to spend a great deal more time with his or her parents, regardless of his or her own needs or wishes.

3. *"You're ruining our lives."* This grabber is used by parents whose lives were not very happy to begin with, so they seek an outside source to blame. A common subtheme of this grabber is: "You're breaking your mother's [father's] heart." To return happiness to the parents' lives, all the son or daughter must do is make them happy according to their definition of happiness. Then all will be well—at least until the son or daughter does something else that grossly displeases the parents.

Guilt-grabbers: Children Grab Parents

1. *"Why did you have children, anyway?"* For maximum effect, this should be asked in a matter-of-fact, non-hostile way. The idea here is that the child feels that the parents spend too much time with each other and not enough time with the child. The hidden question is: "If you think spending time with me is such a drag, why didn't you remain childless and just enjoy yourselves?" The parents are supposed to feel guilty for "neglecting" the child. The parents can show "good faith" by spending less time with each other, by staying home all the time, and by being at the beck and call of the child.

2. *"Why are you so old-fashioned?"* The word "old-fashioned" may be substituted for by "uptight," "distrustful," "conservative," "insecure," "overprotective," or "out-of-it." This grabber is seen in comments such as: "Jim's father trusts him. He's letting him get a driver's license, and he's only sixteen." Or "Cathy's mom is really understanding. She lets Cathy stay out until midnight on Friday nights." To qualify as being "modern," "understanding," and "neat," all the parents have to do is let their children do whatever they please. Until then, these parents are ex-

pected to feel guilty for being less good parents than their neighbors.

3. *"Why didn't you prepare me better for life?"* This is a grabber used by late adolescents and young adults. The son or daughter is experiencing problems with school, work, love, or relationships, and finds the parents to be an easy scapegoat. As long as these problems are the "parents' fault," the son or daughter does not have to change anything about his or her behavior. Parents who get hooked by this grabber will do anything to help their child solve the problem. They give money, lodging, and anything else as a way of "making up for past sins." Of course, the more the parents try to assuage the child, the more they are actually feeding into the child's problems by helping him avoid facing reality and accepting the consequences of his behavior.

Other Guilt-grabbers

The following "grabbers" are often used between adults.

1. *"You love them more than me."* This is said by a person who equates love with dependence: "If you love me you will need me as much as I need you." This person is incapable of realizing that one person can deeply love another and yet choose to get some needs met by someone else. This individual offers the ultimatum: "It's me or them—take your choice."

The recipient of the grabber is on the sharp horns of a dilemma. If the individual "gives in" and attempts to get all needs met with this one person, it will create great frustration and resentment because no one person can meet all the significant needs of another. If the individual insists in maintaining other meaningful relationships, he can feel guilty for being "selfish," "exploitive," and "rejecting."

2. *"But I had my heart set on it."* This is usually said by someone who never told the other person what his "heart was set on" until the last minute.

A husband comes home after a difficult day at the office and just wants to relax and have a quiet dinner. His wife meets him with: "Dear, let's go out to a restaurant for dinner. Looking forward to going out tonight got me through the day."

A husband says: "Can I spend half our vacation money on that set of golf clubs? I've had my heart set on those particular clubs since I was a boy."

A friend says: "When you visit Boston you must stay with my parents for the week. It's been my dream that you get to know each other."

The real message in these examples is: "You mean you would break my heart by not doing what I want?" The recipient of the "grabber" is going to either "break a heart" and feel guilty, or accede to the wishes of the other person and be miserable.

3. *"What are my friends going to think of me?"* The message here is: "If you don't do what I want, I will look stupid in front of my friends—they'll lose respect for me or ridicule me."

A husband wants to buy a very expensive car. His wife feels that it is a waste of money. The husband says: "What do you think my clients think of me when I have to drive around in this clunk I have now?"

A wife says: "Dear, couldn't we remodel the downstairs? I just feel so ashamed to invite my friends over anymore."

An engaged person says: "You can't break up with me. I'll never be able to face my parents and friends again if you do."

In each example, the recipient of the "grab" is faced with the guilt that comes from "publicly humiliating" someone he loves or with giving into an unrealistic demand.

Unfortunately, guilt induction is a part of everyday life and is almost habitual with most of us. Hardly a day passes when we don't set up some situation so that another person will feel guilty if he doesn't do what we want. If there is one sign of true love, it is allowing another person to function freely in our presence.

Guilt is an ever-present emotion. We always seem to be experiencing some personal guilt, feeling guilt as a part of a life role, or being controlled or controlling others with guilt. The more we can understand the nature of guilt and be aware of its traps, the more we can use guilt as an instrument of growth. Atoning for personal guilt can heal us and make us stronger than ever. Understanding the guilts of marriage and parenthood should relieve us of much unnecessary guilt. Refusing to use guilt as a manipulative instrument or to be manipulated by it will significantly reduce the amount of unnecessary tension in our lives.

Reflection Questions

1. We all feel guilty about something. What have I done in my life that generated the most guilt? How well have I atoned for it?

2. What is the last thing I did that caused me to feel psychological guilt? How did I handle the guilt?

3. Is there something I feel guilty about that my head tells me I shouldn't feel guilty about? If so, where is the true guilt coming from?

4. Of the ten guilt indicators, which one best describes where my unatoned guilt goes?

5. Everyone uses guilt to a greater or lesser degree to manipulate others. In which areas of behavior am I most likely to do this?

Thoughts to Contemplate

1. Guilt is to the psyche what pain is to the body: an indicator that something is wrong.

2. The perfectionist sets unattainable goals for himself and others; consequently, he is continually disappointed.

3. The person who assumes inordinate obligations manages to assume obligations of a type or variety that effectively prevent enjoyment of life. Under the rationalization of being "responsible" or "Christian," this individual ties himself into responsibilities that are in reality either not necessary to assume or are required only in part.

4. Some people use religion as an excuse to suffer and to be unhappy. This is motivated not by a positive at-

titude toward God but by a negative, guilt-ridden attitude toward oneself.

5. Appropriate guilt must be atoned for or it will continue to cause unconscious self-atonement, which is always destructive not only to the guilty person but often to innocent bystanders.

6

WHO AM I?
KNOWING AND TRUSTING MYSELF

One very important, perhaps the most important, basis for mental and spiritual health is psychological identification. A person who has a good sense of self-identity lives life very differently than one whose self-identification is confused or unknown. The person who does not really know himself very well, even though he may be a very talented individual, is like an airplane pilot who can't navigate: he makes beautiful landings, but often at the wrong airports. Psychological identification is just a fancy way of naming the process that begins with the question "Who am I?"

WHAT ARE THE ELEMENTS OF SELF-IDENTITY?

Insight into needs. A person with good identification knows clearly what he needs to grow and to be happy. From the limitless ways in which a person can get security, love, and esteem needs met and meet them in others, this individual charts a very specific path which is congruent with his uniqueness.

Some people spend days or months shopping for just the right suit, but are very haphazard and ignorant about the ways in which they choose to get their psychological needs met. Individuals with good self-identification have a clear and accurate psychological map that, when followed, brings them to many good places. Other people have a clear but inaccurate psychological map which they confidently follow, but it's been plotted on false information. These individuals often end up in the wrong places, a situation they may not discover for many years, if ever. Still others have a confused, contradictory map that frequently causes them to run into stone walls or leads them to move in circles.

Some people, perhaps many people, choose a "contra-need" life-style, i.e., what they deeply need in life is not afforded them in their life style, while often the last thing they do need in life *is* present. For example, some people choose to marry when marriage is a contra-need for them. Other people choose marriage which fits their particular need system, but then choose to have children, which may mangle the need system and, consequently, be destructive to all members of the family. Still others choose to remain single, which for them may lead to premature psychological death.

Individuals may choose "contra-need" careers. Some people who have strong needs to be liked become police officers. Those who basically need to be creative may become secretaries, while those who need direction become self-employed. Many people who need continual encouragement choose to pursue middle-management careers in which they are criticized daily from above and from below. If any one of these people was in touch with his real needs and able to distinguish between what was strongly *needed* from what was superficially *wanted,* he could prevent a great deal of grief.

Insight into motives. A second part of knowing the answer to "Who am I?" is to be in touch with one's deeper motives. We all have two sets of motives: the ones we like in ourselves and those with which we feel uneasy. It is the latter that are usually deeper, because we don't like to acknowledge them.

For example, a man may coach Little League because he feels he can be a good influence on the young players. On a deeper level, he may also enjoy being a "boss" and having uncontested authority, because he has a job that deprives him of this opportunity. There is nothing wrong with this deeper motive. Problems will arise, however, if he denies this motive in himself. When parents want to help (share his authority—*dilute* his authority), his behavior toward them will be rejecting and confusing, even to him.

A person's behavior seldom flows from one motive. The vast majority of human behavior springs from at least two, if not an intricate complexity of, motives. We blithely say: "I married because I was in love"; or "I entered the religious life because I want to serve God"; or "I became a psychologist to help people." On a daily basis, we assure ourselves: "I know I'm hurting you, but it's for your own good"; or "I don't spend a lot of time with my children because I don't want them to become too dependent on me"; or "I'm doing this favor for you because I like you."

None of the above statements need be untrue. But in all of them it is very likely that there is more to the behavior than the self-soothing explanation. The deeper motives may be mixed. For example, maybe I *also* got married because I didn't want my wife to marry anyone else; because I was tired of doing my own shopping and cleaning; because it was a hassle dating somebody new all the time; because I wanted sex without feeling guilty; and because she adored me.

Most behavior, especially significant behavior, is attached to several motives; some are altruistic; some self-fulfilling; some selfish; some destructive. The more we are in touch with all our motives, the fewer problems will confront us and those around us.

Insight into strengths and weaknesses. When I participate in interviews of job candidates, my favorite question is: "Name three of your strengths and three of your weaknesses." The first part of this question sometimes causes consternation, but the second part *often* does. Some people can think of only one weakness, while others begin to describe a weakness, but before they are through, they have transformed it into a virtue. For example, an individual may state: "My main weakness is that I sometimes get depressed. And I get depressed because I want to do so much for people and there just isn't enough time." One job applicant pulled me aside after the interview and confided: "Gee, I couldn't think of a single weakness and had to make up one."

The person with weak identification says: "Oh, I know I have weaknesses; I'm no different from anyone else." But this is merely a token gesture to reality. In fact, this individual lives each day blissfully unaware of weaknesses and how they are causing problems for him and for others. It is not enough merely to know one's weaknesses, but by knowing them, the person can work to strengthen himself. If a known weakness cannot be strengthened, one's life can be planned so that the weakness is activated the least number of times.

It is equally important to recognize one's strengths. Some people contact me and wish to take tests that will tell them their strengths. Some of these individuals are over fifty years of age. Tests can tell someone his strengths in an academic way, but if an adult *needs* a test to tell him his *basic* strengths, his problem is a deeper one—he doesn't know himself as well as he should.

By being in touch with one's intellectual, social, emotional, and moral strengths and weaknesses, one can approach life with more confidence because one already knows the location of the "minefields" and how to avoid them.

Insight into one's purpose in life. This kind of purpose in life is a philosophical one. It is a theme that ties together the individual days in a person's life and makes them into an integral whole. Purpose in life is like the string that holds all the beads on a necklace together. It makes sense out of each day and out of a lifetime. Purpose in life is a goal that one is daily striving toward but can never meet because it is infinite. The person with good psychological identification knows *why* he is getting up each morning, and it is not just because he has to go to work.

A person with less strong psychological identification may have a material purpose in life; e.g., he wants to be a millionaire before he is thirty, or he wants to be president of a company. But there are no philosophical, deeper values involved. A person may lack even a material purpose in life. This individual lives only for what that day will bring him. It is as if he has a broken necklace and has beads scattered all over the place. Today he is going to the ball game, and tomorrow he is going to a nice restaurant for dinner. This is what gets him through the arduous parts of life. These people often remark: "What I do, I do well, but I don't know why I'm doing it." Often as these people approach middle and old age, they feel the effects of the existential vacuum in which they have been residing. To ward off the depression and anxiety caused by this awakening realization, they often seek more "beads" in life, unaware that it is the "string" that holds the beads together that is missing. They try new hobbies, develop new friends, buy more antiques, and join more clubs, but none of this seems to offer anything but temporary relief.

In summary, the person with good psychological self-identification can say the following four sentences:

"I know the specific needs that I must get met if I am to grow into a reasonably effective and happy individual and if I'm going to be able to help others be happy."

"I know what my real motives are. I know when I'm doing something to help myself, when I'm doing it to help another, and when I'm doing it to hurt another."

"I know my strengths and weaknesses and have consciously chosen paths in life that maximize my strengths and minimize my weaknesses."

"I know what I want to accomplish on earth and how to go about doing it. On my death bed I know what final question I want to ask myself, and I know the answer I'm going to give."

WHAT ARE SOME TYPICAL SIGNS OF IDENTITY WEAKNESS?

There are six typical behaviors that often indicate that a person is not in touch with his or her real self.

Emotional distance. This individual tends to live in a "psychological castle" with a large moat around it, and the drawbridge is seldom lowered to allow others to enter. One of the reasons for this is that the individual, at least unconsciously, does not want others to see the vacuum or confusion that hides beneath the facade. A common statement from such an individual is: "If I let people in, they may discover that the outside looks better than the inside.

"Distractability." This individual, often unbeknownst to him, actually creates a plethora of distractions so that he is protected from looking inward. He has so many friends, so many appointments, so many places to go, so many people to help. When he does have a precious little time to look in the psychological mirror and examine himself, he is too exhausted and lapses into a narcotic sleep.

Malleability. A person who lacks at least reasonable psychological self-identification is malleable, i.e., he can be easily sculpted by others. This individual gets his self-identity from other people. The most dramatic example of this is a young lady who sought advice from someone about her upcoming marriage and left the "counseling" session convinced she had a religious vocation.

Such individuals have little psychological substance. They are very suggestible and become what others want them to become. Unfortunately, this symptom is sometimes viewed as a virtue. People who are easily formed are seen as "cooperative," "obedient," and "flexible." They never make waves because they so readily blend with the terrain. Consequently, a psychological symptom is rewarded daily.

Difficulty with decisions. If a person does not know himself, then he doesn't know what's best for him or who he'll be tomorrow. This person worries: "Sure, today I want to get married, but what will I want next month—what will I want *next week?*" Because individuals with weak self-identification can become a different person each new day, they are rightly afraid to make decisions because they are likely to find that the decision that was made by one "self" will not fit the "self" of a week from now.

Over-identification with a role. This person confuses personal identification and role identification and makes them synonymous, the result being that the person *becomes* the role. An example of this trait was present in the old Marine Corps whose philosophy it was to tear down a recruit's personal identification and "make him into a Marine" (role identification). All Marines talked, ate, walked, thought, and slept like a Marine. If you talked to one Marine, there was no need to talk to another.

Many individuals define themselves by their role: "I'm a psychologist"; "I'm a priest"; "I'm Mrs. Smith"; "I'm a professional athlete." One of the problems with this attitude is that if the role loses status or is lost, then the person disintegrates as well. What happens to "Mrs. Smith" when Mr. Smith divorces her? What happens when the athlete is no longer able to play his sport? Role identification should be a thinner layer that lies on the much more substantial layer of personal identification. Then, if something goes wrong with the role, the person still knows very well who he is and what he is about.

Ethereality. Ethereal people glide around a few feet off the ground. They never seem to be quite "here." They appear to be listening to something else with one ear. They have a fragile, angelic quality that protects them from many of life's realities. They are seldom upset because they fly right over upsets. They flit away from responsibilities and skirt being known. Sometimes they are seen as beautiful, but the beauty is an illusion, similar to what occurs when the pink cheeks of a child are taken for an indication of health rather than a sign of the fever that is ravaging the body. Such individuals are so frightened of their deep attitudes and feelings that they dissociate themselves from themselves, thus giving them the "out of touch" aura.

WHAT CAUSES IDENTITY CONFUSION?

Identity confusion is a normal part of development. It is typical for adolescents to go through a period of identity confusion, and sometimes identity crisis. Adolescence occurs generally between the ages of twelve and twenty-two. However, adolescence is a developmental phase not necessarily constricted to an age range. For example, a person may go through adolescence between the ages of fifty and fifty-five. This happens because the individual was deprived of his adolescence during the more typical age range. Some people never experience adolescence, remaining pre-adolescent throughout life.

Identity confusion is the experience of **gradually** discovering who we no longer are, but not yet knowing who we are or want to become. This confusion is related to choosing a career, but it runs far deeper than that. It not only asks the question: "What will I *do* in life?" but also "*Who* will I *be* in life?"

A child's relationship with his parents is the main source (although not the sole source) of psychological identification. As parents or teachers it may be helpful for us to be aware of the pitfalls that would interfere with children developing a healthy sense of who they are.

Three types of parents who make healthy identification difficult in their children are:

1. Strong but split parents. This occurs when each parent is quite strong (*too* strong) and each possesses quite different attitudes, beliefs, and values regarding life. The child is caught in the middle. If the child imitates the father, he loses some of the mother's love and vice versa. Unconsciously, the child makes a deal. When the child is around one parent, he behaves in one way, and when the child is around the other parent, the behavior changes accordingly.

After twenty years of this, the young adult is psychologically half the mother and half the father. The child's own self got lost in the squeeze a decade previously.

2. Over-controlling parents. These parents feel that they possess *the* key to life and want to hand it down to their children. They are overly serious and have a rather rigid value system. They are extremely well-meaning, but equally misguided. They want their children to be "good, hardworking, religious, and successful" but at the expense of other equally important traits. These parents negatively value behaviors such as: relaxing ("wasting time"); having fun ("being childish"); being confused ("straying"); experimenting ("asking for trouble"); risk-taking ("foolish ventures"); being assertive ("bold"); being strong ("stubborn"); and being self-directing ("un-grateful").

Such children may never have a childhood or adoles-cence. They become "miniature adults" early in life and prematurely lock into a mode of behavior and a life role. Unfortunately, school and society reward this behavior because it is "more mature" than the behavior of the child's peers. On the momentum of this pseudo-maturity such children and adolescents often become class repre-sentatives, club leaders, and are regarded as outstanding graduates.

Sooner or later, however—often at middle-age—these people awaken to the fact that they became an image or an illusion and not a real person. It is at this point that they must begin to live the parts of their childhood and adolescence that they lost. Sometimes this necessitates only minor revisions in their lives, and sometimes it means a total revision of life-style. While worse things can occur in life, most of us would wish to prevent this from occurring in our children and students.

3. "Bartering" parents. These parents barter their love to gain the behavior they want from their children. The message is: "If you are who we want you to be, we will love you." The child learns very early that he had better become someone he isn't. The child must learn to behave happier, quieter, smarter, funnier, tougher, holier, more extroverted, complacent, athletic, attractive, or seductive. The child learns to sell his personality as a way of win-ning love and acceptance.

The bartered child grows into adulthood having sold off so much of himself and having borrowed so many traits from others that he may not have the slightest idea of his personal identity.

WHAT CAN BE DONE TO STRENGTHEN ONE'S SELF-IDENTIFICATION?

There are three areas which can help introduce an individual to himself and can strengthen one's sense of self.

1. Speak out. Often people state: "I don't like to say anything because I'm not sure what I feel." The answer to this is to say *something,* even if it is only "I'm not sure of what I feel"—because at least this is a start at plumbing one's depths.

Except for super-repressed people, most individuals are somewhat in touch with what they feel at any given moment. A voice within us says a variation of: "I like what's going on here"; or "I don't like what's going on here"; or "I'm confused with what's going on here." This should be articulated in a way that will invite discussion and feedback. But too often we decline the opportunity to grow, using rationalizations such as: "I'd sound stupid"; or "People would be shocked"; or "It would only cause more problems."

The relationship between speaking out and a sense of self is that when we actually hear what is going on within us, and when we get it reflected back to us in a mirror image, it provides an opportunity to say to ourselves: "This is what I am, and I like it"; or "This is who I am, and I don't like it." In the first case, we receive some positive reinforcement as to who we are. In the second example, we receive some information that can help us grow into who we'd like to become.

2. Try new things. One of the greatest enemies of self-identification is routine. When we do the same thing all the time, we become the same thing all the time. Our sense of self gets lulled to sleep by boredom; we become "automatic."

Trying new things can tap latent interests, abilities, needs, and values. It can also create stress which calls forth new ways of dealing with life. "New things" can be going back to school to take courses in an interesting subject. It can mean developing new hobbies. It can include joining groups for the purpose of bringing new people into one's life. It can encompass travelling, trying new ways of praying, working, or recreating. The most "blossoming forth" I've witnessed in people came from the ventilation of their life-style with new and different people or things.

3. Quiet time. Admittedly, it is difficult in today's world to find time for quiet, uninterrupted reflection. But it is very important to *make* time in order to reflect on all the external and internal data about ourselves that are continually flooding us.

We delude ourselves into thinking that such quiet time is a luxury, that there are so many more important things that must be accomplished. It is paradoxic that a person will religiously reserve a half-hour or an hour each night to read the newspaper to see what's happening in the world, but rarely will reserve the same amount of time to see what's happening inside him. Quiet time is the time to say to one's psyche (soul): "Now it's your chance to relate to me." During this time thoughts, feelings, and questions that were repressed during the day have permission to surface. The fears, hurts, angers, and guilts will surface along with the joys, happiness, warmth, and love.

BUT CAN I TRUST MYSELF?

Sometimes a person can work toward self-identification and still be hesitant in relating with oneself and with others. The basis for this feeling is a reluctance to trust oneself because one isn't *sure* of what will happen in any particular interaction. Yet, it is better to trust oneself and fail at times than to distrust oneself and, consequently, to fail all of the time. Developing self-trust is an attribute which is seldom discussed, and yet it is a very important element in knowing oneself and in relating with oneself and with others.

Many examples of self-distrust can be seen. A person who distrusts himself often seeks managers to direct him. He fails to distinguish between a manager who takes one rein, if not both reins, of a person's life and a consultant who shares information and feedback but allows the person to keep charge of both reins. Unfortunately, many people in the helping professions also fail to make the distinction between being a manager (which is almost always destructive, regardless of the rationalization) and being a consultant.

The self-distrusting person *wants* to be managed because he doubts his abilities and erroneously thinks that his management relieves him of the responsibility for where his life is taking him. Managers want to manage because this is how they have been taught to help people. In fact, some people feel that it is their moral responsibility to manage other people's lives. Managing is relatively simple because the self-distrusting person simply asks the questions, and the manager provides the answers.

A second sign of distrust of oneself occurs when the person tends to relate to others as if they were casting directors. As the manager tells people *what to do,* the casting director tells him *whom to be.* This self-distrusting person's approach to people is: "Just tell me whom you want me to be—what part you want me to play—and I'll do it." This person trusts his goodness and competence so little, he feels that whatever part someone assigns him will be better than playing out who he really is.

This is the chameleon effect in which a person changes his colors to fit the background. Often, the background changes several times a day, so the person becomes several different people each day. (This is quite different from changing superficial behavior to meet the appropriateness of a given situation.) The person becomes such a quick-change artist that after a while he is even fooling himself, to say nothing of confusing others.

Thirdly, the self-distrusting person may distrust others, including God. Unlike the person mentioned above who seems to trust *everybody* more than himself, this person works on the premise: "If I can't trust myself, I'm surely not going to trust anyone else." This person views others as potential mine-fields that could explode if he gets too close to them. "Explode" could mean: Reject the person, break a confidence, exploit the person, or even want to get emotionally close to the person. This person is often wary of people's motives: "Why is he being so nice to me?" "Why is she doing this favor for me?" "Why didn't she speak to me?" The self-made answers to these questions are invariably more negative than positive.

If these people are religious, suspiciousness can invade their relationship with God. These people are backseat drivers to God. They "trust" God, but just to make sure, they are chronically directing him as to what to do with their lives: "God, make me be this"; "God, don't let me do that;" and "God, where are you going with me now?" These persons see God as a puppeteer who has a tendency to forget what he is doing.

Finally, instead of acknowledging to himself and others how deeply he distrusts himself, the person may overcompensate by assuming an air of supreme confidence and bravado. These are the "last people in the world" you would think have grave self-doubts. They "run the whole show." There is never a minute of doubt or hesitation. They take over the reins of other people's lives to prove to themselves that they would never be so weak as to need that kind of help. Their failures are chalked off to the bumblings of others. There are only two kinds of answers: Their answers and wrong answers. People who are genuinely self-trusting trust themselves enough to know that they are human, imperfect, and fallible.

From the above example it can be seen that self-trust does not mean "I have enough intelligence, knowledge, and experience always to be correct in my perceptions, feelings, judgments, and values." It *does* mean: "After I have thought about it, felt about it, discussed it with people I trust, and perhaps prayed about it, I trust that what I shall do will bring about growth in me and/or in others."

There are a number of factors in this definition that need expanding. A person should trust himself if he *thinks* about what he is going to do. This means that he tries to scrutinize what his motives are for doing what he is about to do, and that he considers all the possible consequences, both positive and negative. The time spent thinking should, when possible, be in direct proportion to the gravity of the decision. Knowing a person for a short time and taking only two months to decide whether or not to marry him or her will likely result in a marriage that lasts for two years.

A person should "feel through" his decisions. Decisions based on pure logic often turn out poorly, because they ignore half of the total person, viz., his emotions, his feelings. A person's head tells him he should do only one thing, but his heart tells him something different. Historically, there has been a prejudice against emotions in the decision-making process. Businessmen often ask: "How can I get my employees to think with their heads and not with their hearts?" Yet, there is no reason to believe that one's intellectual abilities alone will bring him to the truth better than his emotions. Most people who study human behavior agree that both intellect and emotions should be given equal consideration.

Discussing an impending decision or behavior with people one trusts can be helpful. But the discussion should have certain qualities. The person with whom we discuss the situation should not have an ax to grind with regard to the situation in question; otherwise the discussion turns into brainwashing. The person making the decision should be completely open about all the details of the situation, not holding back embarrassing parts. Giving selected information will get selective feedback and does not constitute a discussion. Finally, the purpose of the discussion should be to get some objective feedback which can be "taken home" and mixed in with all the other data so that a decision can be made. This is not the same as getting advice from someone and making a decision based heavily on that advice. This is the antithesis of self-trust.

To some people, praying is an important part of making a decision. If prayer is invoked, it should mean asking God for the insight and strength to make a good decision, but not to make the decision for us. Sometimes we secretly know what we are going to do before we pray. Going to God in this instance is merely a token gesture to one's conscience. It is a way of spiritually covering oneself if something should go wrong.

When these four elements are met, one must reasonably assume that whatever the effects of one's decision or behavior are, they will result in growth for the people concerned. The situation may not turn out the way we had hoped. It may even create anguish for ourselves and others. But people can learn from it. Maybe, with the benefit of hindsight, one can see a mistake one made in the decision-making process and be well aware of it the next time a similar situation arises. Maybe the decision-making process was all right, but the other people involved "dropped the ball." Both we and they can learn something from the situation. And maybe the hurt, or disappointment, or guilt that comes from a mistake can strengthen us to face future problems more wisely.

In developing the attribute of self-trust, one is constantly working on the scale from "little self-trust" to "healthy self-trust" to "exaggerated self-trust." Some principles may be helpful in growing toward the middle of the scale.

1. We can trust our judgment and make some mistakes, or we can distrust our judgment and always make a mistake. It is better to go through the self-trust process and to make a mistake, than it is to hand over a decision to someone else and have it turn out well. Under the management circumstances no real learning can take place whatever the results of the action. If our behavior evokes positive results, we can falsely glory in them, but we will never learn all the ingredients that went into the decision or be able to repeat it. If the results are negative, we don't have to assume responsibility for the action (we think) because it wasn't our idea in the first place.

All we have learned in the first instance is that we went to a good manager and will have to use him again. In the second example, we learn that the next time we want advice, we'd better try someone else.

It is far better to make a mistake on our own, discover where we failed, and strengthen those psychological muscles for the next decision than to slide through life never making a mistake because we never trusted ourselves enough to make a decision. On the other side of the fence, we can help others learn these skills by declining to manage them.

2. Good decisions can turn out poorly. It is important to distinguish between trusting oneself and the *results* of trusting oneself. After careful thought and discussion, a girl may decide to accept a marriage proposal from a nice young man. After she is engaged for a year, her fiancé begins to behave selfishly, insensitively, and even cruelly. This continues long enough for the girl to decide to break off the engagement. Did she make a mistake in choosing to get engaged? No. She had considered all the data that were available to her at the time and acted upon them. She had no way of knowing that the closer the boy got to a life commitment, the more terrified he became but lacked the courage to break off the engagement. Consequently, he unconsciously set up the situation so he didn't have to make that decision but still could escape the life commitment. It would be inappropriate for the girl to conclude that she shouldn't trust her own judgment again.

This often happens in life. A person makes the best decision under the circumstances, has it go wrong, and then, at least subconsciously, decides never to trust his judgment again. Obviously, one can err on the other side too. A person can *always* assume that he made a good decision and, when it goes wrong, blame in on "uncontrollable factors."

3. *Not everything that looks like a mistake is a mistake.* For the most part, no one really is in a position to know with certainty when a mistake is a mistake, and when it is a God-send in disguise. A man may enter a seminary and leave after five or ten years. At first glance, it may seem, especially to him, that he has wasted the best years of his life. He berates himself and those involved in the decision for doing such a stupid thing. He asks people: "How can I trust myself to make a life decision again after the way the first one turned out?" Yet it is quite possible that, imperceptibly, the seminary experience allowed him to gain a sense of independence from home, an appreciation for close friendship, an appetite for intellectual pursuits, a deeply rooted value system, and a sense of purpose in life. It is possible that he personally would not have acquired these traits in the same way if he had gone through a traditional education process. It could be that the very experience which he is denigrating is the very one that could help him make a truly sound life choice in the future. It may sound peculiar, but it could be that the good health of his future marriage and parenthood is significantly based on his seminary experience. So, what appears to be a big mistake is, in fact, a cause for celebration.

In summary, without self-trust, there can be no genuine trust of others. People don't either have self-trust or not have it. No one is born with self-trust; it is taught, and it is learned. Self-distrust is also taught and learned. It is never too late to start learning self-trust or to start teaching it. And it is important to do so. As Goethe wrote: "As soon as you trust yourself, you will know how to live."

Reflection Questions

1. What need do I have at this point in my life that I would not necessarily want everyone to know that I have? Why am I ashamed of it? Can I get this need met as long as it's a secret?

2. What are my three greatest strengths and three greatest weaknesses? Am I doing anything to strengthen the weakness, or do I blithely say, "Well, that's just me"?

3. Regarding purpose in life, what epitaph would I like on my gravestone that would best describe my life? What have I done this week that would make that epitaph an accurate one?

4. When is the last time I was a chameleon? Why didn't I trust myself enough to let people see my true color?

5. When is the last time I consciously helped someone grow in self-trust?

Thoughts to Contemplate

1. The person who does not really know himself very well, even though he may be very talented, is like an airplane pilot who can't navigate: He makes beautiful landings, but often at the wrong airports.

2. Some people spend days or months shopping for just the right suit, but are very haphazard or ignorant about the ways in which they choose to get their psychological needs met.

3. Some people, perhaps many people, choose a contra-need life style; i.e., what they deeply need in life is not afforded them in their life while often the last thing they do need in life *is* present.

4. Purpose in life is like a string that holds all the beads on a necklace together. It makes sense out of each day and out of a lifetime.

5. One of the greatest enemies of self-identification is routine. When we do the same thing all the time, we become the same thing all the time.

7

FREEING OURSELVES

There is no such entity as a "free person" or an "un-free person." Freedom is on a scale that runs from "little freedom" to "great freedom." People with little freedom can develop great freedom; and people with great freedom can develop it more fully.

Another important distinction to make is that freedom in itself is not necessarily good, nor is restraint in itself necessarily evil. Individual people, as well as mankind in general, function best with a judicious mixture of freedom and restraint. For example, one should not destructively hurt others under the rationale of "expressing oneself freely." On the other hand, for example, one should not be restrained from a just protest against authority.

A third point is that we should distinguish between personal freedom and societal freedom. Both individuals and society can differ greatly in the amount of freedom they possess. However, there is a tendency in many people who are personally unfree to blame their lack of freedom on society. Their license for an unfulfilling life is that they "got stuck in a lousy society." The truth is, however, that some people have exercised remarkable personal freedom in dramatically repressive societies, e.g., concentration camps.

In my experience, the vast majority of unfree people are self-shackled and not shackled by society. It is with this in mind that the Ten Psychological Freedoms will be discussed.

1. FREEDOM TO BE SELF-FULFILLING

It is helpful to distinguish between three types of people: self-fulfilling people, selfless people, and selfish people.

Who are self-fulfilling people? These individuals realize that they have a "self" and that they should take good care of it. Self-fulfilling people live according to the Christian-Humanistic principle: "Love your neighbor *as* yourself"; *not:* "Love your neighbor *instead* of yourself" or "Love your neighbor *more* than yourself." Such individuals *take* the time that they need to be alone; the time to relax; to pray; and to enjoy life. They protect themselves from the inordinate demands that people and life make upon them.

Self-fulfilling people are not afraid to give of themselves. But, when they do so, they give freely and not because they will feel guilty or be rejected if they don't. They give fully up to the point where it begins to interfere with their own personhood.

Who are selfless people? Unfree people are selfless; they are "totally giving." These individuals never think of themselves, or they think of themselves last. This behavior is often viewed as the epitome of virtue. But selflessness is no more mentally healthy or spiritually healthy than selfish behavior. In fact, it is a disguised form of selfishness.

To begin with, selflessness is inappropriate behavior because the person *does* have a self. To deny its separate existence or to give it over to another is a violation of reality. Secondly, selflessness is a manipulative ploy to gain something that the person feels he could not gain in any other way.

The unfree person's intent, although it is primarily unconscious, is to gain acceptance or love, or to control others. If I give you something at great personal sacrifice, how could you not accept me? How could you reject or leave me after all I've done for you? If I give to you and ask nothing in return, how can you criticize me? or be angry with me? or hurt me in any way? or love anyone more than me?

Thirdly, selfless people are resentful, although the resentment must be well disguised or it will interfere with their design. They are resentful because on some deep level they realize that they must prostitute themselves to gain what others receive in easier ways. Secondly, if the dividend fails to materialize, they feel double-crossed and bitter, as if some contract had been violated.

Who are selfish people? Unfree people are selfish people; they think *only* of themselves, in contrast to the self-fulfilling person who thinks *both* of himself *and* of others. Although the selfish person appears to be in love with himself, in reality just the opposite is true. Selfish behavior states: "I'm so unlovable that if I don't watch out for myself, no one else will." Such individuals equate receiving with being loved and giving with losing love. When an emotional drought occurs, this person cannot tolerate it and develops psychological symptoms often involving anxiety and depression.

Emotional self-fulfillment does not mean that we don't need people; it means that our entire survival and sense of well-being are not dependent on them. It means that we rely more on ourselves than on others for the following:

1. Getting essential needs met. The self-fulfilling person forages to get his needs met and actively approaches the world and sees to it that the emotional groceries are brought home. This is in contrast to the individual who waits passively for people to bring emotional groceries to his doorstep.

The self-fulfilling person has built up a reserve of emotional groceries, so that he can afford to give some away without expecting to be emotionally reimbursed. This person does not have to beg for emotional groceries and can maintain a sense of integrity.

2. Self-definition. The self-fulfilling individual is his own center of gravity. He does not have to use others as a mirror to reflect on who he is. He knows what is good about him and what is not so good and uses this information to guide him without relying primarily on the opinion of others.

3. Direction of one's life. The self-fulfilling individual "calls his own shots" and willingly accepts the consequences. He may consult with others, but he does so to gather data to make his own decisions, not to collect votes as to what he should do.

4. Being complimented. The self-fulfilling person enjoys getting compliments and encouragement from others, but he is not so reliant on others that he functions significantly less well without them. He knows when he has done well, when he has strengthened a weakness, taken a risk, overcome difficult odds, and extended himself beyond what was expected. If someone else also notices and compliments him, it's nice—but not essential.

2. FREEDOM FROM MANIPULATION

Manipulation occurs when one person exerts a force on the other, attempting to blackmail the individual out of doing what he feels to be the proper or desired thing. Unfree people possess a "manipulation button." When people push the right button, the unfree person will do almost anything, if not anything, for the person.

There are several types of manipulation buttons. One common type is the "intelligence button." Some people need to feel intelligent and to be perceived as intelligent more than anything else. So, when another person says: "I know you're an intelligent person, so I know you'll see things the way I do," the person agrees to the situation, despite his deeper feelings to the contrary. A manipulation button can be pushed retroactively, e.g., "I thought you were such an intelligent person, how could you have done that?" The manipulable person then quickly tries to undo the "stupid" thing he did, even though in his heart he doesn't think it was stupid.

Other common manipulation buttons are:

1. "Sensitive" as in: "Being the sensitive person that you are, I know you won't confront Joe with this situation." The non-manipulable person is already aware of how sensitive he is or isn't, and replies: "Well, I think I am sensitive, and I feel that being sensitive to all the parties involved in this situation, I should confront Joe with the problem he's creating."

2. *"Mature" as in:* "I've sought your advice because I've always admired your maturity. Don't you feel that it's my boss's fault and not mine for the difficulties I've been having at work?" The non-manipulable person replies: "Sometimes I feel I'm mature, and other times I'm not so sure. But, from what you told me, it sounds as if both you and your boss are equally creating problems for the other."

3. *"Reasonable" as in:* "Being a reasonable person, I know you'll agree with me that there is only one way to go on this thing." The non-manipulable individual answers: "I do try to use my reason, but I also try to trust my feelings, and the combination of my reason and feelings tell me an alternative plan may be better in the long run."

4. *"Unselfish" as in:* "I know with your generosity you'll bail me out of the mess I got myself into." The non-manipulable individual will respond: "I would like to help you, but you've contacted me at a time when my priorities require that I spend my time and energy in another situation at this particular time."

5. *"Strong" as in:* "I know with your strength of conviction that you won't allow these people to get away with that." The non-manipulable person responds: "Well, as with everyone else, I guess I have my strong days and weak days. I don't know which today is, but I really don't feel the need to stand in the way of these people."

6. *"Attractive" as in:* "Gee, that's a cute dress, and your hair looks darling that way. Incidentally, could you drive me downtown to my dentist appointment?" The non-manipulable individual says: "Thank you; I like the dress too. Unfortunately, I have some shopping that I must do today on the other side of town."

The main thing that makes a free person feel good

about himself is that he is doing what he thinks and feels to be the correct thing. Being "made to feel good" about anything else is secondary.

3. FREEDOM TO BE IMPERFECT

A free person can serenely acknowledge his imperfect state. Imperfections are weaknesses, faults, and mistakes. Free people realize that they were created as human beings and not as angels. A free person acknowledges his imperfect state. A free person can say with ease:

—"I'm confused" versus "Of course, the situation is quite clear to me."

—"I don't know if I'm correct or not, but . . ." versus "I know what I'm talking about."

—"I have no one to blame but myself" versus "If they had helped me the way they should, I wouldn't have made that mistake."

—"I got 'shook' and couldn't think straight" versus "The questions they asked me were so stupid I couldn't understand them."

—"I'm sorry for causing you this problem" versus "You get yourself into these messes all the time."

I gave a talk recently that included a question-and-answer-period. At the end of the presentation, a successful, middle-aged man approached me and shook my hand. He said: "I couldn't believe what I was hearing. Not once but twice during the question-and-answer period you responded 'I don't know.' I learned something today that I never knew—that it's all right to say 'I don't know.' "

Free people understand that the path to perfection is necessarily marbled with imperfection. Our imperfections are the isometrics we need to grow psychologically. To disdain imperfection is tantamount to trying to reach the top of a ladder without using the rungs as levers. The result is a good deal of fruitless exercise and needless frustration.

Acknowledging imperfection is important for the following reasons.

First, acknowledging specific imperfections in oneself is the first step toward psychological and spiritual growth. People who lack this ability have no "braking mechanism" to prevent repetition of the same or similar mistakes.

Recently I asked a man who was twice divorced—although not yet twenty-five years old—what he felt had caused his two failures in marriage. He responded: "Well, I guess I just married a couple of lemons." Within a year he had picked his third "lemon," and I have no doubt that by the time he is thirty he will have acquired an orchard. He had absolutely no insight into his own mistakes and the weaknesses that contributed to these failures.

People who perceive themselves as possessing few or only minor imperfections have no place to grow because their greatest imperfection (lack of insight) is freezing themselves into a state of complacent mediocrity.

Acknowledging our imperfections is important for a second reason: It can increase the depth of our interpersonal relationships. This reaching-out is a very important ingredient of psychological growth because no one can live healthily as a self-contained unit. People who view themselves as perfect or near perfect have little need to relate with others. The more we hide our imperfections, the more destructive our behavior becomes. Hiding faults from others absorbs a tremendous amount of psychic energy.

Probably half the fatigue experienced at the end of a work day results from energy spent camouflaging mistakes, confusions, inadequacies, and ignorance. The less people allocate personal resources to their "psychological defense budget," the more energy they have for creative pursuits.

When we are obsessed with hiding our flaws, we cannot allow others to come close to us. There is the subconscious fear that we will be discovered for who we are. Holding people at an emotional distance eventually results in psychological hunger pains because the emotional groceries others have to offer us cannot be delivered.

Finally, the more we can acknowledge our imperfections, the more empathetic we become. The more we admit that many, if not most, of our problems were created by us—by our failings, weaknesses, errors in judgment, selective perceptions, impulsiveness, selfishness, and insensitivity—the more we can say genuinely: "Yes, I do deeply understand what you are going through, because I have gone through comparable experiences." The way we express this sentiment lets the person know we truly do understand.

In summary, we must dispose of the destructive myth that becoming a complete human being means becoming a perfect one. Psychologist Abraham Maslow states this clearly when he writes: "Self-actualizing people are simultaneously selfish and unselfish, rational and irrational. They tolerate their own inconsistencies and contradictions and see a kind of wisdom in conflicts.... Self-actualization does not mean a transcendence of all human problems. Conflict, anxiety, frustration, sadness, hurt, and guilt can all be found in healthy human beings. In general, the movement with increasing maturity is from neurotic pseudo-problems to the real, unavoidable, existential problems inherent in the nature of man (even at his best) living in a particular kind of world." (*Toward a Psychology of Being*, D. Van Nostrand and Co., New York, 1962)

4. FREEDOM TO STRIKE A HEALTHY BALANCE BETWEEN WORK AND LEISURE

Free people set aside daily or almost daily a few hours during which they can relax and enjoy themselves. They don't feel guilty about doing this, nor do they feel that they must work until they "deserve" to take leisure time.

To the free person, the main purpose of healthy work is to survive materially and to grow psychologically. The unfree person, on the other hand, works for the following reasons:

1. To distract himself from unpleasant or painful feelings, such as fear, anger, doubt, boredom, inadequacy, or loneliness. The unfree worker gradually but steadily loses contact with who he really is; what he really needs and feels; and where his life is really taking him. The net effects of this process can be disastrous.

A middle-aged executive, after two years of "uncovering" in therapy, summarized this problem when he said: "I'm just now beginning to rediscover who I really am. I wonder who I will be when I grow up?"

2. *To avoid emotional involvements with people.* As long as he is too busy, the unfree person cannot become emotionally close to spouses, children, or friends. Invitations to be with people (even loved ones) are met with "I'd love to, but you see I've got this work to do." This begins a vicious circle with a downward spiral. The more emotionally (which does not necessarily mean socially) withdrawn the individual becomes, the more lonely, fearful, and angry he feels, the more he has to work, and so on.

The unfree worker operates on the principle that work is the panacea for all ills. Perhaps the best way to describe this individual is to use an analogy: A person may see his room on fire and, being too frightened to look, he runs outside and begins vehemently sweeping the sidewalk—as if sweeping the sidewalk will make the fire go away. Unfree workers are busy sweeping sidewalks while their houses burn, ignoring the real problems but keeping busy to make them feel they are *doing* something.

In his book *In Praise of Play,* Robert Neale describes well the problems of the unfree worker: "Leisure provokes boredom in the individual who does not know what to do with himself. It elicits shame in the person who must be important by means of business. It gives rise to guilt in anyone who seeks justification by good works. And it provokes anxiety in the many whose free time exposes them to the alienation and meaninglessness of their lives."

The free worker finds time for leisure. Unfortunately, people who make room for leisure time are more often than not viewed as selfish, lazy, or hedonistic. Many of us distinguish only between two types of time: work time and wasted time. People have wasted the most important parts of their lives because they did not want to "waste time" for a few hours. Enjoyment is often considered the sin of the wealthy or a sign of the uncommitted.

As a matter of fact, enjoying leisure pursuits is as important a mental health value as is the ability to work well. And working compulsively is a neurotic trait, though one that is much rewarded.

By leisure is meant unobligated time which can be spent in any way one wishes. The time can be spent alone or with another. It can be spent thinking, reading, listening to or playing music, writing, walking, or painting. Prayer may or may not be a leisure activity, depending on how much "work" it is. Sleep has its own benefits, but it is not a leisure time activity.

This is not to say that one cannot grow in work or ever enjoy his work. Work, in itself, however, can never bring the relaxation, solitude, healthy distraction, refreshment, and contemplation so necessary for psychological and spiritual growth.

It is true that some people cannot afford *financially* to take as much leisure time as others can. But the greater problem is the vast majority of people, rich and poor, who cannot afford *psychologically* to take and use leisure time well.

A psychological basis underlying the need to keep busy is predicated on a partial truism, viz., we tend to measure a person's worth and vibrance, not by who he is, but by what and how much he does. Yet it is clearly a myth that either a person's worth or competence is reflected in how much or how long he works. All things being equal, I would much prefer to be operated on by a surgeon who works six hours a day than one who works twelve; to be taught by a teacher who is relaxed, refreshed, and alive because he has taken time out to get his own needs met; and to be loved by someone who views life as a celebration rather than as a debt to be worked off.

As psychologist Rollo May writes: "Aliveness often means a capacity not to act, to be creatively idle—which may be more difficult for most modern people to do than to do something."

5. FREEDOM TO SUFFER

The free person does not enjoy suffering. But the free individual realizes that suffering is an inherent part of life and that great knowledge and strength can come from suffering. By the same token, free people are slow to abate another person's suffering prematurely, lest the person be deprived of a precious opportunity for growth. Being "present" to one who is suffering is far more helpful than rushing in with emotional Band-aids that only serve to complicate matters.

The following are some typical causes of suffering that most, if not all of us, face. The question is: Will we suffer them well, or will we suffer them poorly?

Suffering can be caused by failure. This comprises the experience of giving something our "best shot" and having it fall short. One's failure may be as a lover; it may be academically; it may be at work; it may be as a parent. The free person realizes that, statistically, the more things he tries in life, the more he will fail. But he decides that he'd rather try ten things and be successful in six than to try only four "sure" things and settle for less. He does not equate a failed attempt with being a "failed person." In fact, even in failure he can congratulate himself for taking a risk.

The unfree person avoids failure like a plague. Consequently, the dividends in life are minimal, and the excitement of life is muted. If the individual does fail, he cannot accept responsibility for it. It is someone else's fault, or "It wasn't *really* a *failure*," or it was "God's will." Such defenses contribute nothing to the future growth of the person.

Suffering can also be caused by rejection. This occurs when we love someone but the other person does not reciprocate. It can occur when we give something of importance to another, and it is not appreciated. The free person suffers through the rejection, whatever its source, learns something about himself and life because of it, and continues to hold a relatively positive attitude toward life, in spite of the hurt.

The unfree person refuses to accept rejection. He bribes, clings, pouts, blames, and threatens revenge. He may cater to others in ways that preclude the possibility of rejection. Unfortunately, this requires selling the most precious commodity a person possesses, namely his selfhood, for the acceptance of another person or institution.

Another cause of suffering is the gradual or acute realization that we are not the person we would like to think we are. We often realize that we are more jealous than we'd like to think; more competitive, narrow, judgmental, threatened, selfish, manipulating, boasting, angry, fragile, ignorant, and self-deceiving than we had expected someone of our inherent goodness to be.

The free person audibly groans as each realization seeps through consciousness. He eventually laughs at himself: "Well, my friend, who *did* you think you were, anyway?" He can then pinpoint weaknesses and work on them.

The unfree person precludes suffering the pain of self-realization by denying shortcomings. He goes through life banging into things and people and wonders how they got in the way. Unfortunately, one day this person may step over the edge of an abyss and be swallowed up in it before he has a chance to blame anybody.

Suffering is also experienced when other people discover who we really are. This could be a situation in which a son discovers that his dad wasn't really a war hero, or a star athlete, or the "boss of the whole company," or that dad isn't always right, always unselfish, always in control, or always strong. Gradually, as the son matures, he cannot help but send the message to his dad: "You're not as good as I once thought."

The free person's attitude to this type of message is: "As we grow closer, you will discover things about me. For every discovery which will cause rejoicing, there will be one which will cause disappointment. But know me for who I am."

The unfree person does not allow himself to "come into the range" of another person. He keeps a plastic shield between himself and others to prevent discovery and the consequent pain. Such individuals go through life half-starved emotionally and rarely realize it. All they know is that something seems to be missing.

Finally, suffering is caused by letting go of a loved one. Seeing our children leave us to enter adulthood, needing us less, and finally not needing us at all, can be very difficult. Suffering results from letting go of a lover who needs to grow in ways that do not include us. These and other instances of letting go include the pain of loss of the past and the pain of fear of the future. Who or what is going to replace what we've let go? How will we exist now?

The free person allows himself to endure and to grow through this pain. He realizes that this pain is analogous to the pain of a scab coming off a wound. It hurts, but it is also the precursor of new growth.

The unfree person cannot let go. He hangs on tenaciously, battering himself and others in the process. These people define letting go as the worst thing that could happen to them—an event that will cause psychological death. Ultimately, the unfree person may capture the other person and both live in emotional captivity, or the other person finally escapes but at great expense to both people.

6. FREEDOM TO LET GO OF THE PAST

The fields of psychology and psychiatry are probably the most to blame for the misconception that people are "stuck" with their pasts, that whatever bad or good happened to them during childhood, or even adulthood, has left an indelible imprint that will program their behavior for eternity.

This myth was born from early, untested hypotheses about human behavior. We now realize that childhood experiences, and even traumas, almost never constitute a sufficient cause for problematic behavior in adulthood. They represent a *potential* for adult problems, but potentials can be overridden by any one or several of the psychological competencies mentioned in the first chapter. I know adults who presently have no more problems than anyone else, yet who, as children, witnessed one parent slaying another; had prolonged incestuous relations with a parent or sibling; were heterosexually or homosexually raped; lived their entire childhood in an orphanage; were severely beaten by adults; or were drug addicts and prostitutes as teen-agers.

Nevertheless some unfree people feel that they are prisoners of their past. They go through life carrying a "clinic card" that says: "I can't help my behavior; my par-

ents were alcoholics"; or "Of course I'm frightened of sex;
I was molested when I was nine"; or "Naturally, I can't
get close to people; my parents gave me away when I was
five"; or "How am I supposed to know about how to make
a marriage happy; my mother was divorced three times."

"Clinic card" carriers excuse their present difficulties by blaming the past. The inappropriateness and futil-
ity of doing this is seen in the following monologue:

> One client "tells how he has always felt his
> family was to blame for all of his difficulties,
> and then adds, 'But now that I understand all
> they've done, I guess it's up to me.' " In me, the
> knowing "It's up to me" comes about in this
> way: When I understand "all they've done" (to
> me), I also understand "so this must have been
> done to them." Through knowing the way that it
> came about in me, I know how it must have
> come about in them. Then the whole thing goes
> back and back, each generation having been
> "done to" by the preceding one. There is no one
> to blame, and all that I can do is get to work on
> myself *now* and break the chain, so that I won't
> do unto others what has been done to me. It is
> not enough that I simply *know* this. I can *know*
> without any action taking place either within
> me or outside me. (The one follows upon the
> other.) I can feel superior to someone who
> doesn't *know* what I know, without being one
> whit a better person for my knowing. I have to
> *undo* what has been done to me, by *doing* in an-
> other way. That's where the scary part comes in,
> in my experience: I can find it comforting to
> *know,* and almost terrifying to *do.* But it is in
> the doing that I change, and in my changing,
> my relations with other people change too."
> (Carl Rogers and Barry Stevens, *Person to Per-
> son,* Real People Press, 1967, pp. 73–74.)

Other unfree people carry "charisma cards." These
originate from having been born into a privileged family
or having earned certain successes in the past. These

cards tell you who the person *was,* but are not updated to tell you who the person *is.* These people inform others: "I'm the son of the president of the National Bank"; or "I went to Harvard"; or "I made a half-million dollars before I was thirty"; or "I was a colonel in the Army." A type of charisma card is the "runner-up card," as in: "I was almost a Rhodes Scholar"; or "I was Miss Congeniality in the State beauty contest"; or "I was an alternate javelin thrower in the 1956 Olympics."

The individual with the charisma card attempts to coast through the present on the momentum of the past. These individuals plead: "Don't look at who I am now, but look at who I was—who I could have been." They get daily sustenance from an "emotional scrap book" that has been preserved and cherished through the years.

Both the carrier of the clinic card and of the charisma card are unfree. Neither exercises much, if any, free will. Both feel that the past is determining the present and will determine the future. Their main activity in life is to "flash their card," and their fantasy is that people who were in their way will now stand aside to let them pass.

The harsh reality is that almost no one respects these cards. Most people view them as counterfeit, and rightly so. The only people being fooled are the card-carriers themselves. The pleasant reality is that while our past *influences* the present, it does not *determine* it. Cards can be destroyed once and for all and ex-card-carriers can take charge of the present and make necessary changes. They can accept the fact that their present is their past of tomorrow.

People who wish to overcome a pernicious past can do so. I've seen people tear up clinic cards that they were using for a "free ride" for thirty years and do very well in life. And I've seen people burn their "emotional scrap book" and update their competencies so that they begin to handle the present instead of trying to seduce it with old trophies.

All free people had either a mostly pleasant or a mostly unpleasant past. It is not the past that makes a person who he is; it is the present which makes the free person who he will be.

7. FREEDOM TO DISAPPOINT OTHERS

One of the most difficult things we can do is to disappoint another person, especially someone we admire or who admires us. To understand disappointment, it helps to look at the word itself: dis-appoint. In other words, someone "appoints" or "selects" us to fulfill some role or expectation. But sometimes it is necessary, both for our overall well-being as well as those closest to us, to "un-appoint" ourselves which, in turn, "disappoints" others.

When we don't care about someone, it is easy to disappoint them. But, when we love someone dearly, it can seem impossible to feel free enough to disappoint them. There is a very strong myth in our culture that holds that a true lover never disappoints a loved one. And this myth has caused more emotional problems than perhaps any other myth.

Our parents may "appoint" us to go to college; to live at home until we are married; to marry the "right" person; to pursue the "correct" career; to live close to them and visit them frequently; and to view religion as they do.

Our spouse may "appoint" us to accept a promotion at work that we really don't want; to buy a home that we really don't need; to socialize in ways and with people with whom we feel uncomfortable; to relate with our parents in ways which we find difficult; to love our children in specific "approved" ways.

Our son or daughter may "appoint" us to always be right; to always be strong; to never fail; to always "be there" when they need us; to always love them and never hurt them; to make life decisions that best meet their needs; to be "special" in the world of adults; and to always be worthy of their pride.

Our friends may "appoint" us to always be around when they wish us to be; to go on vacations with them; to share the same social and religious values; to be the kind of person they originally thought we were; to agree with them on issues that are important to them; and not to choose the company of other friends over them.

Our bosses and supervisors may "appoint" us to be inordinately dedicated to our work, which often requires working overtime or on weekends, and often for no compensation except our "love for the work"; to "buy the program" that management hands down; to "blend in" with the values of the organization; to accept all work that may lead to advancement; and never to leave the organization except for retirement.

A typical example of the lack of freedom to disappoint is the following: John's dad owned the family store which had been in the family for three generations. John hated the store for how it had consumed his mother and father for as long as he'd been alive. John had been "appointed" by his father to be the next proud proprietor of the store. Although John wanted to attend college and enter a profession, his father assured him that he could run the business quite well without a college diploma.

Because John couldn't disappoint his "poor dad," he gradually took over the store. John got married, had three children, and worked twelve hours a day at the store six days a week. Each day his anger and resentment grew. At first he was angry with his father who "made him take the store." Then his resentment began to include his wife who "enjoyed life" while he slaved at the store. So, he decided she should help at the store on weekends. He then gradually realized the deep contempt he had for himself. *He had taken* the store—he *could* have said "NO." He had forced his wife to work on the only two days she had to relax, and he knew he did that out of resentment, not necessity. He became sexually impotent with his wife, but found he could enjoy sex with some of the female customers.

John's wife could not allow herself to refuse to work at the store. She did not wish to disappoint John or John's family who had long awaited the day when she would choose to join them in their enterprise. After a while, John's wife got tired of her husband who was married to the store, and with whom she had not slept for a year, of a job she hated, and of the psychological problems her children were having as an obvious result of the tension and unhappiness of the home.

After many heated arguments and threats, she divorced him and took the children. John was shocked, humiliated, hurt, and furious. He "suddenly realized" that his father had "caused" all this grief. John had a few drinks one night, barged into the half-full store, and screamed at his father all the hateful things he had felt toward him since he was fifteen years old.

Now, John has lost his wife whom, at one time, he loved deeply. He has lost his children whom he adores. He has lost his father, his job, and his self-respect.

One wonders how different things would be now if, ten years ago, John had been free enough to disappoint his father and had gone to college.

One wonders how different things would have been if John's wife had been free enough to disappoint John and his family by declining to work at the store. Perhaps if she had, her strength would have been contagious and an impetus for John to face his own need to break away.

As it was, both John's and his wife's lack of freedom to disappoint one person temporarily caused several people to be damaged for a long time.

8. FREEDOM TO ASSUME RESPONSIBILITY FOR OUR BEHAVIOR

The relationship between freedom and responsibility is a close one. Freedom does not only mean a lack of restraints; it also requires us to accept the reality of who we are and what we do. It is a false freedom that declares: "As a free human being I can be and do anything I want."

True freedom says: "As a *caring* human being, there are certain things I am and certain things I am not; certain things I do, and certain things I do not do; and I am willing to stand by these things and to admit when I've failed in them."

Freedom without responsibility is a dangerous weapon, whereas freedom with responsibility is a tremendous source of growth. Responsible freedom begins when the individual is willing to assume personal ownership for his behavior. There are three ways that the free person does this.

First, the responsible person is willing to own his or her *messages.* He or she is unafraid to use the pronoun "I," as in "I am angry at you." The unfree person says: "You make me angry"; or "That makes me angry"; or "It makes me angry."

The free person can say "I love you." The unfree person states: "You are very lovable"; or "Do you love me, too?"; or "Don't you already know how I feel about you?"

The free person states: "I think you made a mistake." The unfree person will say: "Do you think you made a mistake?"; or "It seems a mistake has been made"; or "Somebody made a mistake."

Secondly, the responsible person is willing to acknowledge ownership of his *motives*. The free person states: "I'm helping you because I like you." The unfree person states: "I'm helping you because you have too much work"; or "I'm helping you because it will make things easier for both of us"; or "I'm helping you because I have nothing else to do anyway."

The free person states: "I'm not giving you a letter of recommendation because I don't feel that I can honestly recommend you for the following reasons. . . . " The unfree person can only state: "I must never have received your recommendation application; where did you put it?"; or "I can't write you a letter of recommendation because I don't feel that I know you well enough"; or "It's my policy not to write letters of recommendation because I feel it's all a game anyway."

The free person can state: "I'm not going out with you tonight because I want to hurt you for what you said to me today." The unfree person can only state: "I can't go out with you tonight because I'm too tired"; or "I can't go out with you tonight because I promised I'd help my parents"; or "I can't go out with you tonight because I think it would be good for us to be apart for a while."

Thirdly, the responsible person owns the *consequences* of his behavior. The free person can say: "I made an error in judgment that resulted in this problem." The unfree person states: "What problem? That's not a problem"; or "Oh, they didn't make it clear to me what they wanted"; or "I was so distracted by all the injustices I was burdened with that I couldn't think straight."

The free person says: "I considered the short-term consequences, but I obviously overlooked the long-term consequences." The unfree person says: "I can't control *everything*"; or "How was I to know they'd take me so literally?"; or "That's *their* problem."

The free person says: "I made a premature decision because I wanted to solve the problem fast, but I can see now that I should have waited until all the data were in." The unfree person says: "They forced me to make the decision so they'll have to 'eat' the consequences"; or "It serves them right, maybe they'll learn something from this"; or "I don't care—they're idiots anyway."

When we are willing to own our messages, motives, and the consequences of our behavior, there is a more honest and pertinent encounter. I am dealing openly with who I am and you are dealing openly with who I am. When we deny ownership of what is rightly ours, the encounter is replete with dishonesty, hedging, and pseudo-issues, all of which militate strongly against personal growth and a successful resolution of problems.

9. FREEDOM TO ALLOW CONTRARY FEELINGS TO EXIST SIMULTANEOUSLY

Unfree people lack the confidence and the strength to acknowledge contrary feelings within themselves. They want to appear "integrated," but erroneously think that "integrated" means "unanimous"; i.e., they force themselves into feeling only one feeling toward a person or a situation.

They either love a person or hate him.
They are either proud of another person or jealous of him.
They either believe something or disbelieve it.
They feel either brave or frightened.
They feel either generous or selfish.
They feel either hope or despair.
They feel either free or unfree.
They feel either polite or rude.
They feel either respectful or disrespectful.
They feel either trusting or distrusting.
They feel either intelligent or stupid.
They feel either beautiful or ugly.
They feel either joy or sorrow.

The fact is that we are almost never "unanimous" in our feelings, especially when we are relating with some-

one who makes a difference to us, either positively or
negatively, or when we are faced with an emotionally involved situation.

As Paul Tournier writes:

> We are all seething with contradictions; it is
> only with difficulty that we admit the fact to
> ourselves, and we take great care to hide it from
> others. It is perhaps as a form of escape from
> the vertigo which the full knowledge of this
> tangled complexity within us would cause, that
> we compose for ourselves a simpler personage.
> We do not have to explore the unconscious to
> find these contradictions, they are obvious
> whenever a man speaks to us frankly about
> himself. (*The Meaning of Persons,* New York,
> Harper & Row, p. 42)

Serious problems can arise when an unfree individual forces an emotional unanimity that does not truly exist. The problems lie in three areas.

One problem is that the "vetoed" feelings do not disappear but quietly remain to haunt the situation. A woman may feel tremendous pressure from her parents to
raise her children in their religious faith. She truly loves
her parents, but also deeply resents their subtle and obvious intrusions. She feels she must "veto" the resentment
because how could a loving daughter feel resentment to
such well-intentioned parents?

As an effect of the vetoed resentment, the woman increasingly finds she is too busy to visit her folks. She
knows that she misses the more frequent visits, and she
knows that her parents feel hurt, but what can she do? Or
she finds with increasing regularity that her planned visits are preceded by headaches or stomach problems that
force her to stay home. Or she may find herself saying
hurtful things to her parents, things she "doesn't mean."
She can't understand "what's got into her" and returns
home guilty and down on herself, taking it out on her husband and children.

A second problem of unfree people who demand emotional unanimity of themselves is evident. By vetoing a

contradictory emotion, they frequently deprive themselves of the very tension they need to grow. Growth cannot be achieved by canceling or prematurely terminating emotional tugs-of-war.

A person's love is only as genuine and strong as his capacity to hate. Love and hate are not opposites, but are polarities that rub against each other creating a heat that energizes. The opposite of love is not hate but indifference. "Pure love" is an artificial substance distilled by filtering out important parts of reality. It should be labeled "hazardous to your health."

A person's faith is only as strong as his capacity to doubt. Faith and doubt are also polarities, not opposites. The opposite of faith is not doubt, but disbelief. Doubt can motivate a person to grapple with his beliefs and shake out the unrealities. With regard to religious belief, Gordon Allport writes: "We may then say that the mature religious sentiment is ordinarily fashioned in the workshop of doubt."

The third problem is that unfree people who demand unanimity of emotions within themselves bind others by demanding it also from them. The message is: "Love me or hate me—take your choice"; or "Trust me or distrust me—take your choice"; or "Believe it or don't believe it—take your choice."

These unfree people continually skewer others to "either-or" dilemmas. And unfree people, to avoid tension, will respond "All right, all right, I LOVE you." Free people will respond: "There are some things I love about you, and a few things I don't. And there are some times I love you very much, but other times when I don't." This free person, however, will probably have just lost a "friend."

Free people invite the tension created by contrary feelings. They employ the tension generated by polarities to grow larger within themselves and closer to others. Free people can also admit emotional polarities to themselves: "I love my dad, but sometimes he bugs the heck out of me"; or "I believe a good deal of what my religion holds, but there are some things I just can't accept"; or "Most of the time I really enjoy being married, but sometimes I wish I weren't."

The free person can communicate these polarities to

others: "I like part of what you're saying, but I'm having difficulty with another part"; or "Part of me feels like taking the risk, but another part of me is scared to death"; or "I can trust you in most areas, but there's one area that we really need to work on."

Free people understand that "integrated" does not mean an absence of tension, but that the almost omnipresent tensions are bridled in the direction of growth.

10. FREEDOM TO FACE OUR MORTALITY

The thought of dying, of ceasing to exist in our present form, is not one most people entertain with enthusiasm. Although nothing is more obvious than the fact that in an eye-blink of time we will no longer be a human being, most people live each day as if they plan to be immortal. The closest we come to acknowledging the end of life is when we look forward to retirement. But we fail to carry the thought one small step further and acknowledge the fact that if we retire at sixty-five, statistics tell us there is a good possibility that we will be dead in three years. We look with enthusiasm toward retirement from work, but completely exclude the thought of retirement from life.

Most of us cannot acknowledge the inevitability of death because the thought petrifies us. For people who view life as merely a time to have fun, death represents an intolerable intrusion. For people to whom life is a heavy burden, death represents the termination of a life that was never begun.

The unfree person has an attitude toward life much like that of a millionaire toward one-dollar bills. He doesn't pay attention to individual days but squanders them, loses them, forgets them. The unfree person often sweats incidentals. A simple concern such as getting to the hairdresser on time can ruin the better part of a day. A man may spend many hours over the period of a month worried about whether he will be assigned the new company car or the one with 40,000 miles on it.

To the unfree person, religion is a fragilely constructed belief system to alleviate existential anxiety. However, existential anxiety is the very substance which, when used properly, makes life truly livable. The unfree person's religion reflects one of two extremes. It may be Pollyannish, based on the simplistic principle: "If I'm good, I'll go to heaven." Since most people define being "good" as merely refraining from being "bad" (rather than *doing* good), and since most people rationalize "bad" behaviors as being "good" anyway, the daily life of this individual is no different from anyone else's and perhaps less fruitful than that of many others.

On the other extreme, the unfree person's religion may be based on the neurotic principle: "If I suffer enough in life, I'll get to heaven." Life for these people becomes an exercise in self-punishment, which destroys the beauty in each day both for themselves and for the innocent bystanders around them.

In contrast to this, the free person keeps in touch with his mortality. It is not a morbid preoccupation with death, but a comfortable awareness that today is the last today of one's life. The free person's mortality is the benchmark against which he consciously or sub-consciously measures much of what he does. He asks himself: "On my deathbed, am I going to be furious at myself for spending this time the way I am?"

The free person absolutely refuses to waste time on unimportant trivia (some "trivia" are important). He jealously protects the use of his time and energy so that they will be properly invested in the values that are important to him. He appreciates the fact that he might never have been created, or that he could have been created a rock, or a cloud, or a cow. He is willing to invest himself in life in appreciation of this fact.

The free person uses his religion to glean more out of each day, both in terms of giving to life and of receiving from life. Religion makes life more "alive"—more meaningful, beautiful, and enjoyable.

The free person remains close to the realization of death and, because he does, he lives a fuller life. As Rollo May writes:

> The possibility of death jars us loose from the treadmill of time because it so vividly reminds

us that we do not go on endlessly. It shocks us
into taking the present seriously; the Turkish
proverb employed to rationalize procrastination,
"Tomorrow also is a blessed day," no longer
comforts and excuses; one cannot wait around
forever. It makes more crucial for us the fact
that while we are not dead at the moment, we
some time will be: so why not choose something
at least interesting in the meantime? (*Man's
Search for Himself,* Signet Books, New York,
1967, pp. 22–23)

In summary, it is helpful to remember three points:

1. We are responsible for freeing ourselves. The individual who states that he could be free if only other people would allow him to be free is deluding himself.

2. Freedom is not always "free," but frequently demands a price. The more free we become, the more we assume responsibility for our own behavior, and the less blameworthy other people become. When we succeed, we take the credit; when we fail, we take the blame.

3. The more free we are, the less we attempt to bind others. Developing our own psychological freedom will give us the strength to allow others to find their own freedom.

Reflection Questions

1. Almost everyone has a "manipulation button." What is mine? How can I become more aware when it is being pushed?
2. What is my favorite way of avoiding the normal sufferings that are a part of life?
3. Who is the one person in my life that I find the most difficult to disappoint? What can I do to become more free with that person?
4. What are the two contrary feelings that I experience that create the most anxiety in me? Why?
5. In a relatively short time, I shall be lying on my

death bed. What do I want to be able to feel in my last conscious moment? What am I doing to make that possible?

Thoughts to Contemplate

1. The self-fulfilling person enjoys getting compliments and encouragement from others, but he is not so reliant on it that he functions significantly less well without them.

2. Free people understand that the path to perfection is necessarily marbled with imperfection. Our imperfections are the isometrics we need to grow psychologically.

3. Enjoyment is often considered the sin of the wealthy or a sign of the uncommitted.

4. A person's love is only as genuine and strong as his capacity to hate. Love and hate are not opposites, but are polarities that rub against each other, creating a heat that energizes.

5. We look with enthusiasm toward retirement from work, but completely exclude the thought of retirement from life.

8

UNREAL EXPECTATIONS

One of the true marks of a mature person is that he can accurately distinguish a realistic from an unrealistic expectation. As a result, this person's daily life is significantly less fraught with hurt, disappointment, frustration, and resentment, thus freeing him for more creative endeavors.

An unrealistic expectation is one in which a person expects or anticipates a certain good when such is unlikely to occur. It does not mean such a good won't happen; it is just *unlikely* that it will. It does not mean that a person doesn't have the *right* to expect that the good will occur, but what is right and what is real are not always identical. It does not mean adopting a cynical attitude toward life, since cynicism is as unrealistic as naiveté or wishful thinking.

Realistic expectations flow from an honest appraisal of oneself, of the people involved in a situation, and of human nature in general. Unrealistic expectations are programmed more by needs, hopes, and naiveté than by an accurate estimate of reality. Unreal expectations are found in all areas of life. Some of them deal with general attitudes toward life while others develop particularly in the family—in the expectations of parents regarding their children or of children toward their parents.

UNREAL EXPECTATIONS OF LIFE

1. We should be shown appreciation at work. Appreciation means support, concern, affirmation, and gratitude.

Expecting appreciation from a boss, fellow workers, and the people toward whom we render our service—customers, clients, parishioners, patients—is often an unrealistic expectation.

The reality is that work can provide three kinds of reward. The first is material reward, i.e., money, benefits, power, prestige. The second kind of reward is a sense of inner satisfaction which flows from the feeling that we are doing a good job and/or the feeling that we are helping another in an important way. The third kind of reward is the expressed appreciation of those with whom and for whom we work.

The agreed-upon reward in most work is material reward. Almost no job promises more than this. In effect, this is the only agreement and, therefore, the *only* realistic expectation.

Some people are fortunate enough to have a job that offers both material reward and a sense of inner satisfaction. But inner satisfaction is never part of a job description. In fact, some jobs, by their very nature, provide no inner satisfaction.

There are very few people who have a job that includes appreciation as a reward. This is true because bosses typically feel that a paycheck is an adequate sign of appreciation. Bosses are also distracted by the overall functioning of the organization and tend to pay attention to individuals only when there is a problem. This is not ideal, but it is understandable and natural.

Co-workers are not likely to show each other appreciation because of the competition present in many job situations. To affirm a fellow worker often means giving him an advantage which most people are disinclined to do.

The people toward whom we render our services are unlikely to show appreciation because, like bosses, they feel they have shown appreciation by the money paid for the service. Some jobs cause anxiety in the recipients of the service who thus are not disposed to show appreciation. Occupations such as police officer, judge, dentist, teacher, and therapist rarely afford signs of appreciation, because most of the work consists in causing others pain of one sort or another.

When we unrealistically expect to be shown appreciation at work, our morale declines and gradually we feel cheated and resentful. We are tempted to quit the job and find a more satisfying one, only to discover that work is not a realistic place in which to look for appreciation.

Appreciation is more apt to be found in friendships and love relationships. As a statement in a teacher's magazine reflects: "If your students grow in skills, confidence, and self-direction under your tutelage, you can feel that you've been a good teacher. If you want to feel *loved,* too—get married."

2. *We should progress at work according to the quality of our work.* This is an unrealistic expectation because there are several factors that make a person successful at work, the quality of the work being an important one but not the only one.

A person's attitude toward authority is an important factor. Some people have the attitude: "I know more than my boss, so I don't have to pay any attention to him." Whether or not an individual is more skilled than the boss, such an attitude will cause antagonistic feelings in the boss.

It is possible for an employee to be more qualified than a boss, but this does not necessitate a contemptuous, cynical attitude toward the boss. Sooner or later, the boss is placed in the position of preferring an equally competent worker or even a less competent worker with whom he can relate smoothly.

A second factor relevant to success at work is the worker's ability to relate smoothly with fellow workers and the people for whom the worker provides a service. A person may be an excellent surgeon but relate in an arrogant or irritable way with colleagues and patients so that his services are no longer desired by partners or the hospital staff. A person may be an excellent classroom teacher but treat parents with disinterest or contempt. A college student may get all "A's" in academic courses but be so abrasive that the professors decline to write good letters of recommendation. Sometimes people protest: "I'm a lawyer—not a diplomat," but most jobs require both skills and the ability to relate adequately with peo-

ple. To expect that a particular skill alone will be sufficient in our work and will compensate for everything else
may often result in unemployment.

*3. Our problems can be solved by the passage of time and
by changing our environment.* It is unrealistic to expect
that the mere passage of calendar dates will have a therapeutic effect. Time may heal wounds, but it does not solve
problems. So many of us work on the principle: "Things
will be better next year." When someone has the nerve to
ask: "Why?" we respond: "Because they couldn't get any
worse." Problems "go" only one of two places: They get
solved or they incubate and become larger. The elapsing
of time only crystallizes the problem so that it becomes
more deeply embedded. The vast majority of serious
problems—personal problems, marital problems, school
or work problems—were once simple and easy to attack
and solve. It was time that entrenched them.

Changing one's environment means making a significant change in one's life. When we are unhappy, it is terribly tempting to look for a simple solution. Some hoped-
for panaceas are: falling in love (finding the right person); getting married or divorced; having a baby; changing schools or jobs; buying a summer home or going to
Europe; becoming more religious or entering psychotherapy.

Each of these could be a constructive step in growth.
But to view any one of them as the solution to a problem
is foolhardy. If I'm unhappy here, I'll be unhappy in Europe. If my marriage is not good now, the addition of a
baby is likely to make it worse. If, deep down, I don't want
to confront my life directly, psychotherapy will be merely
a token gesture.

Each behavior may bring some temporary relief because it distracts us from our real problems. But soon the
newness wears away, and we often discover that we not
only still have the original problem, but it has been com-
pounded by the "panacea." For example, now I not only
still have marital problems, but a new baby. Or now I not
only am depressed but unemployed; or now I'm not only
angry but guilty because of my affair.

When a house is on fire, watering the lawn will not extinguish the blaze. While this is obvious, many people operate exactly in this way; they feel inadequate so they get married; they are angry so they get divorced; they feel lonely so they have an affair.

Certainly there are some situations in which adding something or subtracting something from one's life will solve a problem. But in making such decisions, we must be careful that the solution is clearly linked to the problem and not just a stab in the dark.

4. We should be able to behave in certain ways but not experience the consequences. We often participate in cause-and-effect behavior and expect that the effect won't follow the cause. The following are some common examples of unrealistic expectations in this area:

—I want to be a private person but still have people care about me. These are mutually exclusive wishes. People can care about me only to the extent that they know me, and people can love me only to the extent that they care about me. In reality, one must choose one side of this coin or the other, but can't enjoy both.

—I want to please people and have a sound sense of who I am. When we highly value pleasing others, we are forced to wear many masks, all of which have a smile. After years of our wearing pleasing masks, bits and pieces of the masks become grafted to us. After a while, we lose track of who we really are. We look in the mirror and see a confusing and sometimes grotesque collage of many conflicting needs, values, hopes, and dreams. Realistically, we must choose between habitually pleasing people or habitually being who we are.

—I want to appear perfect and enjoy close relationships. If I wish to appear perfect—or near perfect—I shall have to hide my weaknesses and failures. This will necessitate a crust of subterfuge that is located between myself and the other person. The thicker the layer, the more cumbersome it is to touch and be touched by the other person. No matter how positive people feel toward me, these feelings get absorbed by the layer of subterfuge so that few reach the deeper parts of me. The more I allow my weakness to be seen, the more possibility there is for rejection, but also the more possibility there is for genuine intimacy. The problem is we must choose one or the other and not be surprised if the results are disappointing when we try to do both.

—I don't have time for fun, but I want to be happy. The main source of happiness is fun. Yet, so many of us don't have time for fun, or we ridicule fun as being for children but not for mature adults. It never ceases to amaze me how many people come to me complaining of fatigue, pessimism, apathy, and general unhappiness. When I ask them to relate the last time they really had fun, they answer: "Once last year"; or "When I was in college fifteen years ago." And they answer with a look that says: "What does *fun* have to do with anything?"

For many people fun is a memory. We should decide which way we want it. If something is more important than fun, we must accept the boredom and unhappiness that may go with it. If we want happiness, we have to sacrifice whatever it is that is usurping the time for fun.

—I want to violate my deeper values and still feel good. For anyone with an adequate conscience, this is an unrealistic expectation.

A man sees no relationship between his extramarital activities and his depression.

A woman sees no relationship between her dishonesty to her husband and her sleepless nights.

A college student sees no relationship between his cheating on exams and increasing disinterest in school.

A shop owner sees no relationship between overcharging his customers and increasing headaches.

As the adage goes: "If you want to dance, you must pay the piper." If we don't want to pay the piper, then we must stop dancing. Unfortunately the piper is a very wealthy person.

5. *When a person promises something, he will keep the promise.* In reality, the chances are about 50–50 that a person will carry through on a promise. If the person cares about us, the odds are a bit higher that the promises will be kept; the less the person cares about us, the lower the odds.

The following are some typical situations in which one is likely to be disappointed:

A friend says: "Don't worry about it; I got a job for you—it's all sewed up."

A roommate says: "Don't plan anything for this weekend, and we'll go on a picnic Saturday."

A classmate assures us: "Sure, I'll lend you my notes over the weekend."

A son or daughter says: "I'll have the car home by six o'clock sharp."

A boss says: "You'll be getting your promotion on July 1."

A teacher says: "If you work hard, you'll get an 'A.'"

A neighbor says: "I'll leave your house key under the door mat."

The unrealistic person accepts every promise with complete good faith, placing "all eggs in one basket." When the bottom drops out of the basket, there is nothing in its place but disappointment or, depending on the gravity of the situation, panic. In matters that make a difference, the realistic person divides the eggs into at least two baskets, so if the bottom drops out of one, a workable option will remain.

Why don't people keep their promises? Some people are sincere about their promises, but become distracted and forget. Others are half-sincere because they have mixed feelings about us and unconsciously "forget" the promise. Still others make a promise because they lack the strength to say "No," but have no intention of keeping it.

One need not be distrustful of people, but one should not be pollyannish either. The realistic person assesses the situation and, if it is important, makes auxiliary plans in case the promise is not kept.

6. *Somebody—somewhere—has the answer to our problems.* The truth is that no one has the answer to anyone else's problems. There are only processes that we can go through to arrive at *our own* answers.

Some people are forever shopping for a savior. They expend great amounts of time, energy, and money searching for the person who is going to bail them out of their difficulties. They hop from one friend to another and from one expert to another. Each new savior is ushered into life with adulation and hope. But gradually it becomes evident that it is the person alone who can rescue himself.

Sometimes people come to see me professionally and state after four or five visits: "I thought this was going to be simple—that I would tell you what's wrong with my life, and you would tell me how to make it better—like a doctor gives pills to make pain go away."

An analogy may help clarify the importance of process in arriving at one's own answers. A child asks his parent to help him with a multiplication problem: 360×360. The parent who does not understand the principles of learning responds: "Here, the answer is 129,600." This parent has confused two separate concepts: helping the child learn a process and giving the child the answer. Giving the answer is easier and faster, but this child will continually return for help because he did not go through the process personally and therefore is no better off than he was before the parent "helped."

The situation becomes even more complex in human behavior, because, unlike arithmetic, there are no universally correct answers. What is a correct answer to my marriage problem may be an incorrect one for yours.

Other people—friends, relatives, and experts—can help us progress through a process, and this requires time and work. The longer the problem has existed, the more time and work it will take. A marriage problem that has existed for two years will not be solved in five or ten discussions. One that has lasted for five or ten years will not be solved in twenty or thirty discussions.

There *is* somebody—somewhere—that has the answer to our problems: US. We can, and often should, avail ourselves of relatives, friends, clergy, and psychologists for help with the process, but none of these people has THE answer.

7. *If we do all the "right" things, everything should be all right.* Often people say: "I did everything right—just the way everyone said it should be done—and now look at the

mess I'm in." This sentiment could be describing a friendship, a romatic relationship, work, marriage, or parenthood.

There are two major difficulties with this type of expectation. One is that we believe there is a "right way" and a "wrong way" of doing things. We believe that there is one right way to communicate, to love, to have sex, to pray, to share bad news, to be a spouse or parent, to be accepted, to feel happy, and even to die. For the most part, there *are* right ways and wrong ways of doing any of the above, but there are *many different* right ways and wrong ways, not just one. A physician may inform five different patients that their illness is terminal in five different ways, and each may be the right way for the individual patient.

It can be helpful to consult others as to how to do something in a good way. Hopefully the person we consult, be it friend or professional, will offer at least a few options for us to consider. The next step is to distill these options through our own personality and through the situation, sifting out the options with which we feel uncomfortable or that are inappropriate for our situation. It is this distillation of options that will increase the likelihood that our behavior will be effective.

A second problem occurs when a person tries too hard to do the right thing and loses sight of the overall situation. Some newlyweds try so hard to be expert spouses that they become marriage technicians, which eventually chases the warmth and humanness out of the relationship. Some people try so hard to be proficient sexual partners that they get an "A" in mechanics and an "F" in love. Some parents try so hard to be excellent parents that they rear well-behaved but resentful children.

Whatever is the "right thing" we are trying to do, if it detracts from the freedom, honesty, or love in a situation, then it's not the right thing for us.

8. If I'm good to God, God will be good to me. When people build their lives on this hope, they are likely to be disappointed. And when they are disappointed, two damaging reactions occur. First, they become resentful of God, because God is perceived as having double-crossed them. Secondly, they enter a state of despair because when God lets you down, where else is there to turn?

This expectation is unrealistic for three reasons.

First, "being good" means different things to different people. For many people, what they consider to be "good" behavior is actually unhealthy behavior. And unhealthy behavior, even when it is engaged in under the banner of religion, will eventually cause both psychological and spiritual negative consequences.

For some people "being good" means not expressing anger toward loved ones. For others it can mean being selfless, never allowing one's own needs to get met. "Being good" can mean remaining in a life commitment such as marriage or the religious life even though it has become irreversibly mutilating. It can mean interpreting every negative event in one's life as "God's will," precluding the necessity of reevaluating and changing one's own behavior. It can mean having such a "complete trust" in God that one does not exercise ordinary precautions and prudence in making important decisions. If "being good" means any one or all of these attitudes, then, sooner or later, the person's life is liable to cave in on top of him.

Second, this expectation implies that God is only outside of us. It assumes that if we please this being outside of us, it will protect us. The problem is: How do we know what pleases God—what does God want us to do? The answer is that we can look to the Bible or the church or to daily events that, if interpreted correctly, will give us clues to what we can do to please God.

In so doing, we ignore the presence of God in ourselves, the fact that God can speak to us just as surely through our own needs, fears, desires, angers, and hopes. This results in disastrous situations such as a woman saying "I don't want to remain a nun, but that is what God wants me to do"; or "I don't want to break off this engagement, but I think that is what God wants"; or "I don't think we can cope with one more child, but obviously God wants us to have as many kids as he sends us." For these people, paying attention to their own wishes, feelings, common sense, and needs is viewed as "selfish" and displeasing to God. The attitude "I am nothing, and God is everything" can cause much needless and destructive suffering. Furthermore, it is not even theologically correct, because most of these people also believe that a human being is a creature made in the image and likeness of God. If this is so, man is surely not "nothing."

Third, this expectation reflects a "slot-machine" approach to God. If we invest a certain number of good works in God, God will reward us accordingly. This is an uncomfortably anthropomorphic view of God which makes God's love sound very conditional. God becomes the father who protects us when we please him and rejects us when we displease him. Since even good fathers don't operate like this, it is unlikely that God does.

A more realistic expectation involves understanding that sound mental health principles do not contradict sound religious principles, but complement them. What's good for the psyche is good for the soul, and what's bad for the psyche is bad for the soul. To the extent we ignore or sacrifice our deepest needs, wishes, and hopes for any reason, the more will we become psychologically and spiritually emaciated.

UNREAL EXPECTATIONS IN THE FAMILY

Two kinds of conflict occur in families. One is *unavoidable*, a natural result of human beings living closely with one another. Conflicts of this type create tension, which, when used constructively, is a necessary fuel for family growth.

The second type is *avoidable* conflict, which occurs when family members fail to understand some important principles of behavior. Add avoidable conflict to unavoidable, and the resulting tension often overloads the family's psychological circuits. Relationships become frayed and damaging.

Most avoidable conflicts stem from the unrealistic expectations family members have of each other. When father expects from son, or son from father, or sister from brother, a certain type of behavior which is unlikely to occur, the result is usually tension, frustration, conflict.

The behavior is unlikely to occur for one of three reasons: (1) A level of maturity is expected that is simply beyond the individual, given his or her age, intelligence, and life experiences; (2) The expectation is for *ideal* behavior which is the exception rather than the rule in human interactions; (3) The expectation asks the individual to behave in a way that would be detrimental to self-growth or the growth of another family member, so the person eschews the behavior.

While many of the expectations which family members have for each other are realistic, perhaps as many are not. For this reason, it is helpful to identify some common unrealistic expectations that occur primarily in the family, to discuss their causes, the problems they create, and the ways to avoid them. The two dimensions that will be discussed are the unrealistic expectations that parents have of their children and that children have of their parents.

PARENTS' UNREAL EXPECTATIONS OF THEIR CHILDREN

All parents have unrealistic expectations of their children. The term "children," as it is used below, includes adolescents and young adults. Following are three such common unrealistic expectations that are manifested almost daily.

1. Children should always be sensitive to the needs and feelings of others in the family. Sensitivity to others is both a beautiful trait and a necessary one for genuine love and happiness. Thus, most parents are disturbed to see their children being insensitive to those around them.

We expect our five-year-old to share his toys with his three-year-old sister, and when he doesn't, we scold him for being selfish. We expect our eight-year-old daughter to realize we have a headache (especially when we *tell* her that we do) and become furious when five minutes later she is playing the piano. Our ten-year-old tells his fourteen-year-old sister she is "fat" in front of her friends, and she retaliates by replying "At least I'm not stupid" in front of his friends. Our fourteen-year-old wants dad to play ball even though it should be obvious that dad had a bad day at work. Our sixteen-year-old waits until we plan our evening and then asks us to drive her to a dance across town.

In the ideal realm, none of these children should have behaved so insensitively. But in the spirit of respecting reality, we can expect insensitivity to occur for the following reasons.

First, as parents, we often display insensitivity toward our children. When our children are in the midst of a game or doing homework, how often do we casually drag them away to do something that *we* want? We protest that what *we* want them to do is "more important." But the principle we are teaching is that if an individual feels his needs are "more important," this gives him the right to be insensitive.

How often do we scold or berate our children and adolescents in front of others? We argue that the "others" are only his brothers and sisters or friends—but we don't apply the same principle when our children embarrass us in front of our family or friends. When our child is feeling tired or irritable, do we curtail the things we want to do, or do we become irritated with our child's irritability?

Our eighteen-year-old son forgets to tell us to return a phone call, and we can't understand how anyone could be that unconcerned about others. Yet it was only last week that his girl friend phoned, and we forgot to tell him. We explain, "But *our* call was *urgent*," failing to realize that to our son his call was equally urgent.

Children are often insensitive for a second reason. Sensitivity is related to cognitive sophistication which is based on neurological development and affects how keenly we perceive the world. In childhood, development from one year to the next makes a significant difference in cognitive sophistication. For example, a five-year-old should be much more perceptually aware than a four-year-old, and an eighteen-year-old more so than a fifteen-year-old. Yet, almost unconsciously, we ignore this reality. We sometimes expect our children to possess the same degree of cognitive sophistication as we do. And we *often* expect our children to be more sensitive than their cognitive sophistication could possibly warrant. We scold our three children for lacking sensitivity in a situation in which two out of the three may lack the neurological development to support that sensitivity.

Because insensitivity in children is to be expected, it should be treated as any other behavior that is normal but that needs changing. Scolding and punishing our children for being insensitive causes a paradoxic effect. When children (or adults for that matter) are attacked, they turn inward, "licking their wounds" and resenting the people that caused them. So, instead of becoming more sensitive, they become more impervious, and this creates a vicious circle.

It is more helpful to teach sensitivity by *being* more sensitive daily to our children and to their childlike needs and fears; by being sensitive at the particular time that our child reacts insensitively; by discussing the reasons for the behavior with the child in an empathetic rather than in an angry manner; by showing the child the harmful consequences of the behavior; and by helping the child realize more sensitive options for handling a similar situation in the future.

2. Children should not argue and fight. If parents have a peaceful home as their goal, then it is true: Children should not argue and fight. But if we want a healthy, growth-producing home, some arguing and fighting should not only be expected but encouraged in a family. This is so because three important psychological skills can be learned in normal arguing and fighting.

The first is the ability to be assertive. Being assertive does not mean being aggressive, intimidating, or selfish. It means having the skill and the confidence to reach out for what is rightly ours; to say "no" to unreasonable requests; and, when necessary, to fight in a constructive way for what is essential for our growth and happiness. This ability is important because without it our children will deprive themselves of the "emotional groceries" that are necessary for their growth. Arguing and fighting are natural testing-grounds for developing this ability.

The second psychological skill is the ability to acquiesce to another when it is appropriate without loss of self-esteem or feeling a need for revenge. It is easier to learn to *always* acquiesce (thus avoiding conflict) or to *never* acquiesce (thus avoiding loss of self-esteem). But the two-fold challenge is to teach the child how to acquiesce *only* when it is just and reasonable, and to view such yielding to another as a sign of maturity and not of weakness. This can be learned only through years of "supervised" fighting and arguing.

The third trait which normal arguing and fighting can teach is the ability to tolerate tension. Many adults have never learned to "handle" tension. They sacrifice important needs and values for the sake of preventing tension. And, when tension does arise, they wither under it. It is necessary to teach children not only how to survive tension but also how to think clearly in the midst of it and how to use it creatively. Arguing and fighting are realistic arenas in which to learn this skill.

The problem is that many parents view arguing and fighting as "not nice." These parents fail to realize that it is *more* "not nice" to be an adult who has been deprived of opportunities to learn these skills in childhood. Other parents resent being distracted by the noise and commotion of arguing and fighting. Unfortunately, the price for this "peace and quiet" may be a very dear one for both the children and parents a little later in life. Still other parents exhort their children not to argue and fight but to "settle things in a mature way." These parents fail to realize that mature behavior cannot appear as if by magic, but must be preceded by many years of childish behavior.

It is important for us to realize that learning the three aforementioned skills is no different than learning the academic skills of mathematics, reading, or writing. Ironically, however, many parents reward children's attempts to learn academic skills and are only too happy to tolerate and help them correct mistakes. But when children are learning psychological skills through arguing and fighting, they are often punished and sent to their rooms.

Another important teaching element is the manner in which parents themselves handle arguing and fighting. Some parents refuse to argue and fight, thus depriving their children of healthy models. When parents are *always* arguing, or arguing and fighting in destructive ways, they act as negative models. Some parents, when they argue with their children, never acquiesce to the children, even when it would be appropriate. This teaches children that arguing and fighting are good only if you "win." Healthy parents realize that it is human and normal to argue and fight and do so in ways that are not only helpful to them but a positive learning experience for their observant children.

A helpful and realistic approach is to view arguing and fighting as a learning experience and to tutor it as one tutors academic exercises. When the dust clears from an argument, each child should be one degree closer to handling a conflictual situation in a more constructive way. When this is done a reasonable number of times over the course of twenty years, our children will be much better able to live life the way it should be lived.

3. Children should assume the same values as their parents. Parents want their children to become good and happy adults. Most parents feel that this will occur only if the children live according to the same values as the parents. But this expectation generally is unrealistic and is the greatest cause of tension between parents and their children who are in adolescence and young adulthood.

To view this issue realistically, it is important to distinguish between primary values and secondary values. Primary values are basic values which have inherent worth and which pertain to all situations and all ages. Actually there are relatively few primary values. The main ones are: It is good to love oneself and to love others; it is good to be honest with oneself and to be honest with others; it is good to be just with oneself and just with others.

Secondary values do not have inherent worth, but derive their worth to the degree that they help a particular individual live out his primary values. Some secondary values are: patriotism, obedience, respect, success, commitment, work, loyalty, and prestige. Any or all of these may be virtues or liabilities, depending on how much growth or damage accrues from them. For example, patriotism is a virtue when it represents an allegiance to a country that is furthering primary values (love, honesty, justice). But it is a liability when a country is violating primary values. Commitment in one situation may provide an individual added resources to actualize his growth potential. But in another situation, it could act as a "noose around one's neck." Obedience is a virtue when the authority is reasonable and growth occurs. But it is a liability when the authority is unreasonable or when it retards growth and causes resentment.

A secondary value may be a virtue up to a point but, past that point, it becomes a liability. For example, work may bring about personal growth, but overwork or compulsive work interferes with and stunts growth.

Secondary values are also often time-related and change with the years. Some years ago, for Catholics, to refrain from eating meat on Friday was an important value, but it no longer is. It was a value for women to be demure, passive, and dedicate their lives to making men happy, but it no longer is.

Conflicts often arise in a family when the parents fail to distinguish between primary and secondary values and lump them into one value system. We often want our children to internalize *both* our primary *and* secondary values because both were instrumental in our growth and happiness. We fail to realize that, while primary values should remain the same, children must learn to choose which of our secondary values will be helpful to them and which will prove a hindrance in living out their primary values.

Almost all value conflicts between parents and children involve secondary values. We often want our children to be obedient for the sake of being obedient and to work hard for the sake of working hard. Whether or not it will further our children's growth and happiness, we want them to dress in certain ways; to go to college; to pursue a particular career; to imitate our specific religious values and practices; to earn money and have prestige; to love only certain people only in certain ways; to "give us" grandchildren and to live nearby. We assure ourselves and our children that we are asking "very little" as a sign of appreciation for all we've done for them when, in fact, we may be asking them to contort their lives as a sign of gratitude.

Sometimes parents even teach secondary values over primary ones. For example, we may use special influence to get our child into a school or a job (a secondary value) even though such preferential treatment is unjust (a primary value) to the others competing for the same position.

Some parents identify so strongly with secondary values that they almost *become* them. This offers the children the unenviable choice of accepting the parents' secondary values, which will damage the children, or of rejecting the parents, which will cause the children great guilt. In cases like this, we parents are violating a primary value (love) in order to enforce our secondary values.

It is realistic to expect our children to assume primary values to the extent that we have taught them by the way we live. But it is unrealistic to expect that our children should automatically assume all of our secondary values because they are not we, and the world they live in is not ours.

In summary, it is unrealistic to expect our child to develop into a sensitive adult when we are insensitive to the child; when the child is expected to relate on a level of sensitivity beyond his maturational level; and when we punish a child for being insensitive, instead of teaching the child more constructive ways of handling the situation. In fact, these behaviors will do much more to effect insensitivity than sensitivity. Our children will become as sensitive as their maturity allows them to be, and their parents teach them to be.

It is also unrealistic to expect our children to grow into strong adults when they have been consistently deprived of opportunities to develop strength in the home. We cannot forbid and punish normal arguing and fighting and, at the same time, expect to have children who will be capable of handling the daily give-and-take and resultant tensions of adulthood. While arguing and fighting are disruptive to the "harmony" of the family, a reasonable amount must be allowed and supervised so that critically important life skills can be learned.

Finally, it is unrealistic to expect our children to develop sound value systems if we coerce them into pursuing our secondary values merely to make us happy or proud when one or more of these values may be toxic to their psychological and spiritual systems. When parents teach primary values by their everyday behavior and expose their children to a wide range of secondary values (not just their own), the children will develop a sound value system.

CHILDREN'S UNREAL EXPECTATIONS OF THEIR PARENTS

Children also have unrealistic expectations of their parents. Sometimes these expectations are contagious, i.e., the parents gradually acquire these same unrealistic expectations for themselves. The following are three common unrealistic expectations that children have of their parents.

1. Parents should dedicate their lives to their children. Children often feel that the only reason their parents were placed on earth was to be their mother and father. This expectation is the tail-end of a larger myth that many people have in our society. This myth holds that when people get married, they should divest themselves of their personal needs and individuality and somehow melt into the personality of the marriage partner, becoming "as one." In other words, one's personal identity should be forfeited to the marriage relationship.

The second part of the myth holds that when the married couple has children, the marriage relationship should become subjugated to the parental role. The following is a graphic representation of the weightings of each of the three roles as measured by the amount of time, energy, and interest expended in families with this attitude:

The ideal situation should appear this way:

INDIVIDUAL   WIFE   MOTHER

INDIVIDUAL   HUSBAND   FATHER

In other words, the individual's time, energy, and interest are equally distributed to each life role, bringing a much healthier balance to the entire family.

An individual should not disown his personhood for the sake of marriage or parenthood because these roles can be only as strong and healthy as the PERSONALITY on which they rest. Consequently, it is important for most people to have their own friends. One should also maintain and develop interests and hobbies and have leisure and quiet time to oneself. The obstacles to maintaining one's individuality are: It appears "selfish"; it is misconstrued as reflecting discontent with one's marriage or parenthood; or it causes jealousy in the spouse who is not involved in the particular source of enjoyment.

It is equally important that parents spend quality time with each other in their marriage relationship. Quality time means time alone with each other which is uninterrupted and unhurried. The time may be spent quietly, or in honest, deep communication, or in play. It is necessary to set aside at least a few such times weekly. A weekend once every six months is not nearly enough.

The obstacles to this togetherness are a fear of intimacy in which the children become a convenient distraction; being "too busy" with other chores; and feeling guilty that the children are left "all by themselves." Children can also foster this guilt: "Are you and mom going out *again*?" It is also important that single parents maintain personal close relationships with adults outside of the family.

Parenthood is a great responsibility and demands enormous resources from the parents. But to ignore one's individual needs and to squeeze one's marriage relationship between the demands of the children, is to invite many problems that will contaminate all three roles.

2. Parents should be "perfect" parents. It is typical of children to expect their parents to be perfect—or at least near perfect. This means that parents should rarely, if ever, make a mistake, act arbitrarily, lose their tempers, be irritable or unkind, fight, or have emotional problems. It also means that parents should always—or almost always—be loving, patient, fair, interested, energetic, joyful, and provide all the major benefits of life.

Children expect perfection for at least three reasons. One is that they are children and have not yet tempered their idealism with reality. Secondly, the modern generation expects perfection in its parents because these children watch television families who embody every virtue imaginable and expect their parents to be the same. A third reason is that parents expect *their children* to behave perfectly, and the unrealistic expectation boomerangs back to the parents. Many parents also expect *themselves* to be perfect because they read pseudo-psychological literature that offers prescriptions on how to be the ideal parent.

In fact, "perfect" parents (as children define "perfect") would be terrible parents because the children would be woefully ill-prepared to live in the real, imperfect world. A thirty-year-old person recently told me: "I grew up in a perfect family. It was absolutely 'germ-free.' But when I graduated from college and left home, I fell apart because I had built up no resistance to the 'germs' of anger, injustice, insecurity, and tension."

When children meet negative experiences, they instinctively withdraw (run away from the situation, quit, become helpless, resentful, or depressed) or attack (hit, scream, ridicule, and hurt). Many adults react to negative experiences in the exact same ways because they came from "perfect" homes and were deprived of learning to handle frustrations. Or they came from homes where there were a sufficient number of negative experiences, but in which parents failed to take the time or learn the skills to help the child discover more constructive ways of handling them. As a result, these adults find life much more difficult than it need be.

The best parents are those who, by their everyday behavior, offer a representative sample of the world the child will have to deal with at twenty, thirty, or fifty years of age. Of course this is not to say that *steady doses* of anger, injustice, and rejection provide any better preparation for the real world. But learning to face an imperfect world is a skill that can and should be learned in the family.

What differentiates good parents from ineffective ones is not necessarily that good parents make fewer mistakes. But, when effective parents make mistakes, they help the child handle the negative experience as constructively as possible. The good parent says: "All right, it wasn't fair; now how are you going to handle it?"

Parents can help their children avoid the unrealistic expectation of "perfect" parents in two ways. First, parents can realize that children must be allowed a certain "margin of error" appropriate to their level of maturity. The more reasonable this "margin of error" is, the more the children will automatically allow a margin of error for the parents, thus preventing unnecessary tension and disappointment.

Secondly, children can be helped to realize that being a parent does not imply or necessitate perfection. Children can be taught that the main responsibility of parents is not to provide a utopian home but to prepare their children to live effectively in the real world.

3. Parents should be "modern" and not "old-fashioned."
This unrealistic expectation in children usually begins at about nine years of age and lasts until adulthood. From the child's point of view, there are two kinds of parents: old-fashioned and modern. For parents to qualify as "modern" all they have to do is allow the child complete freedom. Sometimes the child is so persuasive or, more accurately, the parents are so insecure, that the parents ignore their common sense and abdicate their responsibility in order to "earn" the title of "modern."

Many children expect their "modern" parents to completely trust them, i.e., not to check up on them; to allow them to come and go as they please; to allow them to make all significant decisions by themselves; to allow them to behave any way they wish; to defend them against authority; to give them enough money so that they won't be "embarrassed" to go out with their friends; and, finally, to realize that the children are better prepared to handle life than the parents.

Contrary to what is implied in this unrealistic expectation, the opposite of "modern" is not "old-fashioned." The opposite of "modern" is "effective." Effective parents realize that it would be detrimental to rear their children according to the exact same principles with which they were raised. On the other hand, they realize that it would be equally destructive to be a "modern parent."

Effective parents realize and help their children to learn that no matter how intellectually bright or sophisticated the children may be, they have some basic needs that are crucial. If these needs are not met in childhood and adolescence, problems will be created in adulthood.

"Modern" parents often fail to meet the following five basic needs because they want to avoid unpleasantness and want their children to "approve" of them.

A. The need to feel that the parents truly care about their children. When parents give in to their children against their better judgment, it teaches the children that the parents are more interested in being liked by the children than in doing the correct thing for them.

B. The need to feel that their parents are strong. When parents are manipulated by their children into acceding to unreasonable or inappropriate requests, they are not teaching the children that they are "neat parents" but weak parents, and weak parents rear weak children.

C. The need to develop frustration tolerance. Parents who want to give their children every freedom and material benefit possible and who are afraid to say "no," rear children who, when they cannot get what they want as adults, quickly fall apart.

D. The need to receive honest feedback. Children need an accurate "mirror" because they often think they are creating a positive impression when they are presenting a negative one. Parents are in the best position to help their children correct their perceptions and modify their behavior accordingly. But if parents are reluctant to give negative feedback, they are depriving the children of a chance to make necessary adjustments in their behavior.

E. The need to learn and accept the consequences of their behavior. Children need to be taught that negative behavior (behavior that is inappropriate, dishonest, or harmful) brings negative consequences. But, when parents teach that negative behavior brings no consequences, or positive consequences, or only *occasionally* brings negative consequences, the child is taught no inner controls and no sound reason not to behave negatively. Thus these children of "modern" parents will find the world a very unfriendly place in which to live.

In summary, it is necessary that both children and parents understand that parenthood is *one* role in life and is not synonymous with "life" itself. The more parenthood is overvalued at the expense of one's private self and one's married self, the weaker the parenthood will be. People whose *main* purpose in life is to be "good parents" are doomed to failure because they are not taking advantage of many of the resources that make parents truly effective.

Children and parents should realize that the more parents strive to be "perfect," the more imperfect they will become. Effective parents strive not to be "perfect" but to be *real*. Real parents present life as it really is and teach their children how to deal with it constructively. While this requires more time and energy and creates more tension within the family, it will help the child develop strong "psychological muscles" with which to handle a world that is more imperfect than perfect.

Finally, children and parents can see that being "modern" has the same pitfalls as being "old-fashioned." In each case, parents are regulating their behavior according to outside norms and not according to their own experience, common sense, and intuition. No matter how intelligent a child is; or what sophisticated subjects he is learning in school; or how big or mature he is, there are certain basic learnings that supercede all of these factors. These learnings, for all practical purposes, can best be taught by parents.

Reflection Questions

1. What is perhaps my greatest unrealistic expectation about myself, others, or life in general? What can I do to modify it?

2. What is happening in my life that I hope will get better in a year or so? What am I actively doing to bring that about?

3. What is the largest unrealistic expectation people have of me? What can I do to extricate myself from it?

4. If I'm a parent, what expectation do I have of my children, that, if I'm to be perfectly honest, is unrealistic?

5. Looking at my parents, what expectation do I have of them that, considering their background, is really unfair?

Thoughts to Contemplate

1. The vast majority of serious problems—personal problems, marital problems, school or work problems—were once simple and easy to attack and solve. It was time that entrenched them.

2. For many people fun is a memory. We should decide which way we want it. If something is more important than fun, we must accept the boredom and unhappiness that may go with it. If we want happiness, we have to sacrifice whatever it is that is usurping the time for fun.

3. As the adage goes: "If you want to dance, you must pay the piper." If we don't want to pay the piper, then we must stop dancing. Unfortunately, the piper is a very wealthy person.

4. There *is* somebody—somewhere—that has the answer to our problems: US. We can, and often should, avail ourselves of relatives, friends, clergy, and psychologists for help with the process, but none of these people has THE answer.

5. What's good for the psyche is good for the soul, and what's bad for the psyche is bad for the soul.

9

THE FORGOTTEN VIRTUES: UNDERSTANDING, FORGIVENESS, AND HOPE

In the midst of establishing "meaningful relationships," of striving to "communicate," and of searching for "modern approaches to life," many virtues are disregarded as being old-fashioned. Yet, a study of many of these "forgotten virtues" can provide much food for psychological growth. Three important virtues are understanding, forgiveness, and hope. Each of these attributes is important in personal development and in interpersonal relationships.

UNDERSTANDING

Understanding another human being is an extremely basic and important art. It is important theoretically because understanding is the necessary link between communication and love. The more we communicate, the more we create a potential for understanding. The more this potential becomes actualized, the closer we are drawn to the other person in respect, concern, or love.

Understanding is also important humanly. When we look back to the people who helped and influenced our lives the most, almost invariably the main descriptive term used is "understanding." We feel truly blessed if we have an understanding father, mother, child, teacher, clergyman, physician, or therapist. Obversely, some of

196

the severest hurt that we have experienced occurred when our hopes for being understood were left agonizingly unmet.

What is meant by understanding? It is the art of realizing two things: first, *how* a person perceives a situation or situations, and, secondly, why he thinks what he thinks; feels what he feels; and does what he does. What on paper seems to be a simple process is, when transposed to the vicissitudes of day-to-day living, a very difficult art to learn and to practice. Yet, if we wish to develop healthy relationships, we must practice it arduously every day.

There are at least three barriers that interfere with understanding.

The main obstacle to understanding another person is that we simply do not wish to understand the other. Some people openly admit this. Others say: "Yeah, well, I understand, but...." Teachers, for example, know well the difference between a student who *invites* an answer to a question and one who *dares* the teacher to answer. The first student is genuinely interested in understanding the teacher so as to make an informed decision; the second is interested only in proving to himself that the teacher is not worth understanding.

The main cause of not wanting to understand another is fear—fear that one will be changed in some way that one views as harmful. It would be better if one felt secure enough within himself to open himself up to another's being, anticipating some gain rather than some loss.

Confusing "understanding" with "approval" or weakness is a second barrier to understanding another person. Some people feel that if they allow themselves to understand a person, a belief, or a life style, somehow such understanding will convey approval. Yet, in reality, this need not be the case. A variation of this is the feeling that understanding connotes weakness. If we are seen as understanding, we will be viewed as a "pushover," or as "naive," or, to put it another way: "If we start understanding them, the next thing you know we'll be becoming like them." So, we place ourselves in bell-jars which are very safe but very sterile.

Attributing motives and intentions to another's behavior provides another obstacle to understanding. Ambiguity is very difficult for us to experience. We have almost an innate need to clarify ambiguity—to seek explanations that will eradicate confusion. The need is so strong that we will create explanations to clarify an issue. As a result we find ourselves exclaiming: "I know why my daughter's boy friend says those things to her; he is trying to weaken our influence over her." "I know why that conservative theologian said that: He wants to hang on to power." "I know why that liberal theologian said that: He's not strong enough to live by the rules of the traditional church."

So, on and on it goes. *Now* we know! And as soon as we "know," there is no need for further dialogue or understanding. We create a caricature of another person and "understand" the caricature. To do more than that requires confidence and courage that all of us are capable of achieving with the help of some realizations and hard work.

The difficulties involved in understanding others can be overcome by developing abilities such as the following.

1. The ability to perceive a situation from the viewpoint of the other. This means trying very hard to "get behind the eyeballs and nerve-endings" of another, to see and feel the situation the way he does. It is only then that a person's confusing or aggravating behavior can make sense so that we may react in appropriate and helpful ways. Some examples may be helpful to explain this situation.

Two couples attend a party together. The first couple decides to let the other couple "go off on their own" so that the second couple will not feel "tied down" to them. The second couple notices they have been "left" by the first couple. They feel hurt or angry because they think the first couple must have found them boring or "not good enough" to be seen with. The second couple has two options: They can ask the other couple why they "disappeared," or they can maintain their misperception and do damage to the friendship.

A second example is a boss who chooses not to attend

a party given for one of his employees because he perceives that his presence would put a "damper" on the fun. The employees, noting that the boss has "bowed out" of the party, perceive him as aloof, disinterested, and as frowning on them for enjoying themselves in this manner. The employees don't give the boss an opportunity to describe his perception of the situation, either because they "already know" why he failed to attend the party, or because they are afraid to broach the subject with him. As a result, distance increases in the relationship when closeness should have occurred.

A situation similar to those described happens many times in human nature, and it's sad that it does, because so many people suffer because of it. If we can realize how important it is to understand another person's point of view in a situation, our attitude will be less: "Why did you *do* that!" and more: "How did you *view* that?"

2. *The ability to recognize where another person is coming from.* This requires the ability and willingness to interpret another's behavior in the context of his overall growth and not as a separate piece of behavior devoid of all developmental ramifications.

Much of the behavior that we view as upsetting to us is what might be called "middle-step behavior." This is behavior that is not as good as it could be but not as bad as it was. It may be, for a particular individual, both a necessary phase in his growth and the only behavior available to him at that point in time. It is a "lesser-of-evils" type of behavior on the road, hopefully, to the ultimate "better-of-goods."

The following are sometimes examples of middle-step behavior. Harsh anger is sometimes a person's clumsy attempt to stand up for himself. It is not as good as being smoothly assertive, but it is better than being agonizingly non-assertive ("I'd rather switch than fight"). Middle-step behavior is sometimes seen in conceit (which may be a step up from feeling worthless); selfishness (which could be a notch up from being neurotically sacrificing); insensitivity (which may be better than being an "emotional hemophiliac"); cynicism (which may be growth away from an unhealthy idealism); and disrespect (which may be a step up from unthinking obedience or crippling fear).

This does not mean that we must approve of middle-step behavior; we can help the individual assess the results of his actions and help him learn ways to express his feelings more constructively. By the same token, if we squelch middle-step behavior, we may cause the other to regress to "first step" actions and prolong or extinguish growth in a particular area.

Middle-step behavior is never a final goal, but it could be a temporary and necessary sub-good for some people. Understanding and accepting this behavior (which does not mean "approving" of it) can enable us to be helpful to another person who would ordinarily be upsetting and possibly repulsive to us. Anybody can relate well with the "beautiful people" (good, fun, healthy, etc.). It is more difficult, but very necessary, to relate helpfully to people who upset, confuse, anger, and dumbfound us.

3. The ability to see beyond superficially negative behavior to its positive or neutral base. Whenever people behave in a negative way, i.e., in a manner that results in our feeling angry, upset, or frustrated, there is an underlying reason for this behavior. Often the deeper reason is positive or at least neutral. For example, some people, especially young people, behave in negative ways to get our attention because they like us. Some of the most "obnoxious" students I have taught I gradually became good friends with when I understood they were "throwing rocks" at me to get me to pay special attention to them and not to hurt me. My choices were two: to throw rocks back at them (where everyone gets hurt) or to lead them to the realization that there were more positive ways of gaining the same attention.

Sometimes people behave negatively toward us to test us, even though they may not realize that they are doing this. The more we espouse moral or mental health values, the more we are open to this attitude. The gist of the challenge is: "OK, you say all those nice 'good' things; let's see how you fare in the heat of battle!"—or more colloquially: "Let's see if you can put your money where your mouth is."

If we view the basis of such a challenge as negative, i.e., as an attempt to hurt us personally, then we shall likely react in an unhelpful manner. If we view the basis as positive, i.e., the person is saying: "I like your values, but I want to see if they're *real, living* values or just cheap talk," then we should welcome this opportunity to affirm who we are under difficult circumstances.

A neutral base can also underlie overtly negative behavior. We know that people often strike out at other people when they have suffered a real or imagined threat. This angry reaction is really motivated more by fear than by anger. For example, if we look back at the last time we were really angry with someone, the chances are very good that we will discover that they threatened us in some way. They "made us" feel less intelligent, less sensitive, less reasonable, less mature, less strong, or less generous than we like to feel about ourselves. But, instead of dealing with the *fear* that the threat created, we instinctively cloak it in anger to throw the spotlight off of us and onto the other person. So we say "I'm *angry* with *you*" rather than the more realistic "I'm afraid of what you made me feel about *myself.*" So, if we can "read" also that most anger that is directed toward us is based on fear, it can open up many more constructive pathways of communication.

4. *The ability to realize that "a few notes don't make a melody."* What this means is that we tend to make superficial—and sometimes lasting—judgments of another on the basis of hearing a few of his ideas or listening to a few sentences from his mouth. For example, a teacher may have worked for a school principal last year who said: "We are very interested in you as a person and hope that you will view the faculty here as part of a larger family." This sounded very good until the teacher gradually realized that he was expected to sacrifice large portions of his life to the school—in a way that only his own family would have a right to expect. So he changes jobs. The first day at the new school, the principal calls him in and says: "We're not only interested in what you can give to the school, but we are interested in what we can do for you—like a big family." The teacher then says to himself:

"Here we go again." So, whether he wants to or not, the teacher shifts his psyche into a gear that states loud and clear: "You won't get one ounce of work out of me that I don't get paid for." This eventually reflects in his attitude and work, and his performance is evaluated as "poor." The teacher then may perceive this as proof that this principal wants only slaves and not professional teachers.

This whole unpleasant scene could have been avoided had the teacher realized that many different types of people can say the same things—or have certain personality traits—but be "coming from quite different places." It is only after we allow the other person to play out the entire melody that we can make a reasonable judgment of him and his motives.

FORGIVENESS

C. S. Lewis writes: "Every one says forgiveness is a lovely idea, until they have something to forgive." Like understanding, forgiveness is a difficult ability to acquire, yet one that is essential to the development of good interpersonal relationships.

What does forgiveness mean from a mental health viewpoint? The word that best defines healthy forgiveness is "pardon," i.e., "to release a person from punishment." The important idea here is that we actively decide to stop punishing the individual who has hurt us.

The opposite occurs when we initiate a program of ongoing punishment of someone who has hurt us. We may do this *actively* by saying things to the person to make him feel guilty ("rubbing it in"), or we may actively interfere with his life as retribution. Other ways of continuing a punishment are *passive* in nature. We exclude the individual from our goodness—we ignore him, cut him out of our lives, or we forgive him in ways that make him feel inferior to us and therefore distant from us.

There are some important distinctions with regard to the concept of forgiveness that have more than mere semantic implications. For example, I would not see the concepts "to forgive" and "to excuse" as being synonymous. Most hurtful behavior should not be "excused" for several reasons. One is that it often would be inappropriate, e.g., the thought of excusing a man who murdered his wife is an uncomfortable one, and rightly so, under most circumstances. This means his children could come to a point of forgiving (pardoning) him, but not of excusing him.

Secondly, excused behavior is often repeated. In other words, when people are excused from experiencing the consequences of their hurtful behavior, they are likely to repeat the same behavior again, especially if they lack maturity.

So, it is possible and even probable that one may forgive another person but not feel coerced to excuse his behavior as part of the pardon. In my experience, confusing the two has hindered forgiveness because often an individual feels that excusing is an integral part of forgiving. Since he can't excuse the behavior, he feels he cannot forgive the person.

A second definition of forgiveness that I feel is contrary to mental health is: "To renounce anger or resentment against." In most such cases, "renouncing" means repressing or denying. In other words, some people feel that to forgive ("pardon") another, they must "push down" their negative feelings toward the person. It might be helpful to distinguish between "pushing down" negative feelings and "working through" negative feelings.

In the former, the problem is that "pushed-down" feelings don't disappear, but become buried to create more profound emotional and spiritual symptoms. The latter concept represents working (communicating) with the individual-to-be-forgiven to gain some insights that will help the forgiving process be a natural and wholesome one. But it is also important to understand that, because we are human beings, it is likely that we shall experience negative feelings during and even after the forgiving process. Part of the communication process in true forgiveness is sharing the angry and hurt feelings so that warm and loving feelings can resurface naturally without being forced prematurely to the surface.

In other words, a person can forgive another for a misdeed and still have residuals of anger and hurt feelings toward the person. These feelings will subside *during* and *after* the successful resolution of the forgiving process. To misunderstand this—to feel that one must "work up" positive feelings toward the person *before* forgiveness can be accomplished—is to artificially tamper with one's nature and therefore to confound the forgiving process.

Most of the time, forgiveness becomes an issue when we perceive that another has hurt us. Then we must decide: "Shall I forgive this person who has hurt me or not?" But, if we examine the circumstances carefully, we sometimes discover that though we feel hurt, there is really nothing to forgive.

Three questions can help us discover whether or not forgiveness is a legitimate consideration.

Was the hurt I experienced at the hands of another a justifiable injury or an unjustifiable one? If the hurt was justified, there is nothing to forgive.

An example of a justifiable hurt is the following: A young woman wishes to move to another city to pursue her profession—or to be near her fiancé—or just to "get out on her own." But her mother, a widow, has built her whole life around the daughter, taking it for granted that they would live together for many years. The daughter's departure causes the mother great sorrow and hurt, and she perceives her daughter's behavior as selfish, ungrateful, and cruel. The issue for the mother is: "How can she forgive this hurt perpetrated on her by her daughter?"

The mother has no right to expect the daughter to alter her life to accommodate the mother's problem. A more appropriate solution is for the mother to get help with her problems and free the young woman to pursue her life in a way that she feels is necessary.

The principle is that a person has not only the right but the moral responsibility to disallow others from making unrealistic demands that will significantly interfere with his growth and happiness. And when he does this, "to forgive" him is fatuous.

Was I responsible for getting myself hurt? Sometimes, often without knowing it, we initiate a fight in which we ultimately get hurt. For example, a school principal resents the fact that he has been forced to hire a teacher merely because the teacher had political "pull." On the surface, the principal welcomes the teacher and is friendly; on a more subtle level, the principal's resentment manifests itself in a rather distant and uncooperative attitude. At the end of the year, the teacher asks the school board for a transfer. The principal views this as a deliberate and ungrateful attempt to embarrass him.

The point is, the person who starts a fight is not in a position to forgive the person who retaliates. Forgiveness, in this instance, is a decoy issue. The real issue is the person's responsibility for setting up the situation in which he eventually got hurt.

Am I manufacturing or nurturing a "forgiveness" situation in order to excuse some behavior in myself? An example of this is the "My parents messed me up, and it's hard to forgive them" syndrome. We assure ourselves: "If only they had been different, I wouldn't be so emotionally distant with people; or be so anxious about sex; or feel so guilty; or lack self-confidence; or have authority problems, etc., etc." It's difficult to "forgive" these people because of all the suffering they have "caused" us. Yet we can observe other people who have been in comparable situations and who do not share the "problem."

What we have done is manufacture a scapegoat for our problem and then struggle as to whether or not to forgive the scapegoat. Thus we avoid the more threatening struggle—the acceptance of responsibility for our own problematic behavior.

If a legitimate cause for forgiveness exists, one can consider five principles in the forgiving process which will enable a healthy relationship to develop or continue.

1. We should distinguish between "genuine" and "false" forgiveness. Genuine forgiveness flows from the attitude: "I forgive you because I have hurt others [and perhaps you] in comparable ways. Consequently, I can understand how someone could hurt another—either through ignorance, lack of sensitivity, or maliciousness born of weakness and fear." False kinds of forgiveness are: *selfish forgiveness* which is based on the attitude: "I forgive you because good people forgive those who hurt them, and I want to view myself as a good person"; or "I forgive you because I can't stand the anxiety caused by your being distant from me." In both cases, the forgiveness is for the benefit of the forgiver and only incidentally helpful to the offender.

Manipulative forgiveness. This attitude says: "I'll forgive you if you promise to make it up to me in some way." For example, a husband says to his wife: "I'll forgive you for forgetting to pick me up at work, if you let me go golfing tomorrow instead of taking you and the kids to the beach."

Hostile forgiveness is seen in an attitude such as: "I forgive you, you poor thing, because I realize that you have not reached the same pinnacle in life as I, so you couldn't really understand what you have done." This attitude can be "spiritualized" into: "God just hasn't blessed you with the same gifts as he has me, so I can forgive you for what you've done"; or "I forgive all sinners, including you."

2. Forgiving is a process, and the deeper the hurt, the longer the process. True forgiveness is not simply a matter of "shaking hands and making up." Forgiving a deep hurt may require feeling and talking with the offender over a period of a year or two before one feels a sense of completeness about the process.

3. One great obstacle to forgiving another is one's reluctance to forgive himself for past transgressions. If, deep down, we fail to forgive ourselves, it is unlikely we shall be able to forgive others. The refusal or inability to forgive ourselves is not a virtue, but, in fact, is egocentric. What it says is that we cannot admit that we are so imperfect as to hurt someone deeply. It is saying we shouldn't have been that imperfect, even though it is obvious that we were. It is more realistic and healthy to realize that all of us are capable of doing great harm and that, in an average lifetime, we will hurt more than a few people, some of them deeply.

4. Another obstacle to forgiving another is that, deep down, we really don't want to forgive. When we say: "I can't forgive you," we are often saying: "I *don't want* to forgive you." There are four reasons for not totally wanting to forgive another.

First, if we forgive someone who has hurt us, it reestablishes the person on an equal footing with us. But, if we have been very hurt by them, we don't feel they *deserve* to be taken back into our good graces. Maybe if they apologize and atone enough for hurting us, we'll consider elevating them to the place they previously enjoyed in our lives.

Secondly, when we are still harboring a good deal of resentment, we may want to make the offender suffer as much as we did. We withhold forgiveness until we feel they got the point.

Thirdly, if we forgive someone who has hurt us, it brings us closer, and that's exactly what we may not want, because we don't wish to be that vulnerable again.

Finally, as long as we withhold forgiveness, we don't have to examine the possibility that we contributed to the problem and may have been partially to blame for the hurt eventually perpetrated upon us.

5. *We should realize that forgiving someone, especially one who has hurt us deeply and often, is perhaps the most difficult thing for a human being to do.* The ideal of true forgiveness may not be possible for a particular person under specific circumstances.

If we have truly tried and find forgiveness impossible, it is not helpful to ruminate and brood about our failure. To do so only compounds the problem and affects other areas of life unnecessarily and destructively. We can learn something about our frailty and perhaps gain some empathy with others who are also unable to do things they "should" be able to do. Then we should move on with the business of living and loving.

HOPE

In discussing the concept of hope, Karl Menninger writes: "The Encyclopaedia Britannica devotes many columns to the topics of love and many more to faith. But hope, poor little hope! She's not even listed." Charles Péguy reflects on the same loss: "Hope, little Hope, moves forward between her two big sisters and no one ever notices her."

As a psychologist, I am in very close contact with the workings of hope. Any therapist's files are filled with variations of the following, not uncommon, example. A few years ago, a twenty-year-old girl wrote to me: "Today is the last day of my life. I cannot go on any longer. Everything is hopeless. I am useless and want to rid the world of the ugliness of me. The worst thing is that I am even too terrible to go to hell." After two years of therapy, she wrote the following note to me, a few weeks before her graduation from a university: "Thank you for hoping in me when no one else did. No one thought I was worthwhile, except you. I felt if *you* could honestly hope in me, then there must be something good—something possible in me. It's not only me graduating in two weeks, but it is your hope in me that is being validated. Thank you for the most precious gift you could have given me: Hope." It is after many experiences such as this that I have become a confirmed believer in the power of realistic hope.

The kind of hope discussed in this chapter deals with various things. True hope deals with earthly things that can have spiritual consequences: hoping to have a close friend; hoping that one's husband will admit he has a drinking problem, or that one's wife will realize her coldness is ruining their marriage; hoping that one's prayer life will get better; hoping that one's child will do better in school, or be more confident, or be more relaxed, or be more outgoing. One may hope to find a good person to marry; hope that one's relationship with his parents will become smoother and more understanding; hope to get into college or graduate school; hope to do well in a job interview or in a job. A person may hope that his depression will lift, that his marriage will get better, that his sexual problems will go away, that tomorrow will be better than today.

This hope has three basic characteristics; it must be realistic, active, and spiritual.

Hope is Realistic. Healthy hope is realistic. It does not resort to baseless optimism and is not a vague yearning after an unattainable goal. If hope is to be genuine, it must be based on reality and afford reasonable grounds for confidence in its fulfillment. If it doesn't, it is merely an exercise in self-deceit.

When we bring the process of hoping into a religious context, we must be especially careful. Because we are relating with a God who can do anything, some people are tempted to use God as a servant to do the difficult things that they should be doing for themselves. This unreal hope says: "Keep praying and things will get better." Except for direct supernatural intervention (a miracle), which is the exception rather than the rule, prayer *by itself* is not likely to make things happen. Unrealistic hope uses prayer merely as a magical incantation for wish fulfillment without any personal effort. The wife who prays that her husband will stop drinking, but does nothing else, is unlikely to see her "wish" come true.

A second part of unreal hope states: "Be a good person and you will get your wish." This myth is very strongly embedded in our culture. When people try hard to be good and still experience problems or suffering, they often feel that they weren't "good enough" and thus inappropriately berate themselves. On the other hand, they may feel that they were gypped and thus become resentful and cynical.

The practical danger that flows from each or both of these misconceptions of hope is that if we pray hard and try to be good, our problem should be solved. If our problem still exists, we assume that there is nothing we can do about it. We often make this assumption prematurely without directly and persistently trying to change either our behavior or some of the elements in a problematic situation or relationship.

So, unrealistic hope, whether it uses religion as a basis or not, is what Charles Dickens described as "that very popular trust in flat things coming round."

As a teacher on a university campus and as a psychologist, my office is a virtual clearinghouse for unrealistic hopes. Students "hope" they get an "A" but cram for a final exam during the last twelve hours before the exam. A girl "hopes" to meet a nice boy at college but never makes herself available to meet any boys, expecting them to drop down her chimney like Santa Claus. A boy who acts like a brat with his parents suddenly "hopes" they will realize that he is mature enough to move into his own apartment. A student takes dope and, despite evidence to the contrary that he has observed, "hopes" that it will be a conscious-raising experience *for him.* The wife of an alcoholic who is beaten by her husband for the fifteenth time "hopes" this will be the last because her husband swore it would be. The man who never relates personally to anyone at the office "hopes" to get a promotion. The parents who have only the slightest idea of what being a parent entails, "hope" that their children grow up to be happy and law-abiding citizens. The teacher sees a new assignment as a "last hope" for staying in the profession, but has no intention of changing anything about himself.

So, on and on it goes. Unreal hopes leading to predictable failure and eventually to despair—despair of oneself, of people in general, and of God.

Hope is Active. Edgar Watson Howe wrote: "There is nothing so well-known as that we should not expect something for nothing—but we do and call it Hope." Hope is not a substitute for action, and it is not something you do when you give up trying. Hope is healthy only as long as it generates action. Real hope requires work, change, risk, and a willingness to pay the price for our hopes.

Work: This requires approaching the person or persons capable of helping us realize our hope. When a hope is kept to oneself and "unactivated," it is a false hope. The larger the hope, the more time, energy, patience, and persistence required to actualize it.

Change: If we have been hoping for something for any length of time, and it has not come to fruition, then we can assume that we need to change something, either about ourselves, a relationship, or a situation. Normally, tomorrow will not be any better than today, just because it is tomorrow.

Risk: This element requires a willingness to dare to hope and, secondly, to let others know what we hope for. This opens us up to someone saying: "I am not going to give you, or can't give you, what you hope for." Then our hopes will be dashed, and others will know it. On paper, this does not appear to be much of a risk. But it is too much of a risk for many people. They use "cop-outs" such as "But what if . . ."; or "It won't do any good anyway"; or "They'll think I'm silly for wanting that." These people function on the principle that as long as you don't hope for anything, you won't be disappointed; or they "super-naturalize" their fear by rationalizing; "If God wanted me to have that, he would have given it to me."

Paying the price: Almost no hopes of any magnitude are realized "for free." People like Martin Luther King paid the ultimate price to make a "dream" come true. Few of us will be required to do this, but we will often have to pay some price. Hopes to get into college or to get a responsible job; to be a good spouse; to have a good spouse; to have well-adjusted children—these all have some heavy price tags. Some people *willingly* pay the price; others begrudgingly pay the price, and let everyone know how much it costs. Still others try to sneak through without paying, only to eventually learn that a hope turns out to be only as good as what you paid for it.

The real test of the honesty of our hopes is how much repeated effort we put into their actualization. Anyone who has worked with dying people can tell you something very true and very sad. The people who die the most "bad-ly" are those who lived on hopes alone and eventually starved to death. They fear death because they never lived, or they lived only half a life and hoped for the other half.

Hope is Spiritual. Secular hope states: "Keep hoping—things will get better—you'll get what you desire." Realis-tic hope says: "Things may also get worse and, while you may not attain the material object of your hopes, you can still attain spiritual growth."

The spiritual dimension of hoping is most important and often overlooked. We hope for something that will bring us more money, prestige, power, or good feelings. And if we fail to get it, we either pass it off philosophical-ly, or we are filled with disappointment or resentment. But, for a spiritual person it is after he has realized that he has attained or failed to attain his hope that the spiri-tual growth process begins.

For example, a man may hope very much for a pro-motion at work because it will bring him both prestige and financial benefits. After he achieves or fails to attain the promotion, there will be a short period of reflection on the long-term consequences of his hope. He may decide that the result of his seeking the promotion was beneficial to him and to his family on all levels. Or he may find that his quest has raised some disturbing questions. What has he done to his family over the past months while he was hoping for and working toward this promotion? What did he do to himself—how much dishonesty and back-biting was he willing to engage in to win the promotion?

It was the first time in years that he really prayed—and what did he pray for? An increase in prestige and salary. What skills did he have to nurture in the pursuit of the promotion? Did he have to become a person who is aggressive, tough, unyielding, manipulative, and cunning at the expense of being warm, patient, loving, and understanding? Did he win some important points at work and lose some important points with his family? Is his identity so close to that of being a "worker" that he is becoming less of a lover, husband, father, or friend?

Along with an awareness of the qualities of hope, it is of critical importance to understand and accept the fact that some things are, indeed, hopeless. Then it is necessary to discern what is *genuinely* hopeless from what *appears* to be hopeless and even *feels* hopeless, but is *not* hopeless.

If the two are not clearly separated, some serious mistakes will follow. For example, a marriage relationship may be hopeless beyond any reasonable doubt. Yet, if the partners continually entertain unreal hopes, they or their children may incur increasing damage. Or, on the other hand, a marital relationship may appear to be hopeless, but, with some real effort, risk taking, or professional help, the partners may discern there is a good deal of hope.

A second dimension with regard to hopelessness is that one aspect of a person's life may be hopeless while a related area is not. For example, middle-aged parents may have more than reasonable cause to feel that one or all of their children are hopeless as far as the parents being an influence in their lives, but this does not mean that their faltering marriage is hopeless.

Finally, an individual should distinguish between a situation and himself. He may be involved in an objectively hopeless situation, but he should not necessarily assume that *he himself* is hopeless.

We should also realize that probably 90 percent of hopelessness or despair is irrational, self-created, and self-perpetuated. George Bernanos writes in his *Diary of a Country Priest:* "The sin against Hope is the deadliest and perhaps also the most cherished, the most indulged." The question is: Why do we indulge in something so anguishing and unproductive? The answer is that despair accomplishes important benefits for the frightened and/or angry person that are, for him, worth the suffering.

Despair preserves the heart from future hurt. If we expect the worse, we shall never be disappointed. Either we shall be pleasantly surprised that what occurs wasn't as bad as we had expected (or hoped?); or, if it turns out badly, we can, with some degree of satisfaction, proclaim: "See, I *told* you what would happen." This is a poor man's way of gaining some modicum of satisfaction in his life with a minimum of risk and hurt.

There is a perverse type of strength that comes with despair. It says: "You can't hurt me anymore than I am already hurt." It is a "what have I got to lose" position that makes the experience of more hurt or failure impossible. The power that can come from this position can be used to gain mastery over others, sometimes causing them to shape their lives around the despairing person. This is an extremely destructive situation, with all parties going nowhere. We need not reject people in despair, but we don't have to reward them for it either. It has never been a virtue to allow others to use their despair as a destructive force, either against themselves or against others.

Perhaps the most subtle psychological dynamic in despair is that some people "hope" for things that, deep down, *they really don't want.* As a result, they themselves frustrate their own attempts at attaining the goal. This results in the person feeling disappointed and maybe even desperate on a conscious level, but relieved on an

214 MAKE YOUR TOMORROW BETTER

unconscious level. The cause of this "I hope, but I really don't hope" phenomenon is based on fear.

A person "hopes" for a closer relationship with a friend on one level, but, deep down, is frightened of such a relationship. The individual fears that it may require more effort and inconvenience than he is willing or able to give. Or he may fear that if he allows the other person to get *really* close, the other may see negative traits or reject him. Or he may fear becoming too dependent on the other person, causing him to be jealous and weak. Unconsciously, he creates a barrier between himself and the other person, telling himself, "If it weren't for him, we could have a closer relationship."

One of the key manifestations of self-perpetuated despair is the individual's stubborn and combative reluctance to give it up. He adamantly refuses to see any light at the end of the tunnel because he has invested too much in his despair. For example, individuals despair in the workability of their marriage. They can't talk to their spouse because the spouse never listens. They can't get professional help because it costs too much (though they willingly spend money on luxuries). They can't talk to a priest because "what does a priest know about marriage." They can't get a separation "because of the kids." They can't get a divorce because "the Church is against it." And they can't live with the situation one more day because they are "going mad." The more one challenges them on each of these points, the more they scurry for new material to plug the holes ("Yes, but. . . . "). Such individuals need to be introduced to the true nature of their fears and anger that make despair more agreeable for them than hope.

It is possible, however, to help others in their quest for real hope in a difficult situation. This can be done in several ways.

1. We should be honest in our encouragement of others' hopes, in contrast to unrealistic reassurance in order to reduce their anxiety. It is not being supportive to blithely reassure people ("I'm certain you can do it"; "I'm sure things will turn out fine"), if it does not reflect our innermost thoughts. The harm that comes from failing to temper hope with reality (at least as we see it) is two-fold. First, the more unrealistic a person's hopes are, the less likely it is that they will be realized. This creates discouragement about hoping in general. Second, if the individual had trust and confidence in us, and we are proven wrong ("*You* said it would turn out fine, and *you* were wrong"), the trust may become seriously diminished.

The best way to be supportive is to help the individual evaluate his chances for attaining his hope, to suggest ways in which he may increase his chances, and to help him buffer his hopes so that if they do not materialize, it is not the end of the world.

2. *We should be careful not to link the successful attainment of a person's hope with his value as a person.* For example, in my attempts to encourage a student (or son or daughter), I may say: "You are certainly bright enough, good enough, and mature enough to get accepted into graduate school." The student may then get rejected by all five of the schools to which he applied. His "logical" conclusion is that he is *not* bright, good, or mature enough—that his "person" is deficient. It is important to discuss all the factors that may help or hinder a person's realization of his hopes. Some of them may have little or nothing to do with his worth. Many times, when people are not accepted by a school, potential employer, boyfriend or girlfriend, for a promotion or a prize, it is not because the individual lacks overall quality. Often it is simply that the person does not meet the particular (and sometimes peculiar) needs of the chooser.

3. *We can help an individual discern the true ownership of his hopes.* Doing a title search of one's hopes can be a very interesting and complex pursuit. Sometimes we may discover that what we *thought* were our own hopes were actually grafted onto us by our parents, friends, society, or the church. Not all borrowed hopes are bad. It is only when they go against who we really are or what we truly need to be effective and happy that this grafting can sooner or later cause an "infection."

Striving after borrowed hopes that do violence to our deepest nature (even though the hope, in itself, may be a very virtuous one) creates deep-seated difficulties. The end result is an abiding resentment toward the "lender" of the hope and desperate confusion regarding the nature of one's privately owned hopes.

Sometimes, either inadvertently or out of good intentions, we help a person unravel himself from the burdensome hopes of others only to foist our own hopes on him. A not infrequent type of situation is the following: An adviser helps an impressionistic young woman disengage herself from what is really her mother's hope that she marry a particular young man. While she begins to enjoy the freedom created by this insight, the adviser mentions: "This is very providential, because I think it is God's way of telling you that you have a religious vocation." So, one borrowed hope is traded in for another.

4. *We can help others interpret the meaning of their hopes.* A high school student hopes to get accepted into college. Does this mean that he actually wishes to spend four difficult and expensive years working and studying, or does it mean that he hopes this will finally win him some recognition, respect, or acceptance from his parents? The young person hopes very much to get married. Is this person truly seeking a life-long commitment of giving, or does he just want to feel important, protected, and loved by someone (anyone)?

If an interpretation of hopes does not take place, it is very easy for a person to land in a situation (often a life commitment) only to discover that what he *truly* hoped for cannot be given to him by the person or situation he pinned his hopes upon. It is better to discern this early in a situation, rather than to discover it after twenty-five years, or, worse yet, never to discover it at all.

Real hope is neither as easy nor as magical nor as much fun as other hopes. It demands a mature evaluation of oneself, of one's efforts, and of the situation. But the price is worth the difficulty because it is the only hope that brings with it the possibility of psychological growth.

Reflection Questions

1. What behavior in another person do I have the most difficulty understanding? Why? What can I do to increase my understanding?

2. Of the three barriers to understanding, which one seems to be the biggest for me?

3. What have I done in my life that I possibly have never really forgiven myself for? What can I do to become more healed in that area?

4. Whom have I never really forgiven? What has my failure to forgive done to my sense of self-love?

5. What is the thing I hope for most in my life? What have I done this week to help bring it into existence?

Thoughts to Contemplate

1. Most of the time, forgiveness becomes an issue when we perceive that another has hurt us. Then we must decide: "Shall I forgive this person who has hurt me or not?" But, if we examine the circumstances carefully, we sometimes discover that though we feel hurt, there is really nothing to forgive.

2. Genuine forgiveness flows from the attitude: "I forgive you because I have hurt others [and perhaps you] in comparable ways. Consequently, I can understand how someone could hurt another—either through ignorance, lack of sensitivity, or maliciousness born of weakness and fear."

3. The refusal or inability to forgive ourselves is not a virtue, but, in fact, is egocentric. What it says is that we cannot admit that we are so imperfect as to hurt someone deeply.

4. Thank you for the most precious gift you could have given me: hope.

5. Hope turns out to be only as good as what you paid for it.

10

COMMUNICATION: THE
PSYCHOLOGICAL INTRAVENOUS

Communication is the "psychological intravenous" that keeps us and those around us alive. Like the solution in an intravenous, good communication keeps us alive and robust. Poor communication causes psychological weakness and pain, and a shut-down in communication can cause psychological death.

Communication is the mutual sharing of ideas and feelings. Since a person is not by nature a good communicator or poor communicator, communication skills must be learned and practiced. This chapter will discuss several principles of effective communication and some special problems often experienced in our daily interactions.

PRINCIPLES OF EFFECTIVE COMMUNICATION

The following principles are essential in developing effective communication skills.

Effective communication means listening. Listening is perhaps the most overlooked aspect of the communication process. The word "communicate" almost always connotes talking rather than listening. Yet, no matter how eloquently a person speaks, if no one is listening to him, no communication is taking place.

To become effective listeners, we must be aware of some of the aids that can help us become more active listeners.

What are some barriers to effective listening?

Internal noise. This term indicates that there is so much inner static going on within the individual that it significantly drowns out the bulk of what is being said to him. The listener is so threatened or angered by the situation (either the content of the message, or the sender of the message, or both) that he "cannot hear."

The astute person perceives his listener's tuned-out look, the fact that the listener asks questions that have been answered, or makes irrelevant statements. The communicator then chooses to discontinue his primary message in order to deal with the hidden agenda, viz., the smoldering feelings of his listener. Once the feelings are ventilated, there will be a more open receptivity to the original message. The person wishing to communicate must also listen for his own internal noise and deal with it before attempting to continue with a conversation.

Judgmental listening. Passing premature judgments, whether they are favorable or not, tends to restrict a person's freedom of expression. Even a poorly timed positive evaluation can be inhibiting because it could make it difficult for the individual to discuss mistakes he has made. Premature criticism may ultimately turn out to be unjust and, in any case, can discourage good communication. A good listener sends the message: "Tell me *everything,* and I will react after you let me know you are completely finished."

Authoritarian attitude. If a person feels: "What I have to say is more important than what you have to say," he will be formulating his next words instead of listening. Or he may convey the message: "Tell me only what I want to hear." In any communication, this attitude results in a filtering or cover-up of real problems. Often, the information that is not revealed in this situation will eventually return to haunt both communicators.

Misunderstanding silences. A person who is a good listener realizes that when the other person stops speaking, it does not necessarily mean that he has stopped communicating. Often, a silence is a part of an ongoing communication during which the speaker is re-evaluating to himself what he has just said, or is formulating in his mind how he will present the remainder of his message. To interrupt at that time may demolish the speaker's train of thought and emotional state. It is not when the speaker's mouth stops moving that conveys when he is finished speaking; it is when his eyes "rest" and say: "OK, now it's your turn."

What are some aids to effective listening?

Listen actively. The good communicator's whole demeanor should reflect that he is actively involved in the listening process. His attitude, posture, eyes, and facial expression should make it clear that he is "with" the other person all the way. The active listener asks questions that draw out the other person's ideas and feelings. He also checks up on what he has heard by restating it the way he understands it to validate his perceptions.

If the person's mind wanders, he feels free to say: "I'm sorry; I was distracted for a second. Could you repeat that?" It is also encouraging to the other person to nod one's head periodically and reassure him by saying, "I understand"; or "I could see how you would feel that way." If a good communicator senses some confusion or contradiction in the other person's story, he patiently asks for clarifications, e.g., "I think I missed a step back there," instead of "Hey, wait a minute; you just contradicted yourself!"

Listen with the "third ear." A good listener has the ability to go beyond the spoken words to their *meaning* and *feeling* levels. For example, an employee may say to his boss: "I really have to stop all this overtime work; it's creating havoc with my life."

The poor listener who is merely hearing words and not messages replies: "I'm sorry, Bill, but you have to do your part along with everyone else in the company—it's part of the game."

The boss who is an astute listener is aware of the possibility of other messages:

—Is Bill trying to tell me that he and his wife are having problems?

—Is he telling me he is under a great deal of psychological stress and that he is becoming worried about it?

—Are his kids developing behavioral problems because he doesn't see them much anymore?

—Is there something going on at work that is upsetting him?

These are all areas that a good listener will want to gently explore before making a decision within the situation.

Learn to read non-verbal communication. Someone once said that the "loudest" kind of communication is the kind you can't hear. What this means is that an important part of listening is done with one's *eyes.* Facial expressions, gestures, posture, and mannerisms may transmit a message that is not being sent verbally, or may contradict a message that is being sent verbally.

A smirk on someone's face, clenched fists, finger tapping, wandering eyes, looks of boredom or upset, slouched or rigid posture, a smile, all may express messages that a good listener will perceive and pursue in a friendly way. A poor listener will either miss these non-verbal cues or purposely ignore them because he does not wish to "hear" what the messages are saying.

Encourage honest feedback. All three of these words are important for good communication. "Encourage" means that the other person should be invited to share his ideas and feelings. The good communicator's message is: "I'm really interested in what your feelings are on this—what you think about it is important to me."

"Honest" means that we must convey a sense of security that assures the other person that we can take in stride any reaction that he may offer. The message in good communication must be: "There may be some things you agree with and don't agree with. I need to hear both because I want to understand what this means to you." This is in contrast to conveying the thought: "Well, what *I* said makes the best sense, don't you think?"

Feedback in itself is important. It can give us important information which is needed to make good decisions and develop good relationships with others.

Listening pays off in three ways in any communication. It helps the people communicating get all the facts and get a "handle" on the situation. Each person in the communication feels that the other person really cares about him. Finally, each person now is willing to listen with openness to what the other individual would like to say.

Effective communication is direct. When we wish to share some information with another person, it should be communicated directly. This seems simple enough, yet it is one of the biggest causes of failure in communication.

Being indirect is often easier. One can be indirect by communicating by "inference." A boss can protest: "Why should I have to *tell* Bill he's doing a good job? If he hasn't been 'called on the carpet' recently, he should *know* he is doing well." Or a teacher may say: "If Jane can't tell she's got problems around here by the way I have to punish her, she's beyond hope anyway."

Communication can be indirect by being subtle. Subtlety is employed mostly with unpleasant communications. A husband may "drop hints," veiled suggestions, and innuendoes that his wife's housekeeping is unsatisfactory to him. He then says: "I hope she got the point." But there is no place for decoding messages in healthy communication. If the wife failed to *catch* the point, it is because the husband failed to *make* the point.

A third way in which communication is indirect occurs when a person expresses his thoughts about someone else to a third party, hoping that the "word" will filter down to the person for whom it was intended. This is almost always disastrous because the message is often contaminated by the messengers, depending upon their involvement in the situation. The result is that, by the time the communication finally gets to the intended party, it is often distorted in some way. This, in turn, creates a new set of problems in the communication process.

Effective communication is immediate. As little time as possible should elapse between feeling the need to communicate and the actual communication. Immediacy is important for two reasons. If the situation calls for the expression of unpleasant feelings (anger, disappointment, criticism), the longer a person holds in these feelings, the more likely they will be overexpressed (because they incubate), underexpressed (because they wear off), or never expressed. In none of these cases will the other person benefit from knowing how the communicator truly feels; hence, he may overadjust his behavior, underadjust it, or fail to adjust it.

Secondly, immediacy is important because the closer in time a person is rewarded or punished for his behavior (if this is the purpose of the communication), the stronger the linkage between the behavior and the consequences. This is essential for true learning to occur.

The two main barriers to immediacy in communication are procrastination and disturbed priorities. People often put off what will create anxiety within them; they are chronically awaiting the "right time" to convey the message. But in effective communication, there is only *one* right time, and that is the present. Disturbed priorities are evident when a person is "too busy" to communicate issues while they are still "hot." He has letters to write, meetings to attend, things to clean, shopping to do. All of these are, the person thinks, more important than communicating. Interposing other things and avoiding a needed communication can only add distance between the two people who should be interrelating.

Effective communication is clear. Communication should be concise and lucid. Most people talk too much. This is done to camouflage their insecurity stemming from not knowing what they really want to say, or knowing but being reluctant to get to the point.

It is often helpful for a person to phrase mentally the one or two thoughts that he wishes to convey. Then, when the times comes, the person is better prepared to share those ideas in a simple and concise manner. The more words that are used, and the more decorative they are, the more cause for distraction, inattention, and confusion.

There are three common types of unclear message. One is the ambiguous message. A wife tells her husband: "I wish you would show more concern for me—but not too much concern." What does this mean?

Another type of unclear message is an *inconsistent* message. At a faculty meeting, a principal informs the teachers: "Parents are complaining that their children don't have any homework. I think each child should bring home a certain amount of homework each day." A month later, at the next faculty meeting, the principal states: "Parents are wondering why it is necessary to burden the children with homework, if they are doing what they are supposed to do in the classroom each day."

A third type of unclear message is the *double-message.* A parent tells his teenage son: "I'd like to see you get into a good university, but I don't want you to over-emphasize your studies, either."

The good communicator is secure enough in what he thinks and feels that he can afford to be to the point and lucid without being blunt.

Effective communication is "pure." A "pure" communication is one in which the *stated* purpose for the communication and the *real* purpose are identical. A "contaminated" communication occurs where there is a discrepancy between the real and stated purposes.

For example, a boss may advise an employee: "I'd like to talk to you about a few problems with your reports." If the communication is pure, this is exactly what will happen. But perhaps the employer is using the reports as a pseudo-issue. The employer may feel that the worker has been goldbricking lately and is angry with him. So, while the boss's purported motive is to help the employee with his reports, the real purpose is to "stick it" to him.

The results of this contaminated communication are:
The employee is confused because he *hears* what the boss is saying about the reports but he *feels* waves of hostility and punitiveness which seem incongruous and inappropriate.

The employee may feel the boss's wrath but leave the discussion without knowing the cause of his anger. Consequently, he will be unable to make appropriate changes in his behavior.

Other hidden motives can be seen in the following "double-plays":
I want to talk with you about your reports (but I really want to impress you that I know more about your work than you do).

I want to talk with you about your reports (but I really

want you to know that I am your boss, which you don't seem to realize).

I want to talk with you about your reports (but I really want to show you what a nice guy I am so you will like me).

Most hidden motives could be legitimate issues for communication, but should be dealt with as separate topics and not camouflaged by other issues.

Effective communication is constructive. By "constructive" is meant that the purpose of the communication is to better the other person, not to tear him down or destroy him. The message in a communication can be viewed analogously as a brick. A brick can be *thrown* at another person, but this will cause a "fight or flight" reaction in him. Either he will fight, i.e., throw another brick; or he will flee—neither of which creates an atmosphere for effective communication.

But a brick can also be used to build a bridge between two people. A person can express displeasure, disappointment, or frustration in a way that reflects on the other individual's particular behavior but not on who he is as a person. For example, a teacher may state: "I noticed that you have been late for school the last three days, and I'm wondering why"; or she may accuse: "You've been late for the last three days; you seem like an irresponsible person."

"Throwing bricks" can be done in several ways. One is by the vocabulary we use. Referring to people with emotionally loaded labels such as "dumb," "lazy," "irresponsible," "dishonest," accomplishes nothing except to increase the listener's defenses. The more defenses that are erected, the less real listening and thoughtful consideration will be given to what is said.

"Brick throwing" can also be done by use of sarcasm which is a very ineffectual method for communicating. Sarcasm is belittling and hostile, and precludes mutual openness which is a prime requisite for effective communication.

Bringing up old or unrelated issues is another "brick." This is often prefaced by "Now that we are getting things off our chest. . . . " If the side issues are important, they should have been brought up when they were "hot"; if they are not as important, they should not be added to the main issue.

Embarrassing another person in front of others is also a situation that interferes with communication. The message gets lost in the inner static that is created by the feeling of humiliation that the listener is feeling.

Comparisons also are likely to interfere with, rather than to help, the reception of a message. Suggestions such as: "Why don't you watch your sister; *she* knows what she is doing" are seldom helpful. The main effect of such a statement is that the child builds up a resentment toward *both* the *parent and* the *sister.*

Making inferences about behavior rather than focusing on observations can be destructive. For example, it is better to say: "I noticed you had a hard time keeping awake at the meeting, and I was wondering what it meant," than to say: "You were obviously bored stiff at the meeting—what's the problem?"

Attributing motives to someone's behavior can be problematic as well. It is more constructive to say: "You seem to be having trouble doing your chores," than to accuse: "I suppose you think that if you stall long enough, I'll do the chores for you."

Even the most severe criticism can be imparted in non-angry and non-denigrating words. The question a person can ask is whether the aim of the statement is to destroy the individual to whom it is addressed or to open up channels for communication.

In constructive communication, the main attitude should be one of support. One method of accomplishing this is to point out concrete examples of where the person handled something well, so that any mistake may be put into proper perspective.

Criticism can also be a supportive communication if the person communicating shares the fact that he may have made the same or comparable mistakes in the past and elucidates the negative consequences that flowed from it. This leaves the other person feeling "I blew it," but still respecting the communicator as a person. This listener will also be more likely to rectify his mistakes under these circumstances. When mistakes are pointed out in an atmosphere of realistic support and encouragement, the result will be better communication, increased cooperation, and more effective behavior.

Effective communication tolerates disagreement. It is extremely unfortunate that a negative aura surrounds someone who disagrees. Traditionally, if someone disagrees with me on any important issue, it means: He is wrong; he doesn't like me; he is not very intelligent; he is a hostile person; he is trying to stir up trouble. It is no coincidence that we often define a "nice" person as one who is "agreeable" and a "not nice" person as "disagreeable."

Disagreement often can be a necessary and constructive form of communication if it is understood and handled properly. Some disagreement is absolutely necessary to produce new ideas and to question philosophies and procedures. However, it is important to distinguish between constructive and destructive disagreement.

The two most common attitudes in destructive disagreement are the following:

We make a negative evaluation of the person rather than of his performance. For example, we can convey the message: "You are a stupid person if you believe that." Here we are not only disagreeing with the person's opinion but also disparaging his whole self. The reaction this causes in the other person is: "I left feeling not only wrong for what I feel but wrong because I *exist!*"

We exercise an inordinate control over the other person. This occurs when we assume the position: "Might is right." It is seen in situations in which a person states: "I am right because: I've had more experience than you; I'm your parent; I outrank you; I think more logically; I'm more mature." None of these characteristics automatically makes a person correct in any disagreement. There are many things even little children can tell their parents and the lowliest employee can tell the corporation president. A disagreement is never truly resolved by someone pulling his "badge" on another.

The following are some aids to healthy disagreement:

—Assume the attitude that disagreements are to be understood; they are not to be won or lost. Usually when we "win" an argument, it is illusory. What probably has happened is that we have temporarily squelched someone who will be less inclined to work with us in future situations. Rather than view a disagreement as a contest to be won, it is more fruitful to view it as a problem to be solved. Disagreements are caused either by someone not knowing as much as he should about a situation, or by a misunderstanding between people, or because the people have different needs that must be met. In none of these cases will a "victory" by one person over the other effect a satisfactory resolution of the problem.

—Take your time. Before becoming defensive, ask for more information about the situation. No person is ready to listen until he is through talking. Frequently, we hear only the first few words of someone disagreeing with us and we immediately "know" what he is going to say next. If we listen and ask questions we may discover clues to help resolve the conflict. How many times do disagreements end with one person saying: "Why didn't you say that to begin with?" and the other person answering: "Because you got so upset you didn't give me time to finish."

—Define the area of disagreement. Often in disagreements the focus is on the area of disagreement so that it appears that the people involved are poles apart. In reality, in most situations, there is much more that is held in common than is not. This is why it is beneficial to ask: "What exactly do we agree upon and what exactly do we disagree upon?" When we have delineated the specific areas of disagreement, it saves a good deal of time and energy.

There should be much room for healthy disagreement in families and other communities. A home in which there is little disagreement is not a "model" home. It is one in which everyone's unique needs are being artificially tinted so as to blend in with everyone else's. The true nature of harmony is not lack of disagreement but a sufficient amount of healthy disagreement so that everyone in the family or the community is continually reassessing the appropriateness of his behavior, motivation, and goals.

SPECIAL PROBLEMS IN COMMUNICATION

There are some special problems in communication. These are called special problems because they are more subtle and complex than those which have been discussed previously. "Special" does not mean that they are rare. On the contrary, these five problems are neither rare nor benign. Some very good people are living difficult lives because they indulge, unknowingly, in one or more of these behaviors.

Ventriloquism. This is the practice of speaking so that the voice seems to come from a source other than the speaker. Psychological ventriloquism is based on the principle: "I already know what their response to me is going to be, so why go through the hassle?"

The child acts as a ventriloquist when he says: "I'd like to go to summer camp this year, but I'm not going to ask my parents. They'll just say 'You didn't like camp last year; none of your friends is going to camp; and, besides, I think you should stay home and study this summer.' So, what's the use of asking?"

The wife acts as a ventriloquist when she tells a close friend: "I wish my husband would show more affection toward me, but I'm not going to tell him. He'll only say that I'm being silly; that we're not teenagers anymore; and that if I worked as hard as he does, I wouldn't have time to be 'lovey-dovey' either. So, why waste my time?"

A husband is a ventriloquist when he tells a confidant: "I'd like to tell my wife that she's making a big mistake by the way she relates with her mother. But, if I did, she'd fall apart. First, she'd get angry and tell me that it's none of my business. Then, she'd feel guilty and admit I was right. Then she'd get sick for a week, and I'd have to stay home and take care of the kids. So, it wouldn't be worth it."

In all three examples, an imaginary dialogue took place just as if it occurred in reality. In fact, the dialogue is so life-like that it would not be surprising that any of the people mentioned could swear at a later date that the conversation had *actually* occurred. Furthermore, the emotional response toward the person with whom the imaginary dialogue was held can be exactly the same as if the other person had actually said the "ventriloquized" words. For example, the wife may lament: "I really *feel angry* toward my husband because even though I've made it clear I need more affection, he just thinks I'm being childish."

Psychological ventriloquism is never helpful to anyone. First, it is possible that we could be mistaken, and that our fantasized dialogue is different from what the actual response would be. Through ventriloquism *we* deprive *ourselves* of a potential good.

Second, psychological ventriloquism is a "cop-out" from confronting a person and accepting whatever consequences flow from this encounter. With ventriloquism, we can create a dialogue in which we are eminently reasonable and the other person is manifestly unreasonable. If we actually participate in a dialogue, we may be forced to discover that this is not always the case, which would be an unsettling insight.

Finally, some people would prefer to go through life righteously indignant rather than satisfied and happy. Thus, it behooves them to practice psychological ventriloquism almost continually. These individuals habitually put words into people's mouths and intentions in their hearts. They can then smugly assure themselves how crazy and/or evil everyone else is. The ventriloquist is in a position to make a dummy out of everybody. The problem is, life can get very lonely when there are only dummies around, and "righteous indignation" doesn't keep one very warm at night.

Sandwich-board Communication. In the past, restaurants advertised by hiring a man to walk the streets toting a sign with two panels; one that rested on the front of him and one that rested on his back. The panels extolled the virtues and prices of the restaurant's menu.

Many people practice a psychological variation of the sandwich-board by advertising contradictory messages. What is proclaimed on the front-board, which is easily readable to both the bearer and to others, cancels what is advertised on the back-board, which is unreadable to the bearer but obvious to others. "Back-board" behavior is comprised of the subtleties of tone of voice, body posture, facial expression, vocabulary, and the kinds of decisions one makes.

The following are some typical examples of sandwich-board communication:

A person's front-board loudly proclaims: "I want to get close to you." But the back-board states in smaller print: "Keep your distance." This person genuinely wishes to get close to people—to invite people into his life. But the individual's deeper fears can't tolerate the feeling of closeness. And it is the deeper fears that translate into the back-board behavior. This person is frustrated and confused because the people picked as potential friends and lovers are people who are afraid of intimacy. The person doesn't realize that he is the one who is *selecting* people who are afraid of intimacy, or that it is *he* who is fearful of intimacy, not the others. This individual can't understand why the very people he would like to get close to are always frightened and resistive.

A person's front-board may advertise: "You can be perfectly honest with me." But the back-board states in smaller print: "Please don't hurt me." This person is confused and angry because he "does his best" to get people to "speak their mind," but no one seems able to accept the invitation. These individuals are frequently misinformed on important issues, which eventually causes them to make mistakes. They lament: "But why didn't you *tell* me about this? I wouldn't have gotten upset."

Other persons relating with this individual are able to see the fine print on the back-board and know very well that it is better to hide upsetting things from this sign-bearer.

A person's front-board may read: "You can trust me completely." But the back-board states: "Explosives: Beware." These individuals wonder why they are always left on the fringes of things; why they are never included in the "goings-on." The reason is that people know that this person is a "dangerous weapon"; that he can't keep quiet; that he uses information and gossip to personal advantage and to the disadvantage of others; that he has a talent for saying the wrong thing at the wrong time. Often the "explosives" are constructed from a good deal of repressed anger with which the person is laden.

A person's front-board says: "Love me." But the back-board says: "Kick me." These individuals wonder why, although they are so "good-natured," people are always using them and/or letting them down. The "kick me" sign is often painted with unresolved guilt that says: "I don't deserve to be loved." These people set themselves up, almost begging to be kicked, a request that is too tempting for many people to resist. "Kick-me" people are forever plaintively asking "Why do these things always happen to *me?*" An astute observer could reply "Because you want them to."

A person's front-board reads: "I'm not interested in sex." But the back-board reads: "Seduce me." Such people wonder why others are "forever putting the make on" them. All they do is mind their own business and try to do their work and, before they know it, someone is "putting a move on." The world is full of sex maniacs. The sign-bearer is shocked, angry, and perplexed. But the secret part of these individuals is delighted and gleeful and relishes repeating these episodes to interested (or bored) friends. The back-board behavior stems from a conflict between their self-concept ("I'm above sex") and their impulses ("I'd love to get sexually involved"). The result is the contradictory message which in a perverse way gets both sets of needs partially met.

Whenever the same or a similar reaction which we don't understand seems to occur with some frequency, it is likely that we have a back-board of which we are unaware. When this is the case, we need to see exactly how we are giving people a contradictory message, and we need to determine *why* we need a back-board for protection.

Easy-pluses—easy-minuses Communication. "Easy-pluses" means that people are very open when it entails easy positive communication. For example, a husband may tell his wife: "Your hair really looks nice that way"; or a wife may tell her husband: "I'm really proud of you for

winning your promotion." These are "easy-pluses" because the content is superficial and does not require any
risk.

"Easy-minuses" are negative statements that are also
relatively easy to share. A husband may say to his wife: "I
wish you wouldn't vacuum every Saturday morning; it's
the only day I can sleep late." Or a wife may say: "I wish
you wouldn't read the paper before dinner because it
keeps the whole family waiting for you." These are "easy-
minuses" because they deal with superficial behavior.
There is little risk in saying this type of statement and little hurt in hearing it.

"Easy-plus—easy minus" communication is often indulged in by people who define themselves as good communicators. In marital therapy, these spouses agree that
whatever is causing their problem, it is not poor communication because "we are always open with each other."
However, when a magnifying glass is placed over their
communications, it is clear that what looks good at first
glance is, in reality, significantly wanting. What is lacking are two other dimensions of communication which
are especially important to love relationships: "difficult-
pluses" and "difficult-minuses."

"Difficult-pluses" consist in sharing positive feelings
that are very deep, revealing, and sometimes risky. For
example, a husband may say to his wife: "I really enjoyed
being with you this afternoon. I felt a closeness that filled
me with warmth and goodness. I realized how very special and important you are to me. I just want to tell you
that you are very lovable and that I love you very much."
Or a wife may tell her husband: "I watched you playing
with the children today, and it was so obvious to me how
loving you are. You have a warmth and gentleness and
sense of fun that just exudes from you. The children are
so fortunate to have you as their father, and I am very
thankful to have you as a husband."

These "pluses" are difficult because they reveal a
depth, a need, a transparency, and a vulnerability. The
anxiety that "difficult-pluses" evoke can be seen in some
people's reaction to them: they are "mushy," "childish,"
"hysterical."

Rationalizations such as the following are often used to refrain from communicating "difficult-pluses."

"She ought to know by now that I love her. I married her and *stayed* married to her for twenty years. That's all she needs to know."

"He'd just laugh at me, or think I was paving the way to buying a new dress if I said something like that to him."

"When people really love each other, they *know* it; you don't have to put it into *words*."

But inferred love is not very assuring and not very warm. Inferred love is easily erased by moderate or severe stress in a relationship.

"Difficult-minuses" deal with more important, more sensitive, and more threatening issues than "easy-minuses." For example, a wife may say to her husband: "You know, every once in a while I get in touch with how really angry I am at you. I feel that you often treat me like a child, guiding me and protecting me and scolding me. Even when you compliment me, sometimes I feel like a puppy getting petted after doing something cute. But I honestly feel that, when all is averaged out, I'm as capable as you and as strong as you and that I should enjoy the same autonomy and power as you do in our relationship."

A husband may communicate with his wife: "One thing that really disturbs me is that almost everything seems more important to you than I do. You stop and converse with me when there isn't something more interesting to do. But, if the children come in, or one of your friends phones, or your mother wants to go shopping, then you seem very eager to leave me. I feel unimportant to you, and I feel jealous of all the people who attract your time."

Each of these is a "difficult-minus." Both individuals are baring deep feelings and opening themselves to possible ridicule and attack. Both are dangerously encroaching on delicate psychological territory of the other person. But, both "difficult-minuses" and "difficult-pluses" are the necessary mortar that keeps a relationship strong. They provide the depth and the resiliency that are necessary to withstand the natural stresses of a love relationship.

Some relationships have only "easy-pluses" and therefore are "paper-thin." Other relationships have only "easy-pluses" and "easy-minuses"; they have a semblance of health but are so guarded and cautious that they qualify only as functional. Other relationships have only "easy-minuses" or only "difficult-minuses" with no "pluses" to counterbalance them. These relationships are psychologically (and sometimes physically) homicidal. It is the relationship with "easy-pluses," "easy-minuses," "difficult-pluses," and "difficult-minuses" that renders true meaning to the concept of a loving communication.

Translating Psychological Dialects. Not everyone who speaks English speaks the same language. At times, we speak in psychological dialects which makes understanding difficult. Sometimes the dialect is so strange that we don't even understand ourselves.

Psychological dialects occur when we are not in touch with our deepest feelings, so what comes out our mouth is a smattering of our conscious feelings and our deeper, less conscious feelings. Psychological dialects are also caused when we are well aware of what we are feeling, but we are reluctant to put it directly into words.

A good communicator must learn to understand many different kinds of psychological dialects. He must be able to translate the articulated message into what was *really* meant. Sometimes translations will be inaccurate, but discussing even an inadequate translation may lead to ferreting out the accurate translation of a message. The opposite of a psychological dialect is "talking straight," which is an art that few people possess.

There are many different kinds of psychological dialect, but three will be discussed; the dialects of fear, anger, and love. In each case, the first speaker is using a dialect which the second speaker interprets literally and responds accordingly. This is followed by a discussion of the more accurate translation of the dialect.

1. Dialects caused by fear

Husband: "Why do you want to get a job? We don't have any financial worries."

Wife: "Then how come whenever I bring up
taking a trip you say we don't have enough
money?"

What the husband wishes to say and should say directly is: "I'm threatened by the thought of your working.
It makes me feel less like a man because a man should be
the sole provider. Also it will make you less dependent on
me, therefore giving me less power in the home. Moreover, you may meet people at work who are more interesting than I and become dissatisfied with me."

Wife: "Why don't you not work on Saturday, and
we'll go on a nice picnic?"
Husband: "I'm up to my neck in work and *you*
want to go on a *picnic!*"

In reality, the wife is fearful that her husband is
working too hard. What she really means to say is: "I'm
frightened that you'll get sick, which won't do you or the
family any good. I'm concerned that you are becoming
more and more depressed because you are getting no enjoyment in life. Your work is placing such a distance between us that I hardly feel we're even married anymore."

Mother: "I hope you don't come home too late
tonight."
Son: "What difference does it make; you'll be
asleep anyway."

What the mother wishes to say but can't say directly
is: "I'm scared that the later you stay out, the more chance
there is for you to get into trouble. I don't completely trust
your friends, and I think they could talk you into doing
something foolish. I'm worried that you'll get into a situation with your girlfriend where you'll end up having sex,
and she could become pregnant. When you're out that
late, I'm fearful that you might be drinking too much and
get in an accident or get arrested."

Daughter: "Why did you have so much to drink
when I brought my boyfriend home?"

Father: "It's not up to you, young lady, to tell me
how much to drink or not to drink."

What the daughter should say directly is: "Dad, I love
you very much, and I'm very proud of you. But when
you've had a few drinks, you act silly and embarrass me
in front of my friends. I'm sure they talk about it among
themselves, and this hurts me very much. I like to see you
have a few drinks and relax, but when you act the way
you did tonight, it's very hurtful and embarrassing to
me."

2. Dialects caused by anger

Husband: "Dear, I think it's time we left this
party; I'm awfully tired."
Wife: "Why, darling, we've only been here less
than an hour."

In reality, the husband is angry and is using a dialect
to avoid a confrontation. What he really means and
should say directly is: "I came with you to this party to enjoy it with you. But I haven't seen you since we arrived.
You've spent the last hour talking to all your friends
whom I don't know or don't want to know. I feel foolish
standing by myself drinking, and I'm getting angrier and
angrier at you for ignoring me. I'd appreciate it if we
could stay together and mingle as a couple."

Wife: "Did all your friends get as drunk as you
did at the ball game?"
Husband: "First of all, I'm not drunk; and,
second of all, yes, they did."

The wife's dialect has hidden her true message: "You
really bug me. You go out with your friends all day and
leave me alone at home. I was looking forward to going
out to dinner with you, so that I could at least salvage the
weekend, and you come home half-drunk and want to go
to sleep. I don't think it's fair, and I'm really upset about
it."

Daughter: "While you were feeding the cats, my
  dinner got cold."
Mother: "It *couldn't* be cold; I just took it out of
  the oven."

What the daughter wishes to say and should say directly is: "We only get to see each other and talk at dinner time, and the few minutes we have you spend feeding the cat. I enjoy spending some time talking, but it seems more and more I have to make an appointment to see you, and this hurts and makes me angry."

Father: "Why did you invite your girlfriend to
  the game with the extra ticket? What the hell
  does she know about football?"
Son: "I didn't invite her because she knows
  about football. I invited her because I wanted
  to be with her."

The father's dialect has camouflaged what he really wishes to say: "I was hoping we could go to the game together. I haven't seen you much lately, and I thought we could spend a nice afternoon at the game and maybe go out for dinner. I guess I felt you'd rather be with her than me, and it hurt to feel that and made me angry."

3. Dialects caused by love

Husband: "I don't know why you don't quit that
  crazy job."
Wife: "Because I'd rather have a crazy job than
  go crazy around the house."

The husband loves his wife, but feels uncomfortable telling her so directly. His dialect hides what he really should say: "I hate to see you get so upset about work. I think those people are treating you unfairly, and I hate to see you used and hurt by them. I love you very much and would like to see you enjoy your work or quit work and just enjoy life."

Wife: "I wish I were one of your patients; then I
  could get to see you privately for one whole
  hour a day."
Husband: "If you want to pay me the fifty bucks,
  so we can afford to live the way we do, I'll
  gladly cancel a patient and see you during
  that time."

In this case, what the wife is trying to say but cannot
bring herself to say directly is: "I love you very much and
would like to spend more time with you. Sometimes I get
jealous of your patients because I feel you give them your
best self and leave the leftovers for me. Can't we arrange
your schedule so we can spend more time together and
talk and have some fun?"

Son: "I feel sorry for poor Al; his mother is all
  over him like a rash."
Mother: "Well, maybe Al's mother has a very
  good reason for being all over him."

What the son wishes to say and should be saying
more directly is: "I'm sure glad I have you as a mother. I
know sometimes I give you a hard time, but when I see
the mothers that the other kids have, I know how lucky I
am, and I really appreciate it."

Father: "How much did your new hair-do cost?"
Daughter: "A lot, but I paid for it all myself."

This father loves his daughter and wishes to pay her
a compliment. But he uses a dialect rather than saying to
her: "Your hair looks really nice. It's pulled back, so we
can see your face, and that's a very pretty face to see."
It is unlikely that in any of these twelve exchanges
something good will result. The literal interpretation and
response in each case will initiate a lengthy discussion or
argument about a pseudo-issue.
For example, the man who returned from the ball-
game half-drunk will spend a half-hour detailing the exact number of beers he drank along with offering to

prove it with affidavits from his friends. If, after he had a few cups of coffee, his wife had dealt him some straight talk, a good deal more might have been accomplished. The *worst* thing that would have happened is that they would have gotten into an argument, but at least it would have been on the real issue, which would pave the way for future discussion under less heated circumstances.

When we fail to translate, we often miss the point of critically important communications. At other times, we have missed some beautiful messages because we got decoyed by the dialect. As communicators, we can help others translate their own messages ("Dad, what are you *really* saying?"). Equally important, *we* can talk straight, so that our welfare does not rely perilously on the translation skills of others.

Making Messages Palatable. Most of us fall into one of two categories with regard to communicating a difficult thought or feeling; We either swallow it, leaving it unsaid, or we say it in a harsh way that causes unnecessary conflict. There is a third option: We can communicate a difficult message in a palatable way.

Palatable means that the difficult message is couched in a way which allows the listener to hear and consider the merits of what is being said. Palatable does not mean phony; it means that an honest message is being sent, but with no barbs on it. In contrast, when a message is communicated in a harsh way, the listener is likely to reject the message and become deaf to further discussion.

The following are some examples in which a harsh communication is contrasted with a palatable communication.

A high school teacher is annoyed with a student who has been talking and clowning during class. The teacher can communicate the annoyance harshly by publicly saying: "Hey, you open your mouth one more time, and either I or the dean will shut it for you."

The palatable message is conveyed privately after class: "John, you were really distracting me in class today. Are you bored with the class, angry at me, or distracted by something outside of school? Whatever it is, I'd like to help you with it, so that you'll get more out of the class and so that you won't distract me again, because that's not fair to me or to the class."

Employee to boss, the harsh way: "The directives you sent me were vague. What were you trying to say, anyhow?" The palatable way would state: "After reading the directives you sent me, a few questions came up that I'd like to clarify with you."

Teacher Smith to a fellow teacher at a faculty meeting: "Frankly, I can't agree with you at all. I've been a teacher for fifteen years and know by now that your suggestion will bring nothing but chaos." A more palatable communication is: "I'm not sure that I understand all the ramifications of your suggestions, but I'm wondering if one problem that could arise would be...."

Parishioner to priest, the harsh way: "I just heard your sermon, and I think you did a lot of harm. What you said was not only arrogant but heretical." The palatable way: "I don't know if I interpreted what you said correctly or not but I found your sermon upsetting. Would it be possible to discuss it with you some time, because I think it deserves some further thought that perhaps both of us could benefit from?"

Husband to wife, the harsh way: "Why is it that every time I have an afternoon off from work you have to go shopping with your friends? You obviously find them more interesting than me." The palatable way: "The only reason I take an afternoon off is to spend some quiet time with you. I guess I haven't told you that, so you assume that I just want to putter around the house by myself. From now on, I'll tell you ahead of time so that we can save this time for each other. Does that sound all right with you?"

One friend to another: "You told me you were staying home Friday night and the next thing I hear is that you went out with some friends to a movie. Why do you have to lie to me?" The palatable way: "I'm feeling quite upset because you told me you didn't want to go out Friday, and then I heard you went out with someone else. Is it true that you did and, if so, how did it come about?"

There are two common elements in all of the palatable responses: First, they are non-accusatory. The approach is: "We have a problem here that needs resolving," versus "Why are you so dumb?" Secondly, the palatable responses are open-ended and invite a response. The approach is: "This is my concern; can we talk about it?" versus "I'm right, and you're wrong, and whatever you reply won't change that."

Undoubtedly, some people will feel that the palatable responses are too ideal; that in the stresses of everyday interactions one does not have the time to phrase things so neatly. The fact is, however, that it does not take extra time; it merely takes an attitude that says: "My main intent here is not to win a battle, but to resolve a problem." From this attitude the palatable words will flow.

In summary, no problem ever came into existence because of a "lack of communication." Problems occur because people communicate something of which they are unaware or something destructive. The child who refuses to talk to his parents *is* communicating something loud and clear.

The challenge is to become more aware of what we are "saying" everyday to people without even knowing it and to transpose our destructive communications into constructive ones. When this happens, a much more satisfying exchange of emotional groceries can take place.

Reflection Questions

1. Do I actively encourage honest feedback on my ideas, decisions, and perceptions, or do I not only not encourage it but resent it?

2. I'm a pretty good listener, but there are times when it's almost impossible for me to listen and keep my mouth shut until the other person is finished. One of these times is when. . . .

3. What do I find most difficult about communicating immediately?

4. With which person do I find it most difficult to disagree? Why? What can I do to make it easier?

5. Of the five special problems in communication (ventriloquism, sandwich-boarding, easy-pluses—easy-minuses, psychological dialects, and palatable messages),

which one do I need to work on the most? What practical steps can I take to strengthen that area?

Thoughts to Contemplate

1. When we wish to share some information with another person, it should be communicated directly. This seems simple enough, yet it is one of the biggest causes of failure in communication.

2. Most people talk too much. This is done to camouflage their insecurity stemming from not knowing what they really want to say, or knowing but being reluctant to get to the point.

3. Some people would prefer to go through life righteously indignant rather than satisfied and happy. Thus, it behooves them to practice psychological ventriloquism almost continually.

4. Not everyone who speaks English speaks the same language. At times, we speak in psychological dialects, which makes understanding difficult.

5. No problem ever came into existence because of a "lack of communication." Problems occur because people communicate something of which they are unaware or something destructive.

11

BECOMING AN EFFECTIVE HELPER

Perhaps the most beautiful human attribute is the willingness of one person to help another. When one person helps another, and when a person allows himself to be helped by another, there is a mutuality present that is seldom experienced in any other interaction.

We are all in a position to help others, and we are all in a position to be helped. Unfortunately, our society has tended to designate roles as "helper roles" and "helpee roles." For example, parents help children, children do not help parents; teachers help students, students do not help teachers; clergymen help parishioners, parishioners do not help clergymen.

Yet there are many ways (and more than mere functional ones) in which "helpees" can help "helpers." Once I heard a psychologist asked: "What kind of things do you teach your children about human behavior?" He instinctively replied: "Oh, I don't teach them much—I mostly *learn* about human behavior from my children." It is sad that society has often deprived "helpers" of the support they need from others to be more effective helpers.

The chances that any interaction with another person will be a neutral experience; i.e., neither helpful nor harmful to the other person, is probably about two out of ten, while eight out of ten daily interactions will be either a helpful or a harmful experience. This is an uncomfortable thought, because we do not define ourselves as being "harmful" people. Yet, on the average, we probably harm as many people as we help each day. Or to put it another way, we probably help and harm the same individual an equal amount each day. In a home where the parents' "helpful-harmful" ratio is 3:1 in favor of helpful, the children will likely grow into normal adults. In a family where the ratio is 3:3 to 3:5 (weighted in the direction of harmful), the children will grow into adults with mild to serious mental health problems. The same principle applies to classrooms, therapy offices, and confessionals.

What do we mean by the word "help"? *Help means affording another person the opportunity to grow into an effective and self-directing person.* This definition has a number of important points. The helper "provides an opportunity for growth." The helper cannot force the person to grow any more than a farmer can coerce his crop to grow. Like the farmer, the helper sprinkles seeds of care, trust, honesty, strength, and warmth. It is the responsibility of the individual to allow the "seeds" room to grow.

Helping another become effective means the person should grow in intellectual, emotional, social, moral, and spiritual effectiveness. The individual learns to face reality even more squarely and deal with it in order to become the person he wishes to become.

Self-directing means that a person gains more self-confidence. He is capable of relying on others when it is healthy and appropriate, but is not dependent on them for survival or overall well-being. The self-directing person controls "both reins" of life, but is open to counsel and criticism.

Some elements are noticeably absent from this definition of help. The following are not included as basic helping goals: to make a person "happy," "content," "peaceful," or "conflict-free." These states are not included because they could as easily be symptoms of avoiding reality as they could be signs of growth. Some of the most disturbed people I have seen describe themselves as being "at peace with myself."

True happiness and true peace are often the side-effects of becoming an effective and self-directing person. However, sometimes genuine growth creates *more* stress and conflict, the duration of which is often transient but sometimes enduring. A person could be "happy" because he is defending himself so well against unpleasant reality and could become "unhappy" when he is helped to face unpleasant reality. This is why the adage "A person often feels 'worse' before he feels 'better,' " is often true.

Helping should not automatically be equated with making another happy, nor should feeling badly be equated with being harmed. Harming means doing or failing to do anything that sets another person back one degree or more from being a more effective or more self-directing person.

Helping another is somewhat more complicated than most people believe. Being truly helpful requires much more than good intentions and common sense. The majority of the evil perpetrated in the history of man has flowed from good intentions and what is common sense to one person is absolute absurdity to another.

The following are the characteristics of an effective helper.

The effective helper is trustworthy. This is the most important characteristic of a helpful person because everything else rests on it. The basis of trustworthiness is keeping in the strictest confidence what is communicated in the helping relationship. "Strict confidence" means that absolutely no one else will know, directly or inferentially, the elements involved in the interaction. An exception would be that parents should share with each other information regarding their children.

Why do some people find it difficult to keep confidences? Perhaps the most common reason is that confidence is broken with "good intentions." The person trying to help seeks advice from others as to how the situation should be handled, and needs to release the stress generated by being in the helping position. Unfortunately, whatever good that would be accomplished by such sharing of information will be more than undone for two reasons. The first is that the helper knows privately that he broke a confidence, and this guilt will subliminally interfere with the helping relationship. Secondly, it is uncanny how such divulged information can wind its way back to the person being helped. When this happens, the helping relationship is scuttled, and, worse yet, it may be a long time before the "helped" individual will seek help again.

A second reason why people break confidence is that it makes them feel important. Although they would not define what they are doing as "gossiping," this is exactly what it is. For a moment, they have some interesting news that focuses the spotlight on them.

Thirdly, some people break confidence because they suffer from a great deal of chronic anxiety which causes them to blurt out anything that happens to be conscious at the time. While such people are not fully responsible for this situation, this weakness makes them poor candidates for being helpers.

Finally, some people break confidences as part of their passive-aggressive orientation. These individuals are angry people who hurt others indirectly and unconsciously. Such individuals will protest "But you didn't *specifically say* it was confidential!" or "Oh, I'm sorry; I didn't know you were *so sensitive* about what we discussed."

A price that an effective helper pays is that he must carry the burden of handling confidential information in a self-contained manner.

The effective helper is integrated. "Integrated" means that there is a balance between the helper's intellect (the head) and emotions (the heart). Some helpers are more intellectualized than "emotionalized." They think that all problems can be solved with logic and good common sense. They tend to make facile and naive statements, such as:

"Well, if your husband beats you, leave him."

"You should try not to be so hurt by your father."

"If God has forgiven you, certainly you can forgive yourself."

"Since you admit that your boyfriend is just using you, why don't you just break up with him?"

"So you didn't get into medical school; it's not the end of the world—there are many other ways to help people."

All of these statements are logical. And each of them is as unhelpful as it is logical. None of the responses invites the person to get in touch with his deeper feelings or indicates a bit of empathy. Until the welter of emotions dissipates and relative calmness prevails, all the logic and common sense in the world are virtually worthless.

Some helpers are "emotionalized," i.e., they lead with their hearts. Their message is: "Don't pay any attention to reality; just do what you feel is the right thing."

There is a popular axiom today: Trust your feelings. But this advice should be qualified. It is fine for a mentally healthy person to trust his feelings. It is reasonable for a normal person to trust feelings. But it could be catastrophic for a disturbed person to trust his own feelings. For example, if we advise a very hostile person to trust and act upon his feelings promiscuously, this person will meet with repeated rejection, which will serve only to increase the hostility.

The integrated helper possesses a near equal balance between "head and heart" and uses one to temper and guide the other.

The effective helper is real. Being real means being honest. It means reflecting reality the way one experiences and perceives it. The main obstacle to being real is being "nice." Being "nice" means pleasing people: making them comfortable, relieved, or happy. A real helper always tries to be honest. Sometimes this pleases the person being helped, and sometimes it does not. The "nice" helper always tries to be "nice." Sometimes the niceness is honest, and sometimes it is not. In other words, the true goal of a real helper is to be helpful, and honesty is used as the basic tool. The true goal of a nice helper is to be liked, and he uses pleasing as the basic tool.

There is a tremendous premium in our society on being nice—much more than on being honest. In fact, children are often punished for being honest when the honesty displeases adults and are rewarded for being nice, even though it is dishonest. "Niceness" is such an integral part of many people's personality that it takes a very conscious, strenuous effort for them to be honest in a particular situation in which being "nice" would be so much easier.

Helpers who are chronically nice have several characteristics. They nod their heads in agreement long before the other person has said anything with which to agree or disagree. It is as if they are saying "I don't know what you're going to say, but whatever it is, I agree with it."

"Nice" helpers also give assurance when the reality of a situation does not merit assurance, e.g., "I'm sure you're doing the right thing" when there is no reason for such confidence.

Finally, "nice" helpers focus on the positive, pleasant sides of a situation and ignore or downplay the negative, unpleasant aspects, e.g., "Even though your husband has a drinking problem, he's a very good man and that's really what counts."

In a helping relationship, nice helpers can create problems. Most human problems are resolved only by facing unpleasant reality and dealing effectively with it. Since "nice" helpers refrain from reflecting unpleasant reality, they offer no lasting benefit and only reinforce the individual's defenses against looking at the unpleasant reality.

Nice people give invitations to be nice, not to be honest. It is difficult being honest with people who are "so nice." So, instead of the helping contract being "Let's both of us be real," the contract reads: "Let's both of us please each other." Hence the person coming for help is subtly manipulated out of the very honesty needed for growth.

The real helper is an avid yet gentle proponent of reality, at least as he sees it. His attitude is: "I'm not certain that I am correct, but this is what I see and hear, and it may be helpful for you to give it some consideration."

Real people can ask the tough questions:

"Do you think you contribute at all to your husband's drinking problem?"

"Do you think your son's problems at school are related to your being too busy at work to spend much time with him?"

"I hear you saying you want to save your marriage, but is it at all possible that there is a small part of you that would like to try a separation?"

"Is there something in the area of sexuality that is bothing you but that is too embarrassing to talk about?"

"Do you think it's possible that you could benefit from some professional help?"

Nice people rarely dare to ask these questions, and, if they do, they are happy to let hasty denials close the issue.

Obviously, *genuine* niceness includes being real. But there is, and has been, such a fetish in our society on being nice in the superficial, self-serving sense that being real is almost a lost art.

The effective helper is involved. Often people ask me: "How do you stop from becoming emotionally involved with the people you help?" My answer, which initially surprises them, is: "I don't." The reason for this is that uninvolved people, i.e., unconcerned people, cannot help others. But it is important to distinguish between "emotional involvement" and "emotional attachment."

"Emotional attachment" indicates a dependency relationship in which the *basic* needs of the helper are getting met to a significant degree. Certainly it is appropriate that a helper get satisfaction from helping another, but it is detrimental if the helper is reliant on the other person for the meeting of essential psychological needs. When this is the situation, four problems occur.

First, the basic assumption in a helping relationship is that the helper generally views reality more accurately than the person being helped. If this assumption is unwarranted, then the "blind are leading the blind." When a helper is emotionally attached to the person being helped, the helper is not free to be the objective, honest, and strong proponent of reality which is necessary to be of genuine help. This is so because there is always the underlying fear that the person being helped will get upset with the helper and leave, thus depriving the helper of further need fulfillment.

A second problem with emotional attachment is that the helper has a vested interest in the decisions of the person being helped. Consequently, the helper, consciously or unconsciously, angles the other individual into making decisions that most benefit the helper rather than the person being helped. For example, it may be to your benefit to take a job opportunity in the East. But, since I don't want you to leave me, I will discourage you—even though it may be a good decision.

A third problem is that the attached helper is very vulnerable to manipulation. When people are frightened, insecure, or angry, they tend to manipulate others into meeting their needs in inappropriate and sometimes in destructive ways. Some common examples of manipulation in helping relationships are demanding inordinate amounts of time from the helper; asking the helper to intervene in one's life in inappropriate ways ("Will you phone my husband and tell him what you just told me?"); and demanding that the helper stifle his normal reactions and values and retool them to fit the needs of the helpee. When the helper significantly relies on the helpee for need fulfillment, he will be more inclined to rationalize "giving in" to the inappropriate demands and wishes of the person being helped.

Finally, the attached helper must "ride the moods" of the helpee if they are emotionally attached. When the helpee is feeling happy, the helper feels happy, even though there may be no reason in reality for either one to feel happy. When the helpee feels depressed, the helper feels depressed, thus disqualifying the helper from being of any real assistance. The effective helper must act as a fulcrum that remains emotionally stable despite the mood fluctuations of the person being helped.

Emotional involvement, on the other hand, means that the helper and helpee's minds and hearts are *touching,* but they are not *attached.* Each person remains essentially separate and free of the other. The emotionally involved helper genuinely cares about the other person and may even experience warm and loving feelings toward the person. But the emotionally involved helper is free to be objective and honest—to present reality to the individual even when it is painful. The involved person allows the person to make good decisions and holds steady against manipulation. The involved helper's emotional state will be privately owned and not contingent on the people he helps.

These principles are true for all relationships, from formal helping relationships to marriage. An "attached spouse" is a much less helpful spouse than an "involved spouse," and an "attached parent" is much less helpful than one who is emotionally involved. Being "emotionally attached" is often romanticized as being the ultimate in love, but in fact it is a violation of the people in the relationship. Emotional involvement, on the other hand, allows the helper and the person being helped to grow as individuals within the relationship.

The effective helper cares about the person being helped. Humanistic and Christian ideals hold that we should care about all the people all the time. Reality, however, indicates that there are some people we care about, and some people we don't. We may care deeply about an individual at one time and less so at another. This is normal and human, even in the best relationships. Caring is a virtue that we can afford only after we are free from significant pressures. When we are psychologically bleeding, we care little about anyone other than ourselves.

By "care," I am not referring to an "existential caring" as in: "I care about all people." I am referring to a very individualized and concrete care, as in "I care about you personally at this specific point in time."

There are two elements in true caring.

1. When we care about someone we give him quality time. This is to be distinguished from quantity time. Quality time means that we are totally and volitionally present to the other. We are not distracted by outside stimuli or "internal noises." We have saved this part of our life solely for the other person. We are not resentful about giving up the time; we are not in a hurry to move on to more interesting things. We are not half-reading the paper, half-watching television, half-planning what we will have for dinner, or half-wishing we were someplace else. The focus is on the other person. We are not thinking about what we should say next or bursting for our chance to say: "You think *you've* got problems—wait until you hear mine."

Quality time is custom-tailored to the individual; it is devoid of clichés and platitudes. Quality time is *sharing* time with another; quantity time is merely *spending* time with another—it's being geographically present, but that's about all.

2. Caring is also manifested in our willingness to tolerate stress in our efforts to help the other person. A toleration for tedium is necessary because often we shall hear the same laments again and again. A toleration for hostility is also necessary because when a helper is reflecting painful or threatening reality, he is often met with anger.

Caring also requires a toleration for ambiguity because human behavior is infinitely complex, so there will be times when issues and emotions are terribly unclear and confusing. The helper must be able to tolerate watching a person suffer and perhaps suffer with him. Suffering is often a necessary part of growth and to rush in and prematurely or artificially stop it is destructive. A toleration for failure is required because even our best efforts are not going to be good enough at times.

Finally, the helper must have a toleration for ingratitude. Sometimes helped people need to repress the memory of a situation which required help, so the helper gets repressed too. Sometimes people resent the fact that they needed help. So, even though the helper has significantly aided the individual, the person may be unable or unwilling to express gratitude.

Caring, then, means freely giving quality time and freely choosing to endure a certain amount of unpleasantness for the sake of helping another. These are the two largest investments required of a person who wishes genuinely to help another. Many people want to be helpers "theoretically," but are unwilling to, or are incapable of giving time or enduring the necessary stress.

Because we cannot possibly care about all people in the way we've defined caring, and because we cannot even care about a loved one twenty-four hours a day in this way, it is generally better not to try to help the people who, for one reason or another, we don't genuinely care about—or cannot learn to care about. It is better to refer these people to someone who can help them. And, if we don't feel caring at a particular time, it would be better to wait until we can afford to care.

The effective helper reflects. The opposite of reflecting is advice-giving. Advice-giving, in this sense, means telling a person what he should do or how he should feel in a specific situation. For example, a high school girl asks her parents, teacher, or counselor: "Do you think I should phone my boyfriend? I haven't heard from him for a week." The advice-giver replies: "Yes, I think you should see what's happened to him"; or "No, I think you would appear foolish to do that."

Giving advice can be helpful and a learning experience for children, although advice must be given much more judiciously to be a learning experience for those in late childhood. The likelihood of advice being more harmful than helpful increases proportionately as people grow from early adolescence through adulthood. Yet, well-intentioned helpers seem to be forever giving advice with regard to specific decisions.

The reasons for facilely giving advice are three: First, it is tremendously tempting. Most of us "know" we have the right answers, and it is very frustrating to keep this wealth of knowledge to ourselves. It is nice to feel important, needed, and wise. But, using the high school girl's question mentioned above, if she were to ask ten equally "wise" people this question, five would tell her to phone her boyfriend, and five would tell her not to call him.

Secondly, we often give advice because people *ask* for it. Most people in a dilemma think that their problem is that they don't know what to do, but this is merely a symptom of their problem. The real problem is that they lack the self-confidence, self-knowledge, and knowledge of the people and situations with which they are faced to make a sound decision. Many people have the attitude: "Just tell me what I should do—don't waste my time discussing it." But giving advice is merely giving symptomatic relief. This person will return again and again any time a significant decision must be made.

Finally, people give advice because they need to rush in and fix things. A young lady may confide: "I'm depressed because my boyfriend is starting to date another girl." A typical "rush in and fix it" response is: "Oh, I wouldn't get upset over it; if he has any sense, he'll return to you. If he doesn't, he's not good enough for you any way."

What this girl is *really* saying in what *appears* to be a simple statement is:

"I'm *scared* that I am not lovable."

"I'm *hurt* that my boyfriend would do this to me."

"I'm *angry* at him for leaving me."

"I'm *embarrassed* because of what my parents and friends will think."

"I *need* to get all these feelings out with somebody who will understand them."

The effective helper gently invites the girl to get in touch with and share her feelings: "How does this situation make you feel?" "Do you feel anything beside hurt?" "How do you feel your friends will react to the news?" "You seem a little angry, too." "You seem to feel like never dating a boy again." Questions such as these are invitations to emotionally regurgitate the toxins that are eating away at her insides. When this is accomplished, her head will be ready to perceive the situation more clearly.

Giving advice is generally not only unhelpful but destructive because it communicates to the person: "You're right; you're not capable of making your own decisions." It also deprives the individual of the very *process* that is necessary to become a reasonably autonomous decision-maker and shifts the burden of responsibility to the helper. A good general principle is: "The times we are most convinced that giving advice is legitimate and helpful are likely to be the times when giving advice will do the most harm."

An effective helper reflects rather than gives advice. Analogously, this helper is like a good salesperson. He lets the customer choose the different styles and colors of suits and watches while the customer tries on each one. The salesperson acts as an objective mirror and calls things to the attention of the customer that the customer may not have perceived. The salesperson's approach is: "Did you notice this?" or "You'll notice when you move this way, this is what happens"; or "If you choose this fabric, here are some things you might expect to happen." In other words, the effective helper draws out the individuality of the person so fully that the helpee knows what "fits right." There is no such thing as a "nice suit." There are only suits that people feel nice in. The same is true for life's decisions.

The effective helper provides a new experience. When the person who is trying to be helpful functions mostly as an "echo," then he is not being helpful. An "echo" repeats the advice, admonitions, and emotional responses of the person's past. If such repetitions did not help in the past, it is unlikely that they will help in the present, despite the fact that it is *we* who are saying them.

Some typical "echoes" that helpers offer are:

"You need to get your mind off yourself. Maybe you should do some volunteer work with people who have some *real* problems."

"You're too sensitive and take things too personally. You should learn to laugh more at life and not take yourself so seriously."

"You're too possessive and jealous. You must allow the people you love the freedom to live their own lives. It's only then that they can truly love you."

"I know you are grieving about your loved one's death. But he is with God now and suffering no longer. I'm sure he is happier than we are, and you will see him soon."

"Looks aren't everything, and being popular isn't the most important thing in life. You're beautiful inside and God loves you very much."

"You should get your priorities straightened out because you're starting to lose touch with what's really important in life."

And, last, but not least: "Sex isn't everything."

Each of these echoes may be absolutely true. But such statements are seldom, if ever, helpful in themselves for two reasons: One is that words must be wrapped in healing emotions if they are to be palatable. Many people have gone to helpers for empathy and received a lecture; for love and received moralizing; for understanding and gotten an argument; for support and gotten a threat; for warmth and received logic.

An effective helper offers a *new* emotional response. If we look back in our own life to our significant helpers, we will realize that it was seldom something they said that made the difference. It was something they felt or helped us feel that made them different. And it was only after their warmth relaxed us that our ears could open to what they were saying.

The second reason why echoes are not helpful is that people tune out repeated messages, especially when they are unpleasant ones. Parents are forever saying: "How many times do I have to tell you?" as if the mere repetition of a directive is all it takes to help people change.

As we eloquently repeat advice that the person has heard dozens of times (and at least one dozen times from *us*), the person politely listens, but is whispering to himself: "So, what else is new?"

An effective helper offers a new experience. This new experience need not be a dramatic happening. It could be an arm around the shoulder; a smile that says "I know how you're feeling"; a hug that says "You're still lovable"; a demeanor that says: "I'm not too busy to share a part of my life with you"; or "I'm not so upset with my own problems that I can't be present to you"; or "I'm not so insecure that you will be a threat to me"; or "I'm not so needy as to expect something from you in return."

For many people, any one of these behaviors would be a new experience, because the significant others in their lives find it easier to love conditionally than unconditionally; find it easier to reject than to be close; to judge than to empathize; to talk than to listen; to moralize than to understand; to be critical than to be supportive; to be manipulative than to be freeing.

Ten minutes of a new experience that is positive is worth more than ten hours of an old experience.

In summary, the key to being helpful is not what we say or how much we know, but who we are. It is good to possess academic knowledge about behavior and to understand some principles of counseling. It is necessary to have good intentions and common sense. However, these are merely "tools." If a person lacks to a significant degree any one of the aforementioned traits, it is likely this individual will use the tools to perpetrate more harm than good. A person lacking formal, academic knowledge about counseling, but possessing the traits of an effective helper, would be in a better position to help people in many everyday situations than a person possessing great "book knowledge," but lacking the traits of an effective helper.

Reflection Questions

1. What do I find is the hardest part about keeping a confidence?

2. What needs do I have that make it easier for me to be "nice" instead of real?

3. What are some steps I can take to be interested in helping people without becoming emotionally attached to them?

4. The next time somebody asks me: "Well, now that you've heard my story, what do you think I ought to do?" how will I respond?

5. The next time someone says: "This is the third time I've tried this thing, and it's the third time I've failed," what will I respond?

Thoughts to Contemplate

1. Some of the most disturbed people I have seen describe themselves as being "at peace with myself."

2. Helping another is somewhat more complicated than most people believe. Being truly helpful requires much more than good intentions and common sense. The majority of the evil perpetrated in the history of man has flowed from good intentions, and what is common sense to one person is absolute absurdity to another.

3. There is a tremendous premium in our society on being nice—much more than on being honest. In fact, children are often punished for being honest when the honesty displeases adults and are rewarded for being nice, even though it is dishonest.

4. Emotional involvement, on the other hand, means that the helper and helpee's minds and hearts are *touch-*

ing, but they are not *attached.* Each person remains essentially separate and free of the other.

5. Many people have gone to helpers for empathy and received a lecture; for love and received moralizing; for understanding and gotten an argument; for support and gotten a threat; for warmth and received logic.

12

PUTTING SEX IN PERSPECTIVE

Sexuality is one of several important parts of the human personality. Unfortunately, sex is often overrated as being the most important part of one's life or underrated as being of little significance. The areas of sexuality discussed in this chapter are masturbation, homosexuality, premarital sex, motives for sex, and sex in marriage. These topics will be discussed from a psychological point of view rather than from a medical or religious viewpoint. It is important to know why people behave the way they do and to understand the positive and negative consequences of their behavior. Given this understanding, the reader is in a better position to realistically superimpose information from medicine and religion to give a three-dimensional view of sexuality.

MASTURBATION

Masturbation is using one's hands or an object to cause sexual arousal in oneself or another. Although we typically think of masturbation as behavior that adolescents and adults engage in, infants and children also masturbate, i.e., they rub their genitals to obtain pleasure. When parents observe this they often panic: "Does this mean our five-month-old infant is becoming a sex pervert?" When parents actively discourage or punish such experimenting, the child learns very early that certain parts of the body are bad and what you do with them is even worse.

If one were to ask the vast majority of mental health professionals today if masturbation is normal or unhealthy, they would reply that it is normal. And, in my opinion, that would be just as erroneous as stating that it is unhealthy. It seems to me that a more realistic answer to the question is: "It depends."

The same criteria of judging normalcy that is applied to any behavior should be applied to masturbation. Several basic questions can be asked.

First, what is the *frequency* of this behavior? Does the person masturbate ten times a day or ten times a year? The former could indicate an unhealthy situation while the latter could be normal.

Secondly, *why* does the person masturbate? If a twenty-year-old college student masturbates to relax so he can get some sleep before an examination the next morning, it could be considered normal. If a thirty-year-old married man masturbates as a hostile gesture toward his wife, it could be considered unhealthy.

Finally, what are the *effects* of masturbation? If the college student masturbates and the effect is that he can finally get to sleep and thus approach the examination with a clear brain, this would be considered normal. If the same college student masturbates because he is fearful of girls, and if he gets his sexual needs met through masturbation so that he doesn't have to relate with girls, then it would be considered unhealthy.

It is dangerous to label a particular behavior normal or unhealthy without considering the circumstances. Interestingly, sex is one of the few behaviors that we automatically label as good or bad. If I ask a person: "Is homicide good or bad?" I am likely to get the response "It depends. If you kill somebody in cold blood, it's wrong. But if you kill someone who is trying to kill you or your family, it is all right." But if I ask the same people "Is masturbation OK or is it wrong?" or "Is premarital sex right or wrong?" I'm very likely to be told unequivocally that these behaviors are definitely "OK" or "wrong."

To label masturbation as wrong (abnormal, sinful) ignores the possibility that it could be a sign of growth or at least a normal tension release. To label it normal ignores the possibility that it could be a sign of deep-seated fear, anger, or guilt that is not being dealt with constructively.

People masturbate primarily for the following reasons.

To release tension. When a person masturbates to release tension it could be normal or unhealthy. If the tension that is released stems from fear, anger, or guilt that should be used to mobilize the person to face and deal with these feelings, then masturbation is wasting tension that is necessary for growth. On the other hand, the individual may be dealing with fears, anger, and guilt in a constructive way, but still have some residual tension. In this case, releasing that tension through masturbation would not be considered unhealthy any more than is having a martini, a cigarette, an extra helping of dessert, or taking a nap—all of which reduce tension.

To gain sexual gratification. When an individual masturbates as a fantasy sexual encounter, it could be normal or unhealthy. It is normal if it motivates the individual to seek healthy sexual relationships in reality. Analogously, it is healthy for a young person to fantasize himself as a great surgeon if the fantasy serves as motivation to work hard toward that goal. But it is unhealthy if the person gets so much satisfaction from the fantasy that he does not feel the need to transform the fantasy into reality. If a person masturbates because of deep-seated fears regarding the opposite sex that inhibit relating with them, then it would be a sign of an unhealthy situation.

To feel pleasure in the absence of other pleasure. With few exceptions, this is almost always an unhealthy motivation. Normally, this motivation means that the individual is receiving very little satisfaction from life and is reduced to one of the three most primitive satisfactions: sex (the others being eating and sleeping). This indicates that the individual is relating to life in such an ineffectual way that he is on a psychological starvation diet and is living off crumbs. The only exceptions to this would be an invalid whose satisfaction in life is severely curbed by the handicap or someone confined in a prison.

To rebel. Again, with few exceptions, this is almost always an unhealthy sign. This individual has a good deal of pent-up anger, especially toward parents and others in authority. Because the authority figures in the person's life have taught him that masturbation is very bad, this individual uses masturbation as a weapon of rebellion. Secretly, he "gets back" at authority figures for all the hurts and injustices they have perpetrated upon him. It would be healthier for the individual who masturbates out of anger to get in touch with the anger and to learn to communicate it in constructive ways.

There seems to be a general feeling that once a person marries, masturbation is no longer an issue. However, some relatively recent research indicates that almost three-fourths of the husbands in their late twenties to early thirties masturbate with a median frequency of twenty-four times a year while over 65 percent of the women in the same age group masturbate with a median frequency of ten times a year.

The reasons for masturbation in marriage can be benign, e.g., a temporary separation from a spouse; arriving at a climax when the partner in sexual intercourse has already reached a climax; or just needing some tension release but being too tired or too distracted to enter into sexual intercourse. On the other hand, masturbation in marriage could indicate deep-seated fears, angers, or guilts that are interfering with marital intercourse, thus divesting it of satisfaction. It also could indicate a passive-aggressive way of venting one's hostility toward the partner. The message in this case is: "I'll show you that I can get along fine without you." In the latter example, masturbation would be a sign that there are personal or marital problems that need to be attended to and solved.

HOMOSEXUALITY

Homosexuality is a popular topic today, but it rarely is discussed with objectivity. The main purpose of this presentation is to demythologize some beliefs about homosexuality and to offer a realistic and objective discussion of what we presently know about it.

It is important to realize that sexuality is not an "all

or nothing" behavior any more than intelligence or athletic ability. Sexuality lies on a scale with homosexuality
on one end and heterosexuality on the other. In fact no
one is "a homosexual" or "a heterosexual." Men who define themselves as heterosexual may well have males in
their lives that they deeply love, and women who define
themselves as homosexual may have men in their lives
that they deeply love. Consequently, it is more realistic to
think in terms of being more heterosexual than homosexual or more homosexual than heterosexual, although this
concept may make some people nervous. At different
points in our lives we may gravitate more toward one end
of the scale than the other.

It is also important to realize that sexuality can be either psychological or physical or both. The following diagram demonstrates a few of the more common combina-
tions that can occur.

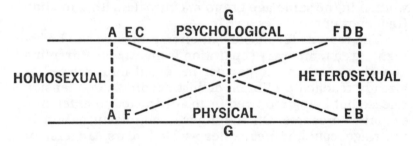

A person (A) could be both psychologically and physically homosexual.

A person (B) could be both psychologically and physically heterosexual.

A person (C) could be psychologically homosexual
but not physically, i.e., have a homosexual orientation but
not actualize it physically.

A person (D) could be psychologically heterosexual
but not physically, i.e., have a heterosexual orientation
but not actualize it physically.

A person (E) could have a homosexual psychological
orientation but engage in heterosexual physical behavior.

A person (F) could have a heterosexual psychological
orientation and engage in homosexual physical behavior.

A person (G) could have a bi-sexual orientation, i.e.,

have both a homosexual and a heterosexual orientation and engage in both behaviors.

Perhaps the question asked most regarding homosexuality is: "What causes homosexuality?"

The cause of homosexuality is not known any more than the cause of heterosexual behavior. There has been research done to determine if there is a genetic factor in homosexuality, and none has been found at this point. Similarly, endocrine research has been done to see if a clue can be found in differing hormonal levels, e.g., if male homosexuals possess more female hormones than do male heterosexuals. No convincing evidence has been found to substantiate this hypothesis. Some studies show more female hormones in homosexual males, but heterosexual males may also manifest these same amounts. There has been a fair amount of research into the family backgrounds of homosexuals to determine if the manner in which the homosexual was reared may account for the homosexuality. After all the data are weighed, it is clear that there is insufficient information to justify the conclusion that the family backgrounds of homosexuals as a group are significantly different from those of heterosexuals.

There are some things we know about homosexuality with some assuredness. We know that homosexuals are no more dangerous or apt to commit crime than are heterosexuals. A child molester is much more likely to be a disturbed heterosexual than a homosexual. The same is true for a rapist. Homosexuals do sometimes kill a lover in a "lover's quarrel" but no more than heterosexuals do.

Studies have indicated that homosexuals and heterosexuals cannot be distinguished on the basis of the presence of abnormal symptoms. Unless one holds that homosexuality is in itself pathologic, homosexuals test out to be no more normal or abnormal than heterosexuals.

We know that homosexuals cannot be easily identified. Some homosexual men, for example, appear very effeminate, while others appear very masculine. Most fall in between these two extremes. The same is true for women homosexuals. Some are very masculine, some are very feminine, and most fall between the two extremes.

People whose hobby it is to spot homosexuals are as likely to be wrong as if they were attempting to spot a computer programmer.

The "prairie-fire" view is that unless we extinguish homosexuality in society, vast numbers of people will become homosexual. History shows that in "open" societies, homosexual behavior never permanently satisfies more than a small minority of people. One could state that since society has become more liberal, there are more people becoming homosexual than ever before. However, it is probably truer to say that more homosexuals are now publicly admitting their sexual preference.

We know that homosexual teachers will have no influence on their students to become homosexuals. Sexual orientation is pretty well formed before the child enters school. Many people have had homosexual teachers at some time in their educational experience, but did not feel swayed to join them in their sexual preference.

The stereotype of the unhappy and promiscuous homosexual is not an accurate description of all homosexuals. One could as easily spend an evening in a heterosexual "body shop" and conclude that all heterosexuals are promiscuous and live in a constant state of sexual frenzy. Or one could reflect that the vast majority of people who commit suicide are heterosexual and conclude that heterosexuals are deeply dissatisfied and unhappy people. The fact is that there are homosexuals who live very effective, loving, and peaceful existences because of, or in spite of, their sexual orientation.

According to the National Institute of Mental Health perhaps 50 percent of predominantly homosexual persons having some homosexual orientation and who present themselves for treatment can be helped to become predominantly heterosexual. For homosexuals who feel comfortable with and enjoy their sexuality, this information is of no interest. But there are some homosexuals who would much prefer to be heterosexual but feel that fate has dealt them a bad card and they're stuck with playing it out. This is not necessarily true.

Two areas regarding homosexuality deserve special mention. One is that having homosexual feelings and attractions is often an important part of sexual maturation.

As Henri Nouwen writes: "When we are still struggling with finding out who we really are, homosexual feelings can be just as strong as heterosexual feelings. There is nothing abnormal about homosexual feelings at a time in which our life has not yet formed a definite pattern. Perhaps the absence of these feelings is more abnormal than their presence."

This is important to realize because many adolescents and young adults experience homosexual fantasies, dreams, feelings, crushes, and behavior. Often their reaction is to panic and assume automatically that this makes them a homosexual.

A second important issue is an ever increasing situation in which parents learn that their adolescent or young adult is a homosexual. This is a very difficult and often painful discovery for parents for three reasons. The parents ache for their child whom they foresee as going to experience a good deal of pain in life because of his homosexual orientation. Second, the parents feel they failed as parents, often blaming themselves and each other for "turning" the child into a homosexual. Finally, the parents feel ashamed in the presence of friends and relatives.

There are some thoughts that may be helpful to these parents. As was mentioned earlier, there is no definitive data that point to the home as the cause of homosexuality. And, even if there were, in most cases the causes would be so subtle that it would be unreasonable to expect the average parent to be aware of them. What makes one child love school, a second child in the same family be uninterested in school, and yet a third child hate school? To explain this by saying that the parents caused each of these different situations and that they should have recognized how and why they were causing them is patently unfair.

Adolescents or young adults who tell their parents of their homosexuality generally do so because they love and respect their parents and want to be loved by them in an honest way. Young people who don't care about their parents—who dislike or disrespect them—would seldom bother to go through this stressful experience. The parents' reaction will cause one of two effects. A positive reaction is one which allows the young person to feel relieved and glad that the information was shared and to feel that he will continue to be loved by the parents regardless of sexual orientation. This does not mean that the parents will not be surprised or even shocked. It does not mean that the parents must deny their own feelings of confusion, anger, disappointment, and guilt. Parents can still love their children and have these feelings generated because of the child's sexual orientation, just as if the feelings were caused by the child's decision to marry someone of whom the parents disapproved; or by the child's quitting college, or moving across the country, or making a career choice which disappoints the parents, or getting divorced. After the initial waves of all these feelings, love can still emerge as the most lasting and strongest emotion.

The other effect that the parents' reaction can have is to make the young person deeply regret having shared the information, making him feel totally rejected, unloved, and without value. Rejection by one's parents, especially when one is young, often causes the person to feel: "If my parents can't love me, who in the world can?" This is not a sound foundation for starting life whatever one's sexual orientation.

In summary, we can react to homosexuality in one of the two ways that we react to anything that we don't understand or that makes us feel uncomfortable. We can tenaciously hold to our fears and prejudices and deny realities that tend to disprove them. Or we can react in ways that reflect our knowledge and understanding of this behavior and allow homosexuals to exist with us in the same way we allow people with differing religions, politics, or life styles to exist without interfering with their rights and their chances for a reasonably happy life.

PREMARITAL SEX

The term "premarital sex" as it is used here denotes sexual intercourse before marriage whether the partners are casual acquaintances or engaged to be married. The questions that will be considered are equally relevant to both situations.

The first question that is often asked about premarital sex is: "Is premarital sex good or bad?" The answer, from a mental health point of view, is the same as it was for masturbation: "It depends."

Rather than jump on a bandwagon to "prove" that premarital sex is good or bad, it is more realistic and helpful to consider some of the issues involved in premarital sex and allow each individual to make his own value judgment.

This section will have two dimensions: issues to consider for those people who are engaging in premarital sex or are contemplating it, and issues to consider for those people who choose not to have premarital sex.

Issues to consider for people engaging in or contemplating premarital sex:

1. Does having premarital sex make you feel better or worse about yourself? This is not the same question as: "Does premarital sex make you feel good?" Feeling good is not a measure for judging the overall benefit of an act. It may feel good to punch someone in the nose, but it may not be a good thing to do.

After having premarital sex, do you feel more lovable, confident, strong, and happy with yourself? Or do you feel used, confused, weak, or ashamed of yourself? This is not a foolproof criterion because defense mechanisms such as denial and rationalization can fool us into feeling good about ourselves when, deep down, we don't. But the answer to this question can give us some information on which to make a judgment.

2. Is premarital sex prematurely isolating? An important part of personality development is to get as many needs fulfilled from as many different kinds of people and experiences as possible. It is not until the personality has matured that one can afford to "specialize" in one or two relationships, and this usually requires twenty to thirty years of varied experiences.

When someone is in the initial or middle stages of psychosexual development and has premarital sex with the same individual, there is a strong tendency to latch on to that person, becoming uninterested in other relationships and activities. As one young man said: "Why should I shop at a bunch of separate grocery stores when I can get all my groceries at one market?" While this may be a sound marketing principle, it is damaging when applied to human growth. Of course, one can enter into a prematurely isolating relationship without sex, but, when sex is present, it can act as a powerful adhesive.

3. Does premarital sex contribute significantly to bonding? Bonding occurs when two people who haven't yet developed a clear and strong sense of identity feel strongly attracted to each other and merge into each other. As the romantics say, they "lose themselves in each other, becoming as one."

From a mental health standpoint, bonding is never good because it results in confusion and slavery. Analogously, it is like taking two batches of wet cement and mixing them together. It becomes very confusing as to which cement went with which batch, and the two batches become so intertwined that they are "stuck" to each other—there is no longer any freedom to separate.

In bonding, needs intertwine as well as do fears, angers, guilts, perceptions, beliefs, values, doubts, and goals. The couple becomes so merged that each becomes a slave to the other and to the relationship. As one person put it: "The relationship is more important than I am. I'd sacrifice my entire self to maintain the relationship."

Sometimes the bonding can become so intense that it can take a year or two after the relationship terminates to regain the foundations of one's identity. Bonding can occur without premarital sex, but, once again, sex is a strong adhesive and can contribute significantly to the bonding.

4. Will premarital sex increase the possibility for extramarital sex? At first this sounds like a silly question based on medieval fears and admonitions. But, under closer scrutiny, it may not be so silly. The possibility exists when a stimulus-response link is created between feelings of attraction and the need to have sexual intercourse. After a while, the "feel attraction—have sex" sequence becomes a powerful necessity and the fact that one becomes married may do little to weaken this link. The problem then arises when the married person meets someone to whom he feels attracted and feels great tension until he has sex with the person to complete the sequence.

The married person who has the extra-marital sex has two options: to tell the spouse, which seldom enhances the marriage relationship, or to keep it hidden, the guilt from which often gradually corrodes the relationship.

Issues to consider for those declining to have premarital sex:

1. Does abstaining from premarital sex create an inordinate pressure on the dating couple to get married? No one knows how many people get married primarily to have sex, but the numbers must be legion. Few people admit this, even to themselves. But after the one-hundredth or three-hundredth act of sexual intercourse, the newness and excitement ebb, and the individuals discover that there is little left to keep the marriage together, except possibly the children.

Declining to have premarital sex can also be a conscious or unconscious manipulation to entice the partner to "stick around" and get married, with sex being the eventual reward. This dynamic is based on the fear, sometimes realistic, that if one "gives" the other partner premarital sex, the partner will have gotten what he wanted and move on to other relationships. Consequently, rather than lose the partner, a subtle contract is agreed upon: "You marry me, and you'll get your sex." Motives such as these seldom reach awareness because they are camouflaged by moral and religious values. If a person has premarital sex, it generally precludes having sex as a primary motive for marriage, although it can create other problems as mentioned above.

2. Does choosing to abstain from premarital sex indicate immature sexual development? Some people, even though they are chronologically, intellectually, and physically eighteen, twenty, or twenty-five years old are only six, ten, or twelve years old psychosexually. Sexually immature individuals generally come from homes that were puritanical and anti-sexual. The child was taught directly or indirectly: "Sex is not nice, so if you want to be a nice boy [girl] and want us to love you, remain non-sexual." The result is that these children grow into adulthood psychologically neuter, although they may have dated and even "gone steady."

People who are pre-sexual do not explain to their partners: "I don't want to have premarital sex because I'm pre-sexual." They garner more acceptable reasons, generally having to do with "values" to describe their position.

Problems can arise when pre-sexual people marry. If both partners are pre-sexual, little tension develops. They may grow together into a mature sexuality, or they may remain stuck at a pre-sexual level for the rest of their lives. This detracts significantly from the marriage relationship, and the couple's negative sexual attitudes will be passed on to the children.

Tension will develop quickly, however, if one spouse is pre-sexual and the other is maturely sexual. The mature sexual person is quite ready for a vibrant sexual relationship now that the couple is married, but soon finds that the spouse is a frightened, hostile, and reluctant participant. The resultant tension will soon cause a myriad of personal and marital problems.

3. Does declining to have premarital sex reflect a psychologically incestuous relationship? A psychologically incestuous relationship means that one or both partners is dating a psychological representation of his opposite-sexed parent, e.g., the boy is dating his "mother" and/or the girl is dating her "father." Psychologically incestuous relationships seem to be quite common in our society. The boy's unconscious attitude is: "My mom was so good; I want to get a mom to live with forever." The opposite can occur, e.g., a girl's attitude might be: "I've never really had a father who loved, protected, and took care of me, so I want to find one and get all those needs met because I was deprived of them as a child."

Although this kind of relationship is satisfying on

many levels, sex is a confusing and anxiety-producing situation because it too closely resembles having sex with one's opposite-sexed parent. The relationship is more a buddy-buddy one than a mature sexual one. The problem is, after this couple marries, they are likely to get their needs for an opposite-sexed parent satiated and discover that they want something more than that. Now they are ready for a truly adult relationship. They may wish to grow into this relationship together, or they may find, as one man told me: "My wife was great as a mother, but I'm not at all interested in her as a wife." When this is the case, the marriage often breaks up.

4. Does choosing not to have premarital sex reflect a deep-seated personality problem? Generally there are three main personal problems that could be disguised in the decision to refrain from premarital sex.

One is that a person could be a passive-aggressive personality, i.e., some people harbor a great deal of unconscious anger toward humanity in general or the opposite sex in particular. Because the hostility is unconscious, it manifests itself in disguised forms. In the context of sex, the passive-aggressive person is unconsciously telling the partner: "When all is said and done, all you really want from me is sex, and I'm not going to give it to you." Superficially, everything else in the relationship may look great. But, looking at the relationship closely, one will find some delicately balanced neuroses between the two partners. If this couple gets married, the problems will become more obvious because there are no longer any "good" reasons for not having sex. I've known some people who refused to have sex for a year or two after a marriage, and when they did eventually have sex, they had it with someone other than their spouse.

A second personality problem is a fear of intimacy. Some people, perhaps many people, have a deep fear of allowing another person to get too close to them for fear of getting known too well; for fear of being hurt, trapped, or rejected. Sexual intercourse for many people is the main symbol of "giving oneself over" to another. Because of the deep fear connected with emotional intimacy, the person cannot participate in the symbol because it would represent placing himself in a frighteningly vulnerable position.

A third personality problem that could be present is latent homosexuality. This shows itself in one or both partners simply not being attracted sexually to the opposite sex. This may be coupled with a sexual attraction to the same sex, but it often is not. (It should be pointed out that pre-sexual people also experience the same kind of disinterest and sometimes aversion.)

In latent homosexuality, the disinterest or aversion is usually caused by a deep fear or hostility toward the opposite sex. In a dating relationship, the latent homosexual may love the person very much but not be able to relate in a sexual way. Heterosexuals may be helped to understand this by realizing that they may have strong affectionate feelings toward someone of the same sex, but are disinterested or repulsed by the thought of having sex with them. Sometimes such individuals get married and gradually, with or without professional help, resolve the fears and angers and can participate comfortably in sex. In other cases, the latent homosexuality becomes more overt and eventually the individual leaves the marriage to pursue a homosexual life style.

In summary, whatever decisions are made with regard to any behavior should be grounded on conscious and healthy reasons. Sexual behavior is no exception to this rule. The problem with sexual behavior is that it is heavily loaded with biological drives, psychological needs, and moral considerations. With these three powerful forces pushing and pulling the individual, clear, honest, and reasonable thoughts and feelings are sometimes difficult to approach and actualize. It is for this reason that pre-marital sexual behavior should be considered with a caution that asks: "Do you really know why you're making this decision?" Caution is the midpoint between fear and foolishness.

MOTIVES FOR SEX

As peculiar as it sounds, sometimes sexual behavior has little or nothing to do with sex, just as drinking in a tavern sometimes has little or nothing to do with thirst. The point is there can be several motives underlying the same behavior.

The proximate purpose of healthy sex is to feel good genitally and to help one's partner feel good genitally. The ultimate purpose of sex is to bring two human beings closer emotionally. To the extent that both these goals are fulfilled, sexuality will be healthy and satisfying. To the extent that only one of these goals is met, i.e., only genital satisfaction but not emotional, or only emotional and not genital, sex will be less than it was meant to be.

It is important to realize that every one of us participates at times in sex when it isn't sex. Because we are human and possess all the conscious and unconscious complexities attendant to being a human being, motives other than sexual and loving ones will creep into our sexual behavior. The better we feel about ourselves and our partner, the less non-sexual motives will be present. But, when we feel less good about ourselves and/or our partner, the possibility of non-sexual motives in our sexual behavior is great.

The following are five non-sexual motives underlying sexual behavior in which many of us engage at one time or another.

1. Sex as a tranquilizer. Both solitary sex (fantasy, masturbation) and interpersonal sex can be used as a tranquilizer—a "sexual sedative." When sex is not used for sex or for love, it is more likely being used as a tranquilizer than anything else. Some research has indicated that "highly sexual" people are actually "highly tense" people who use sex for tension relief.

Sex can be used as a tranquilizer in two ways: First, it can be a good distraction from the stresses of life. While immersed in the sensuality of sex, one is temporarily oblivious to the conflicts at work, the demands of the children, and the stresses of marriage. One sign of sex being used as a distraction is seen in the individual who feels depressed when sex is over. The depression is caused by the sudden invasion into awareness of the unpleasant reality that must now be faced.

While healthy sexuality is incidentally a distraction

from the rest of reality, its main purpose is not to distract but to *share* pleasure and emotions. Unhealthy sexuality's main purpose is to distract; hence, whatever mutual good occurs is accidental.

If a person continually uses sex as a distraction, it gradually will lose its power to distract, as do all distractions. And, since distraction is the main goal that this individual derives from sex, sex will become empty and unfulfilling. This person fails to understand that the problem isn't sex, but the way he is *using* it.

When one partner uses another as a source of distraction from unpleasant reality, he is relegating the partner to a role that could as easily be filled by a good movie, a captivating book, or a hot-fudge sundae. Sooner or later, the partner will intuit this and feel rejected.

As was noted in the discussion of defense activities, sex can be used as a tension release. Healthy sexuality has as one of its characteristics the release of sexual tension. But there are different types of tension: sexual tension, family tension, work tension, social tension, spiritual tension, inner tension, etc. Each specific tension has a specific purpose, i.e., to make a person uncomfortable enough in a particular area that he will identify the source of the tension and then rectify it so that it no longer acts as a barrier to need fulfillment. For example, family tension should be reduced by working things out in the family.

But, if a person takes this family tension and reduces it through sexual activity, he has used sex as a tranquilizer. Two problems ensue: The cause of the tension remains unaltered, thus continuing to create tension, and the sexual partner is relegated to the role of an aspirin. Whenever sex is motivated primarily by a need to release tension, intercourse is merely a disguised form of mutual masturbation.

2. *Sex as a weapon.* Rape is the clearest example of sex used as a weapon. Rape has almost nothing to do with sex and almost everything to do with hostility.

But there are many more subtle "sexual weapons" than rape. Whenever the content of a fantasy or act subtly or clearly degrades, humiliates, mocks, exploits, degrades, enslaves, or coerces another, the fantasy or act is not sexual but hostile. It is important to understand that many sexual problems are really hostile symptoms.

Often a person comes to see me as a therapist because he has "problems with masturbation." But, after the person describes the frequency and intensity of the masturbation; the fantasies or lack of fantasies that accompany it; and the frustrating (anger-producing) circumstances that precede it, it becomes clear that the person does not have a "masturbation problem" but an "anger problem" that is disguising itself in the cloak of sexuality. As this individual is helped to identify the anger and to ventilate it in therapy and, hopefully, with the people who are the targets of anger, the frequency of masturbation often diminishes 80 percent in a few months. Often these people remark: "I can't understand what is happening. All we do is talk about anger, and we never talk about masturbation; yet, I'm not masturbating nearly as much as I was."

It is well known that unconscious anger is an important contributor to premature ejaculation, sexual impotence, and frigidity. It is as if the person is saying to his partner: "I'm not going to give you something that you want very much from me: sex."

Sometimes the opposite is true; i.e., some people are sexually "turned on" the most when they are angry, and sexual behavior provides the same good feeling as a fighter gets when he knocks a punching bag off its hinges.

Even in the best relationships, anger and sex often intermingle. And, when we fail to separate them, neither one will fulfill its proper function. This situation interferes with growth and in some cases causes significant damage to the person and to the relationship.

3. *Sex as a substitute for intimacy.* Sexual activity can be used as a relatively safe substitute for psychological involvement. Unfortunately, "intercourse" and "intimacy" have almost become synonymous. Therefore, it is helpful to distinguish between "physical intimacy" and "psychological intimacy." Physical intimacy means that two people allow their bodies to relate in close and ardent ways. Psychological intimacy involves sharing one's in-

ner and deeper self: one's secret thoughts, feelings, fears, doubts, needs, dreams, and values. And this creates a good deal of vulnerability. The reciprocal part of psychological intimacy is that one is required to accept and deal with the inner self of one's partner. This requires care, time, and responsibility.

Some people fool themselves into thinking that because they are close physically, they must also be close psychologically. But being physically intimate requires infinitely fewer competencies and risks than being psychologically intimate. The only competence that physical intimacy requires is to have sexual anatomy that functions properly. The competencies needed to be psychologically intimate include all of those mentioned in Chapter One and perhaps a few more. In terms of risks, the worst thing that can happen in physical intimacy is that one's partner may communicate: "I don't like you sexually."

But in psychological intimacy a person may communicate, directly or indirectly:

"I don't like your intellect." (You're phoney, dense, arrogant....)

"I don't like your emotions." (You're immature, selfish, insecure....)

"I don't like your social behavior." (You're unassertive, amoral, rigid, shallow....)

A typical symptom of using physical intimacy as a surrogate for psychological intimacy is that boredom sets in once a partner's sexuality has been totally explored. This may take two or three dates or two or three years of marriage. But sooner or later this individual feels the need to move on; to continue the search for the "right person."

4. *Sex as a fiscal enterprise.* Sex has tremendous buying power. Some people can act as "sex brokers" who deal in sex as adroitly as a stockbroker buys, sells, and trades stocks. When a sex broker finds someone who is willing to trade in the same currency, several commodities can be negotiated.

Prostitution is the clearest example of a transaction between a sex broker and a client. The nature of this deal is clear to both parties: sex for money. Unfortunately, most prostitution is more subtle than this, and the currency is much more valuable than money. In "everyday prostitution" the prostitute does not realize that she is a prostitute, and the client does not know that he is a client. They both are under the illusion that they are having sex. Most prostitution does not occur on the bare mattresses of tenderloin hotels but on the freshly made beds of engaged or married couples.

Some of the fiscal ways in which sex can be used are:

Sex as an investment. A wife uncharacteristically agrees to have frequent sex with her husband because somewhere in the back of her mind is the thought that after a few super-sexual encounters she will suggest where she'd like to vacation this year.

Sex as a dividend. A young man agrees to spend the weekend with his fiancée at her parents' home. In the back of his mind is the thought that, when they return to her apartment, she *has* to reward him for "the wasted weekend" by having sex with him.

Sex as a loan. A wife agrees to get more involved in sex while her husband is in the midst of pursuing a promotion at work. She feels he needs more relaxation, but underneath she hopes the relaxation will help him get the promotion because they need the money. As soon as her husband gets or fails to get the promotion, the loan is reclaimed because it is no longer necessary. Sex returns to its normal humdrum place in their lives.

Sex as a down payment. A college boy feels he has very little to offer his girlfriend at this point in his life. So, he gives her his body to keep her until he is able to give her the benefits that will come from his profession.

Sex as payment for a debt. A college girl asks her boyfriend to do her term paper for her and, after she receives an "A", she consciously or unconsciously decides to pay him off in the currency that interests him most: sex. The mercenary basis for the sex is neatly camouflaged by sentiments such as: "Both of us fell into each others arms as if by some hidden signal." The hidden signal was the ring of the psychological cash register.

Sex as a controlling interest. A husband offers intense and exhilarating sex to his wife as long as she pleases him in the other areas of their life. However, when she "steps out of line," he's either "too tired" to have sex, or he goes about it in a mechanical, "wham-bam, thank-you ma'am" way. Although neither partner is aware of it, the husband controls the significant parts of his wife's life through "loving sex."

In these examples, the sexual transaction has been made obvious to clarify the point. In real life, however, few people would agree to such stark and calculated transactions. Both the sex broker and the client are con-vinced that the sexual encounter is truly beautiful or at least a fun experience. It takes some real insight and ver-bal communication to ferret out the latent transactions that appear in even the best relationships.

5. Sex as self-assurance. Many people, especially young people, use sex as an instrument for gaining self-assur-ance. In our culture, especially, there is such an outra-geously high premium placed on sexuality that it takes an extraordinarily secure person to keep sexuality in proper perspective. It is terribly tempting to measure one's total worth solely on the criteria of sexual attract-iveness and sexual competence.

I have seen women who were beautiful human be-ings, warm and sensitive wives, and caring and loving mothers, who felt they were failures because they had never had an orgasm. And I have seen great men, strong yet gentle, concerned and giving, beautiful husbands and loving fathers, who were plagued with the questions about their adequacy and worth because they were occa-sionally impotent.

If one lacks an appreciation for all the dimensions of what makes a person effective or ineffective, lovable or unlovable, one will overestimate the importance of sex-uality.

The reverse of this can also be present. Some people think that if they are good in bed, this automatically makes them good outside of bed. The insecure look to sex-uality as a testing ground on which to prove their worth. It is performance that counts. If I can cause my partner to writhe in ecstasy, then I am a success as a person.

Sexuality is not a good proving ground for anything. It doesn't prove that one is better or worse than one had thought before one had sex. It doesn't prove that one is attractive either physically or psychologically because the most beautiful people in the world have sex, as do the least attractive people. It doesn't prove one's sexual identity because heterosexuals can participate in homosexual behavior and vice versa, and psychologically asexual people can be married and have six children.

The more we try to use sexuality as a proving ground, the more disappointed we shall become. We won't prove what we set out to do because sexual behavior is incapable of proving anything. And we won't enjoy the sexual behavior because we are using it for a purpose other than that for which it was intended. For people who need to "prove" things, it is best done outside of the bedroom.

SEX IN MARRIAGE

Sex does not begin and end in the bedroom. More often than not, it reflects what is happening in the rest of the relationship and is a barometer of the quality of one's life. Specifically, it reflects three areas: the individual spouse's sense of self-esteem; the overall marriage relationship; and each spouse's attitude toward sex.

Sex in marriage is fulfilling when each spouse feels reasonably good about himself or herself. When each spouse feels effective, lovable, and loved, it creates a good impetus for sexual satisfaction. The feeling of being ineffectual at work, as a spouse, parent, or friend, can interfere with self-esteem. A man who is not successful at work or who experiences a setback in his job, may bring his "dented" self-concept into the sexual relationship. A woman may feel that she is actualizing few of her talents, and this causes her to feel inadequate and uninteresting. It is possible she will bring these feelings into bed with her. When *both* spouses have diminished self-esteem, it is very likely to interfere significantly with their sexual relationship.

The quality of the overall marriage is also an important factor in sexual fulfillment in marriage. A good marriage relationship has been defined as one that gives each partner something he or she can't buy. We can buy a housekeeper; we can buy sex; we can buy a cook; we can buy security; we can buy entertainment; we can buy a caretaker; and we can buy a babysitter. A good marriage relationship is more than any one of these commodities and more than all of them put together.

A good marriage has four basic qualities: Each spouse respects the needs of the other; is absolutely honest; is affectionate with the other; and enjoys the company of the other. Ideally a marriage would have each of these four qualities totally present. In reality, because we are human, each of these qualities will fluctuate to a certain degree, but each will be far more present than absent.

The presence of these qualities, combined with at least adequate self-esteem in the couple, will provide a strong momentum for a good sexual relationship. Sometimes, however, there are problems in the marital relationship. These problems may have their source in poor self-esteem which spills over into the marriage relationship.

At other times the self-esteem of the spouses is not a problem, but, when the two selves attempt to relate, problems arise. Each or all of the four love areas can become short-circuited. It may be difficult for a wife to respect her husband because she has reasonable or unreasonable expectations that he can't meet or refuses to meet. A husband may be honest with his wife in most areas, but it is the one or two areas in which he is not that puts a crimp in his ability to be transparent. Or the husband may react so negatively when his wife is honest with him that she is forced to be dishonest.

A wife may have difficulty being affectionate. She lacks feelings of affection because she was never given much affection as a child, or because she is too full of fear or anger which squeezes out the love feelings. A wife may feel affection, but may not be able to express it well because she was raised in a family that did not demonstrate affection. Perhaps, sometime in her past, she did express affection and was deeply hurt in return. Whether or not she realizes it, she made a decision at that time never to place herself in a similar situation again.

A husband may not enjoy being around his wife very much. Whether he realizes it or not, he may have married her for what she could *do* rather than for who she could *be*. When he wants things done, he goes to her. When he wants to enjoy somebody, he goes out with his male friends or looks forward to seeing a female friend. It is also possible that a husband could enjoy his wife, but she behaves in ways that extinguish joy. She may be irritable, demanding, and complaining, which makes her a trial to be near.

The sexual satisfaction in a marriage relationship depends upon how well or how poorly these four qualities are activated in the relationship. Very good sexual relationships have all four qualities mostly present, while the four qualities are mostly absent from poor sexual relationships.

The third factor that relates to sexual fulfillment in marriage is each partner's understanding and attitude toward sex. People who have a positive, healthy attitude toward sex appreciate its unique beauty. They view sex:

As a unique form of fun. There is an old saying: "Sex is the most fun you can have without laughing." The fact that sex is supposed to be fun should be obvious, but it's not obvious to many people. For most people, sex is either dirty or sacred, and the concept of "fun" does not blend easily with either position. At one time it was sinful for married people to take pleasure in sex, since sex was seen to be solely for the purpose of procreation. The image of millions of virtuous couples trying to have sexual intercourse while strenuously attempting to avoid feeling any pleasure is tragicomic. Rather large residues of this type of thinking are still with us.

As a unique way to communicate deep feelings for which mere words are often inadequate. When you hear the words "I love you," you *know* you're loved. But when you sense the embrace, touch, and kiss of love, you *feel* that you're loved. And that's a big difference.

As a unique way of expressing gentleness. No words can express this sentiment as well. If true love is anything, it is gentle. When sex is quiet, unhurried, relaxed, and free, it can make real and observable the depth of one's love.

As a unique way of showing trust. It presents the opportunity to be very vulnerable. It represents one person opening up not only his body but his soul to the other. It is saying I know you, and I want you to accept my being, and I know that you will not harm me.

As a unique way of giving. When sharing one's body represents sharing one's soul, it is the epitome of giving. It is a way of giving deep physical and emotional pleasure to another and enjoying the giving as much as the receiving. The giving is patient and unconditional. It is free and unencumbered with expectations or jealousies.

As the unique way of expressing gratitude. It is a profound way of communicating appreciation for what one has been given and for who one is. It is one of the most precious gifts one person can give to another.

Sometimes a spouse has a negative attitude toward sex. Sex to him or her is "not nice" and is viewed as a necessary evil in the marriage relationship. Negative attitudes toward sex are almost always learned from one's parents. Sex is viewed as dirty, unpleasant, disgusting, primitive. This husband or wife may have healthy attitudes toward the rest of life and may love his or her partner very much. But he or she cannot, or does not want to, shake the negative attitude toward sex. If both partners share the same basic negative attitude toward sex, there will not be much conflict in this area, but there will not be much fulfillment either. Conflict will arise when one partner has a negative attitude and the other has a positive one.

When self-esteem is good, the marital relationship is strong, and attitudes toward sex are positive, sex in marriage will be very fulfilling. To the extent that there is a problem in one, two, or all three areas, sex will be confusing, conflictual, or virtually non-existent.

If there are problems in one or more of the three areas, their solution depends upon the nature and extent of the problem. If the problem is of short duration and not deeply seated, the couple may be able to work it out with open communication, understanding, and cooperation. If the problem is longer-standing and somewhat deep, professional help may be needed to discover the cause of the problem and to help the couple learn to work on the problem in a constructive way. If the problem is essentially life-long or the spouse or spouses have a vested interest in maintaining the problem out of fear, anger, or guilt, then the problem could be insoluble. Such problems are not necessarily insoluble, but the prognosis is at least "guarded."

It is important that married couples realize that normal problems will occur in their sexual relationship. Some couples don't distinguish between normal and abnormal problems, and hence define all problems as abnormal. This increases the tension in the relationship and may eventually lead to abnormal problems. Other couples equate having difficulties with having something wrong with their marriage. Because they don't want to think there is anything wrong with the marriage, they deny and repress normal problems which will often incubate and become larger.

Normal couples have normal problems regarding sex. The following are some normal problems.

1. One of the partners does not feel like having sex at a particular time. This is quite natural. Feeling tired, distracted, ill, or generally upset diminishes the desire to have sex. The tendency is to "emotionalize" the situation based on the myth that a spouse's wish not to have sex reflects a lack of love or interest in the other partner. Having sex is a relatively complicated behavior requiring a fine tuning between the central nervous system, the autonomic nervous system, and the psyche. A person may occasionally be "out of tune" for *any* behavior, pleasant or unpleasant, and sex is no exception. The situation does require the understanding and acceptance of both parties so that it doesn't become magnified. Obviously, if a partner *seldom* feels like having sex, this could be a problem that needs attention.

2. Sometimes sex isn't fulfilling. If sex is seen as being similar to any other behavior, it will help us understand it. No behavior is always and totally fulfilling. We may look forward to a hot fudge sundae and be disappointed. We may look forward to going on a picnic or to a ball game and be disappointed. And we may have sex and be disappointed. Sexual satisfaction, like all behaviors, is very fulfilling sometimes, very unfulfilling sometimes, and mostly falls between these two points. If people don't realize and accept this fact, they look for problems in the relationship that aren't there and this, in itself, can cause problems.

3. Sometimes things go wrong during sex and spoil it. The two most common things that go wrong is that the husband experiences premature ejaculation or the wife has difficulty having an orgasm. As was stated earlier, sex is more complicated than most people think. Like any complicated activity, it takes a great deal of practice, patience, and learning to do it well. Consequently, in the first few years of marriage, sex will not go smoothly all the time, any more than any other behavior will always go smoothly. It may take a couple who has no or limited premarital sexual experience from four to six years before they function more in harmony with each other than not. Once again, however, if premature ejaculation or failure to achieve orgasm shows no signs of improvement over a reasonable period of time and, if the couple views it as a significant problem, they may benefit from obtaining some professional help.

4. Sometimes one spouse doesn't adequately satisfy the other. Often this is a symptom of poor communication. Sometimes people assume that their partner knows, or at least *should* know, how to make them feel good. While this spouse does not fail to ask for things and give directions in other areas of life ("Pass the salt." "Put the lamp on that table."), when it comes to sexual communication the person becomes mute. The problem is that since opposite-sexed people don't share the same sexual anatomy and physiology, they are often clumsy in their attempts to cause pleasure in their partner. Also, what is pleasing to a spouse at one time may not be pleasurable at another. Even couples who have been married for years must communicate in an open and ongoing way what feels good and what does not.

5. Sometimes a spouse does not feel deeply loved during sexual intercourse. Ideally, of course, sexual intercourse is a time for deep emotional and spiritual intimacy, as well as physical intimacy. But sometimes the pressure of the day or heightened sexual excitement cause sex to be more of a tension release than an act of love. Analogously, it is like a person coming out of the desert dying of thirst who gulps down a fine wine without really tasting it or appreciating its quality. This is normal and natural and to be expected. Once again, however, if pure tension release begins to take the place of intimacy, it indicates a problem that needs isolating and solving.

6. *Sometimes sex is boring.* Any behavior, no matter how fulfilling and pleasurable, will become boring when it is repeated in the same way over and over again. Some couples feel uneasy at the thought of varying their sexual behavior. They have related sexually in a way that feels comfortable, and each is reluctant to suggest new behavior for fear of sounding dissatisfied or weird. As Honoré de Balzac wrote: "Marriage must continually vanquish a monster that devours everything: the monster of habit."

There is no sexual behavior that is "weird" as long as neither partner is harmed by it. It is important to try new sexual behaviors and vary them to keep the sexual relationship alive. But it is normal at times for one or both spouses to find sex less interesting than "it should be," to find it routine and mechanical.

In summary, sex in marriage is not a postscript tacked on to the rest of the day. In general, sex will only be as fulfilling as the rest of the day and the rest of the marital relationship. When sex is not good, it's not all that's not good. And when it is good, it's not all that is good.

Reflection Questions

1. How comfortable do I feel with my attitudes toward sex? If I'm not as comfortable as I would like to be, what steps can I take to be more relaxed in the area of sexuality?

2. If I've never masturbated, what does this mean? If I have masturbated, what motive usually underlies it? Do I feel comfortable with this motive?

3. What is the most significant consideration for me with regard to pre-marital sex?

4. When a non-sexual motive enters my sexual behavior, which of the five non-sexual motives described is it likely to be?

5. Of the normal problems in sex in marriage, which one is the most relevant to me? When am I going to discuss it with my spouse?

Thoughts to Contemplate

1. Sex is a powerful adhesive.

2. Psychologically incestuous relationships seem to be quite common in our society. The boy's unconscious attitude is: "My mom was so good. I want to get a mom to live with forever." Or the girl's attitude is: "I've never really had a father who loved, protected, and took care of me, so I want to find one and get all those needs met because I was deprived of them as a child."

3. As peculiar as it sounds, sometimes sexual behavior has little or nothing to do with sex, just as drinking in a tavern sometimes has little or nothing to do with being thirsty.

4. Whenever sex is motivated primarily by a need to release tension, intercourse is merely a disguised form of mutual masturbation.

5. Sex does not begin and end in the bedroom. It is a barometer of the quality of one's life.

13

MATURE LOVE AND ITS COUNTERFEITS

Love is undoubtedly the world's most discussed emotion. Unfortunately, there are no laws governing the use of the word "love," and it often serves to label all sorts of behavior. People kill to prove their "love." They commit suicide because they lost their "love." Individuals live in mutilating commitments for a lifetime out of "love." People manipulate each other because of their needs, feelings, and values—all under the auspices of "love."

This chapter will consider four subjects: the development of love, types of immature love, love within the dating relationship, and some characteristics of mature love.

THE DEVELOPMENT OF LOVE

A person's present loves are greatly influenced by all of his past loves. The truly mature adult is an able lover because his history of loves has freed him to become an honest giver and receiver of love. The less ideal person, which the vast majority of us are, has unresolved feelings left over from previous attachments that influence current attempts at love. It is important to try to understand one's love history in order to be a better lover, parent, and teacher of future lovers.

An individual's love history begins even before birth. Pregnant mothers who, consciously or unconsciously, harbor resentful or rejecting attitudes toward their unborn children give birth to fussy infants with feeding problems. This creates a vicious circle whereby the resentful mother becomes even more resentful as a result of her child's irritability.

The history of our loves evolves through discernable stages. The first stage is "I love *things* that make me feel good." The first things that an infant loves are his food, thumb, erogenous areas, sleep, warmth, dryness, soothing sounds, and safety. It is only after some time that the infant discovers that *people* are the cause of most of these good things. At about a year the infant enters into stage two: "I love you for what you can do for me." The child gradually discovers that parents, siblings, and friends can be instrumental and often indispensable in getting needs met.

At about fourteen years stage three begins, i.e., romantic love, which is a slightly more sophisticated and veiled form of "I love you for what you can do for me." Giving is what differentiates this from the previous state. This giving, however, is not altruistic but of the "I'll scratch your back if you'll scratch mine" variety. The last stage is mature love: "I love you for who you are." The giving here is out of love, and the well-being of the other person is of primary concern.

Our ability to love as adults can be traced directly to how well we fared through these three steps. We all know adults who are still at stage one—adults for whom food and/or drink is the primary love, who still "suck their thumb" when the pressure is on, or whose body is the main source of pleasure.

Some adults still function at stage two. There are those who never outgrew their dependency (or reaction against their dependency) relationships with a mother, father, or both. Other second stage deficiencies can lead to adult relationships which are "buddy-buddy" rather than mature heterosexual ones or those which are narcissistic ("We're both very much in love—with me").

It has been common for these individuals to be criticized as being "infantile" or "selfish." In reality, these persons should not be the objects of derision any more than we blame a person for having a developmental dietary deficiency such as rickets or scurvy. It is important to point out that our ability to love today is the result of the sum total of all our previous loves. And if we experience significant problems in our attempts to love, the causes can be found and in many cases remedied.

When someone with a marked love deficiency enters into a love commitment, immense problems can arise, just as when a man with a significant dietary deficiency chooses to play professional football. The more fulfilling early love relationships are for the individual, the more he is able to consciously and rationally choose his loves. The less fulfilling and the more conflictual the past loves, the more he is driven by unconscious motivations in the choices.

Most people are convinced that they consciously deliberate the pros and cons of their choices before making them. But it is clear that many people do their rational thinking *after* the choice has been made on an unconscious emotional level. If a person needs and wants something or somebody badly enough, he can "con" his intellect into coming up with good reasons to support the choice after the fact.

In his book *The Ability to Love,* Allan Fromme states: "Under the romantic exterior, it may be neurosis calling neurosis which brings two people together and even holds them together. They are not making a choice in their best interests, representative of their most stable values and tastes, but out of the strongest, least controllable forces within them. They seek each other out and cling to each other not out of the luxury of desire, but simply because they cannot help themselves" (Wilshire Book Co., No. Hollywood, Ca., 1972). Many "well thought-out decisions" are the products of such a process.

TYPES OF IMMATURE LOVE

There are several "love" relationships which are typical of people who have not recovered from the debilitating effects of the first two stages.

1. *"I didn't lose a mother [father]; I gained a wife [husband]."* Or "Now, I've finally got a mother [father]." In middle class America, this is a very common basis for

marriage. This person never received the mothering (fathering) needed as a child (even though the person may protest he had "great" parents). Or the individual may have received so much overprotective parental love that he has not learned to live without it and, therefore, does not wish to do so. In either case, the girl is unconsciously looking for a father—someone to protect, guide, and love her unconditionally, and assume many of her adult responsibilities. She needs a shoulder to cry on and a psyche to rely on. A man who would be attracted to this girl has unconscious needs of his own to complement hers. He may have had an overprotective mother who taught him: "The best way to show love is to assume benevolent control over someone." The intense emotions that arise from this mutual delight of finding somebody "just right" will eventually be christened "love." Friends will often describe this couple as "cute together."

The man who is looking for a mother, although he may vehemently deny it, has similar needs: to be taken care of, to slide out from under responsibilities by behaving in a "darling" way, to be free of all but good-natured criticism. When he marries his wife, he assumes not only that she will take care of herself but, much more, that she will take care of him. His aim is to be loved and taken care of—not to give love.

Four problems can arise out of this type of relationship. First, since it is not an equal relationship (one spouse is the "parent" and the other is the "child"), neither is challenged to be an adult. After thirty years of marriage, both partners will be essentially the same; little growth will have taken place.

Secondly, because it is a psychologically incestuous relationship, the sexual part will be poor. It is difficult to have sex with one's "mother" or "father." Whatever sex is experienced is a parent-child soothing relationship rather than a mature heterosexual manifestation of love between equal adults.

Thirdly, children born into such marriages are viewed as competitors by the spouse who is in the role of a child. A subtle but nevertheless intense sibling rivalry begins for the affection and attention of the spouse who is the "parent." If the spouse who is the "child" wins the

competition for affection, the children give up and become depressed, sickly, or get into trouble. If the children
win, the spouse who is the "child" withdraws emotionally
from the family. If the "child" is the husband, he may
withdraw under the franchise that his responsibilities at
work are increasing; if the "child" is the wife, she may
suddenly feel drawn to serve the needs of the community
rather than those of her family.

A final problem concerns the children's experiences
of what they perceive in their parents' marriage. They
are likely to see marriage as merely a continuation of
parent-child relationships and, consequently, they consider the idea of marriage with less than enthusiasm and
excitement.

2. *"This must be love because I need him [her] so
much."* The theme of this relationship is *needing* each
other. For people who don't have much experience in loving (which includes a high percentage of people entering
life commitments), it is easy to confuse "needing and
feeling needed" with "loving and feeling loved." However, there are a number of very important differences.

In mature love the focus is on the other person. It is
demonstrated in the attitude: "What can I do to make you
happy?" In a needy or dependency relationship, there is
pseudo-giving; i.e., what looks like altruism is a disguised
self-centeredness, exemplified in the axiom: "If I give to
him [her], I'll receive in return a hundredfold." Unfortunately, many books on love and marriage actually encourage this philosophy. One test of whether there is true
giving in a relationship is to observe what happens during periods when the dividends don't match the investments on a one-to-one basis.

Mature love is an "oil-spotting" phenomenon which
infuses the individual with so much love that he wishes
to share it with others. In contrast, dependency love finds
the partners becoming addicted to each other. This love is
possessive and jealous. The person in such a relationship
feels: "I want to be the sole source of your happiness. If
you truly love me, you won't need your family, friends,
hobbies, or solitude." Others are seen as intruders and
time spent away from each other as "empty hours." Ma-

ture love, on the other hand, allows each individual to remain separate and free. It proclaims: "I know I can meet only half of your needs, so share yourself also with those who can complement my love for you. My main wish is your happiness—it is not to possess you."

In a dependency relationship, the people cannot be totally honest because it would jeopardize their supply of support and affirmation. Such individuals are easily manipulated and often sacrifice their own values and selfhood for the sake of their emotional addiction. When people are truly in love, their love makes them strong, and strong people are unafraid to be constructively honest with each other and are unwilling to sacrifice any important part of themselves to the other. On the other hand, there is no demand on the part of the other for such sacrifice.

3. *"She's My Prize—He's My Prince."* This type of relationship is quite common because it flows directly from two strong motives in our society: for men, the need to compete, to achieve, and to win; for women, to be admired, pursued, and caught. For the man, his fiancée is a symbol of his talents to get the best. After a long and arduous pursuit, he finally wins the trophy. The wedding is really a victory celebration. He accepts congratulations as if he had just scored a winning basket in an overtime game. But soon afterward he discovers he was never primarily interested in the girl, but he fell in love with the pursuit. When he was competing to win her, it was the happiest time of his life. If only he could keep getting married all the time, he would be a happy man. Getting married was fun; being married is a dismal bore.

The woman in this relationship is also a product of her culture. She has been taught that her worth is largely contingent upon that of the man who loves her. When she is pursued by a man who is a "somebody," she feels ecstatically good about herself. After she awards herself to the winner, she gradually realizes that she is going through the "old trophy" syndrome. At first, she was out front for everyone to see and admire. After a while, she was more in the background and occasionally polished up for company or socially important events. Finally, she finds herself with a house full of unadoring children, and her husband is off chasing other windmills—a promotion at work, big deals, or other women.

4. *"This must be love because I feel so good."* This is the basic theme of romantic love which is the last stage on the way to mature love. While romantic love can eventually grow into mature love, just as often it ends in disillusion and disappointment.

The following are some of the characteristics of romantic love.

Romantic love defies reality. The person romantically in love sees only what he wants to see. The individual falls in love with an illusion sculpted out of intense needs and high hopes. Romantic love is incurious and willfully ignorant. Despite significant personality weaknesses in the partner, or obvious problems in the relationship, the romantic lover can rationalize them into oblivion.

Romantic love is excessive. Individuals who are romantically in love live at the tip of one emotional extreme or the other. Either they are so happy they are going to burst, or they are suffering so much they are about to disintegrate. No barrier is too big to overcome and no sacrifice too great if it means a chance to be together. Romantic lovers view anyone who questions their euphoria either as one who has never experienced real love or as a confirmed cynic. Sooner or later the reality that has been surgically tailored to fit the individual's needs begins to return to its original shape, causing the individual to lapse into despair and possible bitterness.

Romantic love is narcissistic. The romantic lover indulges in love somewhat like a cat. A cat does not caress you—he caresses himself against you. The theme of the love is: "I love you because you love me." Though unable to admit it, this lover is more interested in what the relationship can do for him than in what he can do for the relationship.

Romantic love has a very positive place in the history of our loves. It motivates the adolescent to evolve from being a purely passive recipient of affirmation and affection to a stage where he becomes willing to "barter" with others for affection. It is a precursor of mature love in which "bartering" grows into "giving." The problem arises when life commitments are made on the momentum of romantic rather than of mature love.

5. *"I can't live with him [her], and I can't live without him [her]."* This is the most disturbed of the relationships that have been discussed. In this relationship, the needs of each partner are complex. Each has almost equally strong needs to be loved; to hurt the other and/or to be hurt by the other. These individuals need many obvious demonstrations of love because they did not receive them as they were growing up, especially from the opposite-sexed parent. The need to hurt the other exists because of the deep, mostly unconscious hostility the individual harbors toward the opposite-sexed parent and which is transferred to the loved one. These persons need to be hurt for two reasons: to atone unconsciously for the times they have hurt their loved one and as a way of relating on an intense emotional level without having to get too close to the other person. Some people feel more comfortable being kicked than being held. The ambivalence such individuals feel about hurting and being hurt is seen in the narratives of their battles which are told with a curious combination of outrage and glee.

Because these needs are getting met in a continuous cycle, such relationships rarely terminate. It is typical that such individuals draw outsiders into the relationship; these outsiders often function as coaches. Some are amateur coaches such as relatives, friends, and neighbors, while others are professional coaches such as clergy, attorneys, and therapists. The coach may root for one side (the martyr versus the villain—which spouse is which depends upon who has hired the coach). Or the coach may try to mediate the problem as an impartial observer. Though the coaches are well-intentioned, they are often doomed to fail because the goal of the relationship is not to grow and become happy but to maintain, within tolerable limits, the delicate balance between love, hurting, and being hurt.

DATING: A STEP TOWARD LOVE

There are two ways in which a person can date. One way is to date for the sheer enjoyment that the company provides. It is a here-and-now experience with no further considerations. This can be a very legitimate and healthy interaction. The second way of dating is to get to know someone well enough so that each person can decide whether or not to continue the relationship into a life-long one. Sometimes the first way of dating evolves into the second.

This section deals with some issues that pertain to the second way of dating, i.e., a way of choosing a partner for life. Dating is a very important process because the vast majority of the serious problems that occur in marriage can be traced back to dating days. I don't believe I've ever seen a couple with significant marital problems who did not agree that the "handwriting was on the wall" long before the day they got married. It's sad to hear the couple say: "If only we had recognized the signs, we could have done something either to strengthen the relationship or to dissolve it."

The following is an attempt to prevent others from saying the same thing two, four, or six years from now. In this section a discussion of the phases of dating is followed by a series of questions. In each case, the questions can be used to evaluate a current dating relationship and assess its strengths and weaknesses. For people who are past their dating days or who never have dated, the principles are valid for all relationships and can afford clues as to what areas need strengthening.

The process that leads to a good love relationship has three phases. The first is the infatuation phase. Romance and sex are the key ingredients which, when mixed, create powerful feelings that often override intellect and common sense. These feelings are often stronger and more thrilling than those that flow from the next two, more mature phases.

Analogously, the thrill attached to the first home run a young boy hits will never be surpassed, even by his first or last major league home run, despite the fact that he is then a more fully developed athlete. Unfortunately, many young people mistake the thrill of the first phase as LOVE and make some deeply regrettable decisions.

The second phase of dating is the objectivity and honesty phase. This stage tempers the euphoria of the first with the reality of the relationship. Gradually the partners perceive each other more objectively and relate with a high degree of honesty. The individuals "let their hair down" and discard their dating personalities. Each learns much more about himself or herself, about the other person, about the relationship and the place of that relationship in the real world. This phase is the sobering up after the intoxication of the first. It is a period in which expectations are adjusted, feelings are tempered, and dreams are compromised.

This phase will have one of three outcomes: The individuals will discover that each is not as attracted to the other as was once believed, and thus they will dissolve the relationship in a healthy or a damaging way; the individuals will find that each is attracted to the other, but as friends and not as lovers; or the individuals will discover increasing depth and beauty in the other and wish to continue to grow with each other into the third phase.

The third dating phase is that of altruism; that is, the focus is on allowing the other person to grow and on a willingness to share both the joys and the pains of growth. It is important to understand that although the focus is on the other person, this does not mean that one loses sight of his own needs. Each person is highly motivated to give the other more patience, honesty, pleasure, warmth, freedom, and strength. This paves the way for a relationship that could be infinite because none of these gifts has a limit.

Unfortunately, most people make the decision to commit themselves to a permanent relationship in the middle or later parts of phase one. This decision is dangerous because it presumes that the relationship will weather the objectivity and honesty of phase two, and that the individuals will have the emotional resources to give of themselves as is required in the third phase. The same people who wouldn't bet a nickle on anything less than even odds think nothing of betting their lives on these odds, which are at best risky.

Marriage relationships often break up in the middle or last parts of phase two. The thrill of the first phase is buried in the reality of the second. Sometimes these people learn from their mistakes and, on entering a new relationship, allow themselves to grow through the second phase and into the third before deciding to enter a permanent relationship. Others, however, seek the thrill of the first phase again—they want to "fall in love again." They are bound to repeat the same mistakes continuously.

No one can indicate a period of time that it should take to get into the third phase. This depends on the individuals in the relationship. In general, older, more experienced people would get less delayed by the first phase and be more ready for stage two. On the other hand, it would be highly unusual for young people eighteen, twenty, or twenty-two, and in some cases twenty-five or twenty-eight, years of age to adequately grow through the first two phases into the third in less than four or five years.

A factor that complicates matters is that almost everyone who has ever married or entered into a permanent love relationship was convinced that he had indeed grown through phase two and into three; that each was objective and honest and could focus on the growth of the other. It wasn't until "the other person changed" that problems developed. Generally, the truth is that the only thing that changed was that one or both persons became more objective about the virtues and weaknesses of the other and began to communicate in a more honest fashion.

A thorough understanding of these stages and the principles involved in each can help a person answer the following questions and evaluate his specific relationship.

1. How much do you love yourself? Whenever love of any kind is discussed, this is always the basic question because you can't give what you don't have. A person can give love (which is different from "lending" love) only to the degree that he has it. A young man who was to be married told me: "I can't figure out why Susan wants to marry me—why, *I* wouldn't want to marry me!" When someone feels this way about himself, it constitutes a very weak basis for a love relationship.

People who love and appreciate themselves in a healthy way have several characteristics in common. They treat themselves just as they would treat someone else whom they love: They enjoy life; they refuse to be dominated or manipulated; they make decisions that are good for them; they socialize with people who treat them kindly; they avoid people who injure them; they behave responsibly, thus avoiding unnecessary trouble; they assert themselves and ask for what they need; they are self-respecting, which precludes prostituting themselves for anything or anybody.

A person with self-love has had many years of practice at loving somebody (the self) and can easily transfer some of this love to another. The person who lacks self-love will likely date someone or marry someone to fill a personal void.

This situation is analogous to trying to fill a cup that has a hole in the bottom. As long as a person pours water into the cup at a rate faster than it leaks out, the cup appears full. But the full cup is an illusion. As soon as the person walks away from the cup or slows down the rate of pouring, the cup empties, showing the cup for what it is: an empty cup. When someone without self-love enters into a close relationship, the individual feels wonderful because his cup is being filled with love.

Three problems can arise in a situation in which a person is totally dependent on an outside source for love. First, the individual is so dependent on the person that he dares not behave in any way to cause the pourer to walk away or diminish the flow of love. This causes personality contortions that damage both the individual and the relationship. A second problem is that the individual becomes possessive of the pourer to insure that he does not lose one drop of love. Finally, if the pourer does walk away, the individual is faced with a void and experiences anxiety and depression, sometimes of crisis intensity. The tendency then is to get involved with another person as soon as possible to fill the void, regardless of the appropriateness or health of the relationship.

2. How many friends do you have outside of your love relationship? A friend is not an "associate" or an "acquaintance." When asked how many friends he has, the average person will answer: "I've got lots of friends." But mostly they are describing associates (people with whom they hang around) or acquaintances (people with whom they study or work). A friend is somebody who knows you inside and out. He knows most of your deepest needs, hopes, fears, memories, faults, loves, values, and guilts.

Recently, I asked a college senior who told me he had "several close friends": "Have you told anyone you're coming to therapy? Have you told anyone that you are having anxiety attacks; that your parents are going to divorce; that you really don't want to go to law school; that you wonder why girls aren't attracted to you; that you resent your older brother; that you are confused about God?" The answer to all of these questions was: "No—I couldn't tell anyone that." This pinpointed one of the young man's problems: He had no friends.

The problem with not having at least one and, better yet, four or five friends that one sees often, is that a person is psychologically semi-starved because he receives few nutritional and consistant emotional groceries. On meeting someone he likes or even half-likes, this individual will overrespond to the relationship. Analogously, if a person is starving, the food in a particular restaurant may seem great. The person may then return a week later when only mildly hungry and discover that the food is not very good at all. This individual wonders what happened to the restaurant over the period of a week that caused the quality to decline so rapidly.

When a person is half-starved emotionally, he will overrate the qualities of the other person in the relationship and will become addicted, jealous, overprotective, overreliant, and do anything to hold onto the person. The resulting attitude is "Without you I am nothing," and in a sense this is correct. The person is in love with being loved and not with the other individual.

3. *How many other people have you dated?* When a person tells me: "Jim is the first boy I've ever dated, and I love him so much!" it's very difficult not to respond: "Compared to whom?" It never ceases to amaze me that a person who wants to buy a good used car will check out forty or fifty before deciding on one. Yet, when the same person chooses a partner for life, someone with whom he will live 16,000 days, the first, third, or eighth person dated is chosen. Obviously, the quantity of dates a person has does not make him a good lover. It is the quality of the dates—but the quality needs quantity to become better.

When a person has dated only one or a few people before making a life commitment, two major problems can arise. When one dates only a few people, there is very little frame of reference to judge what one really needs in a relationship. Analogously, it is like a child who is born and raised in a ghetto, who thinks the ghetto is the greatest place because he has never been exposed to another kind of life. In fact, some people feel so secure in the ghetto that they refuse to leave it, even when they have the opportunity.

A young person may find a partner who meets 30 percent of his psychosexual needs, which feels like a windfall compared to nothing. But it could well be that if this individual continued to date others, he could find someone even more compatible who would meet 50 to 70 percent of the person's psychosexual needs.

A second problem with limited dating is that it deprives the individual of numerous opportunities to grow. An important part of a relationship is the challenge it affords the partners to grow in patience, strength, warmth, trust, honesty, and empathy. Dating one or only a few people before making a life commitment is analogous to a baseball player who practices hitting with one or only a few pitchers. The batter quickly learns how to hit the pitchers' best pitches and is fooled into thinking he has reached his potential and is ready to start the season. In fact, the majority of his potential has not been developed, and he never becomes the batter he could have been. Of course, one could go to the opposite extreme and date large numbers of people as a defense against getting deeply involved with any one of them.

A sensible sequence in dating is one that begins with dating at fourteen or sixteen years of age, gradually evolves to dating many different kinds of people during ages fourteen to twenty-five, and then tapers off to dating one or a few people that seem the most compatible. This sequence can be diagrammed as follows:

| 15 yrs. | 25 yrs. | 30 yrs. |

Unfortunately, many people marry the first or third or fifth person they date, and their sequence looks like this:

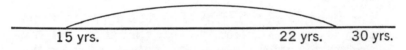

| 15 yrs. | 22 yrs. | 30 yrs. |

The narrower the range of dating experience, the less opportunity the person has to learn about himself, about others, and about life in general. This will greatly influence the person's ability to make an authentic decision regarding a life commitment.

4. Have you developed the psychological competencies to enter into a deep and enduring relationship with another person? Some people lack the competencies to develop a relationship which is both deep and lasting. Others have the competencies to enter into deep relationships but cannot maintain them, while still others can be in a relationship over a long period without deep involvement. A man who described himself as one of these individuals said: "I refer to myself as an 'emotional travelling salesman.' I'll stay the weekend with you and bare my whole soul and listen to you bare yours, but Monday morning I have to leave for my next customer with whom I'll do the same thing."

Entering into and remaining in an intimate relationship requires some specific personality attributes. The following are some of the more important ones.

Confidence in one's ability to remain a free person. The opposite of this is the fear of enslavement. People who know how to remain free in any circumstance or relationship realize that, if the need arises, they can resist and extricate themselves from the tentacles of others. They possess the tools to be intimate and yet to set limits around themselves; to decline inordinate expectations or demands; and to evacuate the relationship if it begins to suffocate them. People who fear enslavement either have been enslaved, usually by one or both parents, or have been an eyewitness to an enslaving relationship, vowing that they would never allow themselves to get *that* close to *anyone.* These individuals, if they enter a relationship at all, do so with one foot only, leaving the other foot outside the door for a quick getaway should an emergency arise. This approach precludes a deep and enduring relationship.

For many people, the fear of being trapped in a relationship is a cover-up for the fear that they will trap themselves. On a deep level, these individuals sense that their dependency needs are so strong that to unleash them would require them to cling to the other person and be at his mercy.

Confidence in one's worth. The opposite of this attribute is the fear of rejection. When people have confidence in their worth, they approach people assuming that they will be liked and accepted until the opposite occurs.

People who fear rejection assume that sooner or later the other person will discover something negative in them and not wish to be with them anymore. When people have confidence in their self-worth, it does not mean that they overestimate their goodness or that they are proud or arrogant. They simply have a serene appreciation for their goodness and recognize that their faults and weaknesses are outweighed by their likability or lovableness.

When a relationship does not work out, the person who fears rejection explains: "I knew that after he got to know me, he wouldn't like me," which reinforces the person's own feeling of rejectability. An individual with a good self-concept states: "It's all right that it didn't work out because the other person wanted me to be somebody I'm not," or "It's too bad the relationship didn't work out, but I feel that the other person is losing as much if not more than I am."

When someone has a poor self-concept, he enters a relationship waiting for the ax to fall. The constant wariness precludes the possibility of entering into a deep commitment.

A basic liking for people. The person who basically likes people does not do so in a Pollyannish way but works on the premise: "I like you until you give me some substantial reason not to do so." The opposite of this is fearing and disliking people, which operates on the premise: "I'll dislike you until you give me a substantial reason for liking you."

Sometimes people who basically dislike others are seen as attractive because they present a challenge. The idea is that if this person likes me, then I must be pretty special because he doesn't like many people. The key consideration, however, is that people who generally dislike others, generally dislike themselves. These people cannot deeply give of themselves because they don't like what they're giving. If the dislike for people is deep-seated, this individual may unconsciously sabotage the relationship to prove his axiom that people are no good.

The ability to receive sufficient stimulation from within. The individual who is stimulated from within has healthily strong and clear needs, dreams, and values that stimulate him to try new things, to take risks, and to accept challenges. The individual finds this process exciting and enjoyable even in the face of occasional failures. When this person enters a relationship, the other person and the relationship become an important medium for this process. When the other person in the relationship has the same capacity for internal stimulation, the power of each combines and results in as much stimulation as any two people can handle. In fact, mentally healthy couples learn that they must occasionally harness the energy or it could run away with them.

The opposite of this attribute is the necessity to rely on outside sources of stimulation: exciting people and situations. Some people have weak needs, no dreams, and unclear values which cause an inner numbness. These individuals either become lulled by their own dullness and lack the necessary energy to enter into and maintain a commitment, or they seek outside people and situations to stimulate and excite them. They are "adrenalin freaks" who need other people to turn on the spigots. These individuals are poor candidates for a deep and lasting relationship because they will eventually become bored with their partner and look for somebody who is "more challenging" or "has more life."

The ability to be consistent and flexible. The opposite of this is being flighty or inflexible. This is an abstract concept, so perhaps an analogy would be helpful. Think of the large doll that children play with that is partially filled with sand so when you punch it, it falls down but is so balanced that it immediately bounces back to its upright position.

If the doll has too little sand, it will fly all over; if it has too much sand, it won't budge. When it has just enough sand, it is flexible but consistent.

The same principle is true with regard to mental health. When people are not sufficiently mature, they won't have enough "sand." They are in love with a person for a year or two, but grow through significant changes and find the partner no longer attractive. Or at one time this individual is "into" love and then goes through a period in which love is "too confining" and only "freedom" is wanted. These changes may well be part of a healthy growth process. The problem arises when the individual makes a life commitment in the midst of this process.

On the other hand, a person, especially an older person (thirty-five, forty-five, fifty-five), may be so full of "sand" that he can't move. The individual doesn't possess the flexibility necessary to have a vibrant and growing life commitment. The average person is probably about thirty years old before he has reached a level of maturity in which he possesses sufficient self-knowledge, emotional security, and purpose-in-life to support the degree of

consistency and flexibility required in a deep and enduring relationship.

5. *Do you recognize the difference between wanting
something and needing it?* Most people think that "wanting" and "needing" are synonymous. In reality, however,
what one wants and what one needs are often contrary.
For example, a child *wants* to eat only ice cream and can-
dy, but *needs* to eat fruits and vegetables. The basic distinction is that we *want* things that make us feel good,
and we *need* things that will provide overall growth and
happiness. Young people often fail to make this important distinction.

Some people *want* to get married but *need* to remain
single, either for a longer period of time or forever. Marriage is not good for everyone, any more than is religious
life or any other life style or career. Some people *want* the
social respectability that comes with marriage or the financial and/or emotional security that marriage can afford. On a deeper level, however, these people *need* the
freedom, the multiple friendships, and the time and mo-
bility to pursue a career to which they are deeply committed. Often people discover the difference between
wanting to be married and *needing* to be married only
after years of marriage and parenthood. This belated insight causes great hurt to all concerned and could have
been avoided if the person had been aware of his real
needs prior to marriage.

Some people considering marriage *want* a partner
who will protect them when they *need* someone to challenge them; they *want* a partner to relate with them as a
parent or child when they *need* one who will relate with
them as an adult; they *want* a partner who will support
their naive and grandiose perceptions of themselves and
life when they *need* a partner who will be totally honest
with them; they *want* a partner who is very similar to
themselves when they *need* someone who is sufficiently
different to be interesting and challenging; they *want* a
partner who will give them great freedom when they
need a person who will make reasonable demands on
them.

If a person is not mature enough to recognize these differences and act upon them, he is not mature enough for a life commitment such as marriage.

6. *How in touch are you with your feelings?* The person who is acutely aware of what he is feeling can control the feeling and communicate it constructively. When a person submerges or incorrectly labels a feeling, or is confused about what is being felt, he cannot control the feeling because there are no "handles" on it. Consequently, it is communicated in a confusing and often destructive manner.

Three emotions cause great damage in a relationship when they are not accurately labeled and communicated: hurt, fear, and anger.

Hurt. What are three things a person could say or do to you that would hurt you the most? Some people confuse feeling hurt with being weak. This causes them to deny they are ever hurt. Others are so frightened of being hurt that they wear a thick skin which causes them to trade off warmth and closeness for safety.

When you recognize that you are hurt, how do you handle it? Some people hide and lick their wounds. Others hurt back twice as much. Still others keep it to themselves, ensuring that they will get hurt again, in the same way, by the same person. Until a person can communicate some version of "Ouch—that hurt. We'd better talk about it," he is not ready to live intimately with another person.

Fear. What three things most threaten your self-concept? Is it when someone implies that you are: stupid, clumsy, naive, immature, phony, insensitive, uninformed, weak, rigid, selfish, unimportant, silly, untrustworthy, incompetent, unattractive, lazy?

How do you typically react to fear? Some people simply deny their fright. Others withdraw and avoid the source of threat. Still others convert their fear into anger and attack the source of the threat. It is not until a person can say: "I'm frightened [threatened] by what you are saying or doing, and we need to talk about it," that he is ready to live with another person for life.

Anger. What three things could a person close to you do to make you angry? If you mention things that *hurt* you, you are confusing the emotions of hurt and anger. If you mention things that *threaten* you, you are mistaking the emotion of fear with the emotion of anger. A person may ask: "What difference does it really make if we don't put the exact labels on each emotion?" The answer is: the same difference it makes when we don't put the correct labels on medicine. When someone says: "I'm really furious at you," when in fact he is actually hurt or frightened, no successful resolution of the problem will be forthcoming. It is possible to have all three feelings at the same time, but even then they must be dealt with separately for them to be effectively communicated and resolved.

How do you handle anger? People with strong needs to be "nice" or to hold onto friends push their anger "underground" where it festers and incubates. Some people who recognize they are angry either pout or attack.

Until a person can say: "I'm angry at you, and I want to tell you about it," he is not ready to face the frustrations that lie in even the best marriages.

7. How well do you know the person with whom you are planning to spend the rest of your life? Strong needs and emotions often cause us to tilt reality in a direction that allows us to feel comfortable. People with good psychological strengths are less susceptible to perceptual tilting than are those with poor strengths. The following questions are meant to prevent or undo as much tilting as possible.

How does your friend treat family and friends? If your friend is kind to family and friends it means that he knows how to show affection. Sharing affection with you would be an easy extension of this trait. If your friend has a good deal of resentment toward his family and either has no real friends or treats others in a demeaning or exploitive manner, then he may eventually find it easy to include you under the same umbrella of resentment and exploitation. In general, it takes more than one relationship to convert a person who is typically unloving and/or resentful into a warm and loving person.

Is there a significant difference between how your friend reacts to you in private and in public? Is your friend equally attentive and thoughtful in both situations, or does he treat you nicely in private but ignore or embarrass you in public—or vice versa? If this is the case, it indicates that your friend's feelings toward you are not very deep, but change according to the situation or to the whims of the moment. This is not a good indication for future happiness.

How reliable or diligent is your friend at work or at school? Does he work in a conscientious and persevering manner? If so, these traits could well carry over into how he works with you in the relationship.

If the individual typically experiences problems at work or at school, the negative traits causing these problems will likely manifest themselves in the "work" parts of the love relationship. The "fun" parts will pose no problems, but since every good relationship requires work, his dedication may gradually wane.

What are your friend's three greater weaknesses or faults? Does your friend know what these faults are and, if so, does he admit them and work on them in a way that shows progress? If the answers are yes, this is an encouraging sign. If they are no, are you willing to spend the rest of your life with a person who has these weaknesses and who seems incapable of recognizing them and/or doing anything to strengthen them?

What are your friend's career ambitions, and how will they affect your relationship if he achieves or fails to achieve them? If your friend is pursuing a full-time or more than full-time career, how will the amount of time, energy, and stress spent on the career affect your love relationship? Many professional careers require fifty or perhaps sixty hours a week for the first five to fifteen years of a marriage. You understand that now *intellectually,* but do you really understand it *emotionally?* The situation is all right with you now, but will it be all right in three or five years, and will it be all right with your children?

Perhaps your friend has aspirations to have a specific career and has dreamed and worked at achieving it for

many years. What will happen to his self-concept and enthusiasm for life if it becomes clear that the goal will
never be achieved and he must settle for what is regarded
as a second-rate career?

*What expectations does your friend have toward you,
and how comfortable do you feel with those expectations?* Does your friend expect you to bring home a good
income, but also want you to spend a good deal of time
with him? How will you manage this?

Does your friend expect that you will become an
integral member of his family even though you can't
stand them?

Does your friend expect to have children, but you
don't feel that you would be good for children or that children would be good for you? Or does the opposite situation exist?

Does your friend expect you to subscribe to his religion or become more involved in religion than you would
need or feel comfortable with (or vice versa)?

Does your friend expect to have a very sexual relationship or a very non-sexual relationship, and how to do
you feel about this?

Does your friend expect that both of you will live
close to his folks, whereas you'd like to be near your own
family or near no one's family?

The romance that is part of dating often renders
these questions unimportant: "If we both truly love each
other, we'll compromise happily." What is often not understood is that superficial needs, dreams, and values can
be compromised without damage to the self, but deeper
needs, dreams, and values, when compromised, can cause
violence to the self that will eventually erode both the self
and the relationship.

*What is there about you that irritates your friend the
most?* Of the hundreds of places where two people rub
against each other psychologically, there must be one or
two or possibly five or six areas that cause friction. This
is true in even the most mentally healthy relationships.
So, if the answer to this question is "Nothing" or "I don't
know; he hasn't ever told me," this means your friend is
repressing the friction before the heat can be felt, or it

means that your friend is afraid to tell you. In either case, this is an area that should be explored before the heat begins to damage the relationship.

Do you like your friend's friends? As trite as it sounds, birds of a feather *do* flock together, even though on superficial observation this may not appear to be true. We choose people as friends who meet our needs, who share our strengths and weaknesses, our beliefs, attitudes, and values. In short, secure people hang around with secure people, and insecure people hang around with insecure people. Sometimes a person will state: "I love my boyfriend [girlfriend], but I can't stand his [her] friends." This is accompanied with subtle or overt attempts to discourage the friend from maintaining the other relationships.

It could well be, however, that your friend shares some of the negative traits that his friends have, even though you need to deny it. If your friend is as lovable, good, or healthy as you think, what *does* he get from these friendships? This is an area well worth exploring.

How does your friend react when prevented from getting his own way? In the romantic stage of a love relationship, the lovers often get what each wants, because neither wants to displease the other. Because this is so, one may have to look outside of the relationship to see how one's friend reacts to frustration, disappointment, and being told that he cannot have what he wants, no matter how strong the need or desire.

The areas of work, school, and home would be the most likely places in which to meet significant frustration. When your friend receives a "C" on a term paper that "deserved" an "A," how does he react? When your friend is told he lacks the required number of units to graduate on time; when he is not given the expected promotion at work, or is criticized by the boss, how does your friend handle the situation? Does your friend threaten to quit or actually quit a situation in which things don't go his way? Does your friend blame everyone and everything but himself? Does your friend withdraw into a shell and pout? Does your friend explore and "tell off" everyone involved in the situation? Does he deny being upset, keeping all the hurt and anger inside?

This is important information to know. Anyone can be loving when things are going the right way. But what will happen when the romantic phase of the relationship becomes increasingly replaced with the reality phase? Unless the relationship is going to develop into a dependency relationship, each person will have to say "no" to the other, even on issues that will cause frustration. It is very likely that the manner in which your friend reacted when he got a "C" instead of an "A" at school will be the way he reacts to you. Perhaps even more so, because he has more invested in you than in school.

The person who says: "Oh, he will react differently in our relationship because he doesn't *love* his teacher or boss," is very likely fostering a delusion. It is unlikely that a love relationship will erase twenty or twenty-five years of habitually responding to frustration in a particular way.

Does your friend have any negative traits or problems that you feel will improve after the marriage? If so, the chances are very good that you will be disappointed. Marriage is like a magnifying glass—it doesn't change the nature of what it magnifies; it simply enlarges it. What was positive in a person becomes even more positive, and what was negative becomes even more negative.

Marriage is not a substitute for psychotherapy. Many people are naive about what it takes to change human behavior. They think that a loving relationship will cure problems with drinking, temper, selfishness, communication, anger, compulsions, depression, anxiety, passivity, laziness, jealousy, sex, suspiciousness, and ulcers. Such thinking is analogous to hoping that a college football player's inability to block will be cured once he enters professional football. Perhaps the saddest words that I hear are: "Well, he had the same problem before we were married, but I thought the combination of my love and the responsibilities of marriage and parenthood would help him grow out of it." This is usually said as the marriage is crumbling.

Negative traits and problems that are significant should be changed *before* deciding to commit oneself for life to another person.

MATURE LOVE

As with all that is beautiful, it is impossible to adequately describe mature love with words. One way to attempt such a description is to relate some of the qualities that seem to be a part of mature love. Two points should be kept in mind while considering these qualities. First, each quality is quantitative; i.e., it can be placed on a scale from zero to one hundred. It is, of course, unreal to expect a lover to score one hundred on all qualities before being considered a mature lover. But it is realistic to expect these qualities to be present much more of the time than they are absent in mature love relationships.

Secondly, as in physical health, it is not good enough that all but one of our vital signs be healthy. So too, it appears that the presence of *all* these qualities is necessary for a truly mature love.

1. Mature love is altruistic. This means that mature lovers give affection, time, and energy without considering what will be received in return. This is not because they don't care whether or not they receive love, since this would be unreal. It is because they feel loved so much for themselves and rest assured in this love. It is like a man who, when he goes to bed at night, does not worry about the sun rising the next morning. It is not that he doesn't care—he just *knows* it will.

Altruistic love is different from "bookkeeper" love, which keeps a strict account of the balance between emotional investments and dividends. It also differs from "slave love" in which the lover will give anything, do anything, and suffer anything just to be kept around.

2. Mature love is freeing. Mature love frees others to be better than they could be in lesser love relationships, and it also frees them to be worse. While the **"freeing to be worse"** may sound peculiar, allowing a person to express what he really feels without fear of rejection is better than using the threat of rejection as a lever to elicit only good behavior. It is through allowing another to *be* as he is, for better *and* for worse, that he can learn to become better. So when a lover protests "You wouldn't talk that

way to the people at the office!" he may be making a very
positive observation.

Mature love also frees the other to do the things he
needs to grow in happiness and efficiency. In this way
mature love is non-possessive and non-jealous. It allows
the other to get many needs met outside the relationship.
These attributes of freedom differ from lesser love relationships that state: "You're free to be anyone you wish [as
long as I approve], and you're free to do anything you
want [as long as I am included]." A mature lover does not
fear "losing" a loved one because he never "owned" the
loved one in the first place.

3. *Mature love is honest.* The honesty in mature love is
bilateral. It declares: "This is who I am with all my
strengths and weaknesses; in all my beauty and ugliness;
in all my knowledge and ignorance. I want you to know
me completely so that when you love me, I know it is I you
love and not an image of me."

Honest love also states: "This is how I see you and feel
about you at this minute in time. Sometimes you will like
what I say and feel, and at other times you will dislike it.
But you will always appreciate it because it is from my
love that I share it with you."

This is different from the false charity that operates
on the principle: Protect those you love from their weaknesses and from your negative feelings about them. Lovers who adhere to this principle are "happier" with each
other. But the dishonesties accumulate until they gradually make the lovers strangers to each other. Then, one
day, something happens that brings this realization
crashing down on top of them.

4. *Mature love is happy, sad, and neutral.* To some, the
term "mature love" conjures up a picture of a man and
woman in their sixties, sitting in rocking chairs, the
woman mending socks and the husband dozing off between puffs on his pipe. In other words, it is as boring as
it is serene. To the contrary, mature love is alive. At times
it is fun, hilarious, and exhilarating; at other times it is
tender, warm, and peaceful; at times it is marbled with
hurt, anger, fear, and guilt. The difficult emotions arise

for two reasons: First, true love requires a person to be open, unprotected, and vulnerable. Secondly, even the best of lovers love with a limp because their past loves were not perfect. The combination of these two factors will inevitably cause periods of pain.

At times, the emotional climate is neutral since plateaus between emotional hills and gullies are necessary for rest and contemplation. But mature love is mostly happy. If a relationship is not primarily happy, then it is some other kind of love, or no love at all.

5. *Mature love is empathetic.* Empathy means "feeling with" another. True empathy is one important mark of a mature person, and only mature people can be mature lovers. Empathy requires four abilities:

The ability to feel. While this may sound obvious, many people are unable to feel adequately. This is so either because they were reared in families that did not teach or allow feelings to surface; because they have been hurt and have discovered that the best way to prevent hurt is not to feel; or because they are "top heavy," i.e., they may *think* feelings, but do not *feel* them.

The ability to feel with another. Many people have easy access to feelings but only those that directly relate to them. I may be able to share my feelings quite explicitly about someone who cut in front of me in a line, but when my wife comes home from the market a week later angry about the same thing, I may respond: "Yeah—by the way, did you buy the beer?"

The ability to "live with" the feeling. This means truly listening to another share feelings without being compelled to immediately *do* something about them. It is well-intentioned but not empathetic to respond to someone who is angry: "Oh, don't let him get to you!" or to someone who is grieving: "You must accept this as God's will"; or the classic remedy for someone who is worried: "Don't worry about it." The most help we can give someone is to listen and accept feelings. Thus the other person can feel there is at least one individual in all of humanity that really understands what he is feeling and why.

The ability to differentiate between empathy, sympathy, and identification. Sympathy is a "feeling for" another, usually a feeling of pity or sorrow. Sympathy is hardly ever, if ever, a constructive emotion for the recipient. It is a dead-end sentiment which declares simply: Poor you. Some people live on sympathy because it is a free ride—all one has to do is be pitiful and get most needs met.

Identification means "feeling that it is happening to me." This occurs in relationships in which two people have become one emotionally. It creates a "yo-yo" phenomenon in which when you're depressed, I'm depressed, and when you're euphoric, I am also. Two problems occur when one person's emotions dictate those of another. First of all, the situation is unreal because whatever is happening to one is, in reality, not happening to the other. Secondly, neither person is free to deal objectively with reality. For example, instead of my wife becoming angry with my boss because I am, it would be much better if she would help me sort out the situation and perhaps realize that my behavior caused some of the difficulty.

6. Mature love is strengthening. This means that both people are growing together, as opposed to one person growing at the expense of the other or both people slipping into a blissful regression and calling it "growth" because it is "freeing and feels good."

The strengths that mature people possess are manifested within the love relationship. Unlike lesser kinds of love, their love does not make them strong; they make their love strong. And if they were not in love with each other, they would still be strong. If the lover dies, they are still strong and full of love for people and for life.

Mature lovers respect and admire each other, which enables them to be strong, honest, trusting, and unafraid in the presence of each other. There are no secrets, no shielding from hurt, no holding back, and no manipulation of each other.

7. Mature lovers are unique, self-defined, and separate. Contrary to romantic notions often seen in both secular and religious writings, mature lovers do not "become as one." This is not a mere theoretical distinction, but one that has very serious and concrete consequences. When

two people "become as one" emotionally, intellectually, and morally, there is no frame of reference—no mirror or source of feedback and correction which is necessary for a healthy balance in a relationship. Numerous problems can occur when two individuals become one psychologically.

First, it is a violation of reality because the persons have different biologies and backgrounds. To attempt to mold two people into one is to ask each to sacrifice important parts of life necessary both for his or her own growth and happiness and those of the loved one.

Secondly, when parents act as one, it provides a serious disservice to the children who are presented with a monolithic structure of what is good and bad, acceptable or non-acceptable, lovable or unlovable. In a healthy marriage there are really three dimensions. There is the husband in all his uniqueness; the wife in all her uniqueness; and the relationship in which the likenesses, the differences, and the contradictions interact to create a third important force. This offers the children many more sources of data, permissions, values, interests, and perceptions which will help them weave their own uniqueness.

8. Mature love is resilient. Mature love between two people has a history of shared experiences which are many and varied. Each experience, regardless of how miniscule, when it is shared and reacted to honestly, builds up a foundation of understanding, trust, and confidence that functions as "psychological shock absorbers" which distribute stress in a balanced way. The opposite of this is seen in less mature types of love in which almost weekly or monthly new discoveries are made about each other that cast serious doubt on the love. Each moderately serious disagreement, conflict, or trauma sends shock waves through the relationship that encourages each person to keep a suitcase half-packed at all times, ready for evacuation. This situation is no better seen than in adolescent crushes in which young people announce once a week that they are no longer in love with their "steady." It is less amusing in people who are married and keep themselves and their children on edge because each argument or failure of any magnitude leads to a total reevaluation of the love.

One cannot realistically look for resiliency in young relationships because there has not been the opportunity to share many and varied experiences. On the other hand, merely putting in time with each other makes no contribution to resiliency; to wit, many people who have been married for twenty or thirty years continually live on the brink of doubt, distrust, resentment, and fear. Time is merely the backdrop that gives people the opportunity to live *with* each other versus merely living *next to* each other. For some people, two years is sufficient time in which to develop emotional resilience, while for others forty years is not enough.

9. Mature love is imperfect. Often people look upon mature love as an ideal that cannot really be attained by human beings. But this is because they fail to understand fully the nature of mature love. If we look in the dictionary, we shall see quite different definitions for the words "mature," which means "fully developed," and "perfect," which means "flawless." For example, a twenty-five-year-old person may be physically mature yet not physically perfect. Mature love denotes a love developed past the point of child and adolescent attachments, but one that is real (versus ideal) and imperfect. In some ways, mature love is more fraught with conflict than is immature love. The reason for this is that immature loves often have so much infatuation and emotional slavery involved that they are relatively smooth-flowing, just as there is seldom conflict between a master and a slave. Conflicts arise between equals: master and master or between slave and slave.

10. Mature love is spiritual. By spiritual is meant nonmaterial and not directly observable. It may include a religious dimension or it may not. In either case, the love surpasses the material. Both immature love and mature love begin at the same place, with an attraction to physical appearance, to personality traits, to deeply shared interests, or to one's popularity or success. Immature love stops there and ceases when the source of the attraction ceases. Mature love includes but then surpasses these traits. It endures because the loved one's spirit endures and is not attached to the vicissitudes of material traits. Because spirit is non-material, its description does not easily encase itself in words. But spiritual love states a sentiment similar to this: "Beyond your physical and social attractiveness, there is you: your sensitivity, strength, vulnerability, humor, and warmth. It is this spirit that I love—that I want to give to and receive from. I carry your spirit within me, and it frees me to be more open, giving, and joyful."

Reflection Questions

1. How much do I love myself? What are the practical implications of my answer?

2. Of the five abilities it takes to enter into and remain in an intimate relationship, which ability is my weakest? Which is my strongest?

3. How freeing am I with the people I love? Do I say, "Do what you need to be happy," or do I say, "As long as you include me in your plans, do anything you want."

4. The hardest thing for me to be honest about in a love relationship is to tell the other person. . . .

5. If the people I love didn't love me, would I still love them?

Thoughts to Contemplate

1. Romantic love is incurious and willfully ignorant.

2. The thrill attached to the first home run a young boy hits will never be surpassed, even by his first and last major league home run, despite the fact that he is then a more fully developed athlete. Unfortunately, many young people mistake the thrill of the first phase of dating as LOVE and make some deeply regrettable decisions.

3. A person with self-love has had many years of practice at loving somebody (the self) and can easily transfer some of this love to another. The person who lacks self-love will likely date someone or marry someone to fill a personal void.

4. As trite as it sounds, birds of a feather *do* flock to-

gether, even though on superficial observation this may not appear to be true.... In short, secure people hang around with secure people, and insecure people hang around with insecure people.

5. Mature love is mostly happy. If a relationship is not primarily happy, then it is some other kind of love, or no love at all.

14

THE EFFECTIVE FAMILY: A BLUEPRINT

The aim of every parent is to have a happy family. Yet it is quite possible for a child to come from a happy family and be ill-prepared for adulthood. What many parents fail to understand is that there are two approaches to happiness in the family. A superficial happiness is achieved when parents stifle conflict and risk-taking and strive only for peace and harmony. A second approach sees happiness in the family as a by-product of growth. Growth, which includes conflict, noise, and suffering as well as harmony and peace, offers a better preparation for living in the adult world.

Most parents, whether they realize it or not, have a blueprint for family living. Either the blueprint is borrowed from their own parents because it worked well, or the blueprint is created by the parents in an effort to correct their own parents' blueprint.

There is nothing inherently wrong with a blueprint if it is based on sound mental health principles tailored to fit the personality of each child. It can act as an overall philosophy which gives direction and reason to raising children.

Many blueprints appear to be based on "good common sense," but are actually fraught with myths and misconceptions about behavior. Some parents tend to compulsively adhere to a blueprint and refuse to deviate from it despite evidence that it is faulty. When things go wrong, they usually feel it is the children or society that needs correcting rather than the blueprint.

Blueprints drawn for happiness and peace in the family leave little space for conflict and tension. The results are similar to those of architectural blueprints based on faulty principles of physics. Either the building will eventually collapse, or it will need continual support and care. Conflicts are the psychological weights that are necessary to build psychological strengths. If the conflicts are too heavy or too light, they cause weakness. But reasonable amounts of conflict, anger, hurt, and sorrow are necessary for both parents and children to grow into more effective people. Happiness and peace are the by-products of this process, but they are not goals to be aimed at directly.

Effective parents have blueprints that are calibrated to the question: "What psychological competencies are necessary for a twenty-year-old person to live his life well?" The answer to this question gives direction to child-rearing from infancy to adulthood. Many parents want their children to be at twenty years of age what they have never given them the opportunity to become.

This chapter deals with the competencies that effective parents include in their family blueprint. The term "children" is used to cover offspring from birth to approximately twenty years of age.

EFFECTIVE PARENTS TEACH THEIR CHILDREN SELF-LOVE

The idea of loving oneself makes a lot of people uncomfortable because medieval notions of love looked upon it as a material quantity. From this evolved the principle that the more a person loved himself, the less he could love others. The ideal was to purge oneself of all self-love in order to completely love others. However, today we know that self-love is the basis of all mentally healthy behavior. When people truly love themselves, they tend to behave in loving ways. When people dislike or loathe themselves, they behave in unlikable and damaging ways.

A second notion was that self-love and narcissism are

synonymous. In reality, self-love reflects our realistic appreciation of ourselves, while narcissism reflects a basic insecurity causing us to look in a mirror continually to see if we still exist.

The most precious gift parents can bestow upon a child is a sense of self-appreciation and love. From this sense flows all that is good in human behavior.

Effective parents teach self-love in several ways. They realize the difference between telling and teaching. Telling a child that he is lovable is helpful only if it is reinforced by many other behaviors. If it is not, then telling means nothing and, in fact, is likely to cause resentment more than any other feeling.

Effective parents teach self-love by touching. We touch things we like and remain distant from things we are disinterested in or dislike. When infants and children are held, stroked, tickled, bathed, and bounced, they develop a sense of lovableness. Touching is particularly important during the early years when a child is not sophisticated enough to hear love—the child must *feel* love. But even at seven, ten, and twelve years of age, children like to be held, rubbed, have their hair tossled more than they admit. As children reach adolescence they still need to be touched, but by people other than family members.

Spending quantity and quality time is another way parents teach self-love. Even small children realize that we spend time with people we like and avoid people we don't like. When a parent's message is: "You're really lovable, but I don't have much time for you," it is unacceptable even to a three-year-old. Quantity time means the parent is spending time with the child, but it is "work" time. Examples of quantity time are waking and dressing the child, preparing meals, eating with the child, bathing the child, driving the child to different places, helping the child with homework, and getting the child ready for bed. As the child grows to middle childhood and adolescence, quantity time is required less.

The main characteristic of qualitative time is that it is "free" time whose only purpose is to allow the people to be with and enjoy each other. Mostly it is private time shared by one or both parents and one child. This gives the child a sense of being individually lovable in contrast to being lovable as merely one of the "Smith kids." It is a time tailored to the individual child. The focus of the parent is: "What would *you* like to do? What would *you* like to talk about?" This is in contrast to the invitation: "We're all going on a picnic and we're all going to have fun, whether you enjoy it or not."

Quality time is uninterrupted by intrusions of other people, phone calls, or suddenly remembered obligations. The time is unstructured and decisions regarding what to do are spontaneous. There may be a good deal of conversation, and there may be periods of silence.

Unfortunately, in today's world quality time is a luxury. But parents who put a high value on it find ways to place a wedge in their hectic schedules and save space for their children. Talk is cheap, but time isn't. When a child receives adequate amounts of quality time, he will experience an important step in feeling lovable.

Effective parents teach self-love when they unconditionally love their children. Their love says: "Whatever you do or don't do, I will deeply love you." This does not mean that parents won't feel anger, resentment, disappointment, and frustration with their children. But it does mean that these feelings are the numerators that always rest on one common denominator: love.

There are two obstacles to unconditional love. One is that parents who do not have sufficient self-love and sufficient love from their spouse have a deep need to receive attention and affection from their children. These parents transmit the message: "I'll love you as long as you need and affirm me. When you don't, I won't love you anymore." This child is in a double bind. If the parent's tentacles are allowed to engulf the child, he will develop self-hatred for being so weak. If the child is strong enough to refuse this emotional extortion, the child will experience self-hatred for "rejecting" the parent.

A second obstacle is that many parents equate the child's worth with performance. When the child gets "A's" on a report card, he is loved. When the child gets "C's" and "D's", the child is less lovable. When a child chooses to go to college, he is lovable; when the child drops out of college, he is less lovable. While all parents deny that they react this way, one need only observe their behavior toward the child to recognize their true feelings.

The child from this family is also in a double bind. If successful according to the criteria of the parents, the child will never know if he is lovable as a person or as a performer. If not successful, the child *knows* he is not lovable because lovability and successful performance are synonymous in the family.

Effective parents teach lovableness by allowing their children to feel important. This is an uncomfortable thought for some parents who think that a child who begins to feel important will want to take over the home. Paradoxically, it is the child who doesn't feel important who needs to control the home, just as it is the people who feel least important who overthrow governments. Important simply means having high value. People who feel unimportant as human beings can not love themselves because we don't love things of little value.

There are several ways that effective parents allow their children to feel important. They allow the children to make decisions commensurate with their level of maturity and to enjoy or suffer the consequences. Less effective parents seldom allow their children to make relatively important decisions or manipulate the children into the "correct decisions." The message to the child is: "We don't value your ability to make a good decision."

Children learn to feel important when the parents allow them a reasonable amount of power in the home. Children are allowed and encouraged to offer input to the parents, and the input is given serious consideration. When the children's requests and complaints are reasonable, the parents make the appropriate changes. And when the parents' and children's opinions are in conflict, the parents defer to the children when reason and justice require it.

Effective parents allow their children to feel important by including them in their lives. Certainly there are times when parents need to be alone together, and when it would be inappropriate to include the children. But sometimes it is just as easy to invite one or all of the children along to share a meal at a restaurant, to go for a walk, a ride, or to a movie. While such invitations often seem trivial to parents, to a child the message is: "We value your company."

Effective parents allow their children to feel important by being honest with them. Most parents lie to their children at times, and some parents frequently lie to them. The lying is always for "a good reason," although when this rationalization is offered by a child to explain a lie, it is never acceptable to the parent. Whatever temporary and pragmatic gains are accomplished by lying, the chances are good that the child will realize that he has been lied to and will receive the message: "You are not important enough to be told the truth."

A child who spends twenty years in a family in which he frequently receives these manifestations of lovableness is ready to live adult life well.

EFFECTIVE PARENTS TEACH ASSERTIVE BEHAVIOR

Being assertive means having the ability to ask for what one needs; to openly argue and disagree in constructive ways; to stand steady against manipulation; and to move aside people who unjustly interfere with need fulfillment. This is a very important competency because unassertive people are doomed to an impoverished psychological diet.

A part of some parents' blueprint is the axiom: Children are to be seen and not heard. These people want their children to stand up for themselves and get their fair share in life. Yet, within the family, these same children are punished for "standing up" and, in fact, are told to "sit down." In other words, children are often told to be assertive outside the family but not in the family. This is analogous to telling a child to learn the English language outside the family but not to practice it at home. These parents view their children who are unassertive as: good, respectful, obedient, sweet, humble, and mature. Children who attempt to be assertive are seen as: rude, disrespectful, disobedient, insolent, and headstrong.

Some parents allow their children to be assertive with each other but not with the parents. The problem with this is that the children are taught that it is wrong to be assertive with authority figures. Unfortunately, half the people we need to be assertive with fall into this category.

Effective parents encourage assertive behavior and reward it. They realize that assertive behavior in the family causes tension—it "makes waves." It interferes with peace and quiet. These parents place a high value on rearing children who will get from life all that they justly deserve. Thus they are willing to pay the price in discomfort, time, and energy.

A teenage daughter may say to her parents: "Gee, this is the third time this week you've asked me to stay home and babysit, and I don't think it's fair." The less effective parent might reply: "Listen to me, young lady. The least you could do is to help us out and not be so selfish. I'm the boss around here, and if I want you to babysit *every* night, you'll do it and like it!" The effective parent, on the other hand, might answer: "You're right. Let's talk it over and see if we can come up with a better plan."

Of course, children will undershoot and overshoot the target as they practice assertiveness. Sometimes they will be too passive and allow themselves to be violated. At other times they will be aggressive and damage the other person. Effective parents realize this and don't punish either type of mistake any more than they would punish a child whose math answer is under or over the correct amount. The child can be taught how he could have handled the situation better, but should never be punished for trying to grow.

EFFECTIVE PARENTS ALLOW EACH CHILD TO BE UNIQUE

One of the most beautiful attributes of a human being is that he is significantly different from any other human being ever created. The more mental health a person has, the more he is unique. The more immature or psychologically disturbed people are, the more they resemble each other. Even within the same family a person should be like a fingerprint, i.e., having some characteristics in common but being essentially different. I think one of the nicest compliments a parent can receive is: "Each of your children has his or her own separate personality." This reflects a warm environment in which each child is growing to his own potential rather than being twisted to conform to some preestablished blueprint.

Each child is unique because each has a separate central nervous system, a separate autonomic nervous system, and, in combination, this creates very individual needs, sensitivities, temperaments, intelligences, perceptions, and energies. When the neurological systems are further mixed with the home and social environments which are different for each child, even in the same family, the result is absolute uniqueness.

Some parents need to treat their children as a matched set. This is done for one or more of the following reasons. For some parents "sameness" means "unity." Other parents are narcissistic and want each child to grow in their image and likeness. For many parents it is easier to treat all the children in exactly the same way.

Many families have a "coin of the realm." If a child does not possess this particular coin, he is not included as an official member of the family. In fact, some parents actually voice this when they say: "I don't know where John came from; I think they gave us the wrong baby at the hospital."

The following are some typical "coins of the realm."

Strength: "Strong Families" are those in which everyone must be tough to survive. Thick skin is the coat of arms, and by two years of age the child must be able to grab the world by the tail. Both boys and girls must "act like a man" or they are discounted.

Behavior such as warmth, tenderness, delicateness, compassion, crying, worrying, and fear are viewed as silly, childish, sissyish, and weak. I once heard a father shout at his son who had just scraped a knee: "John, stop crying. You're acting like a five-year-old!" His son was five years old. Some of the most beautiful traits a person can possess are snuffed out early in this family.

Popularity: "Social Families" are very outgoing, exuberant, and verbal. They love to meet people, entertain, and be popular. These families are almost always going someplace, and when they are home, there is often at least one visitor present. They spend a good deal of time trying to impress others. Children who are shy, quiet, plain, or self-content are viewed as dull, lazy, unpopular, and gradually begin to view themselves in the same light.

Intelligence: "Smart Families" are highly interested in intellectual and artistic pursuits. They read a great deal, love to argue issues, and are fascinated by most academic areas. They groom their children early for college and often *specific* colleges or careers. Children who are of average intelligence or who have high intelligence but are not particularly interested in scholarly pursuits are viewed as stupid, lazy, or of little worth.

Athletics: "Sports Families" highly value athletic activities. In some families, everyone must participate in one or more sports in order to win a family "block sweater" which is the key to acceptance. In other families, only the males are required to be athletes. Children who are awkward, cerebral, artistic, or skittish are ignored or belittled. They try to make the family team, but their attempts are anguishing and humiliating. They gradually slip into feeling and acting like "second string" people.

Religion: "Religious Families" are those that use religion as the main or sole binding force in the family. Everything is tied to religion. Family acceptance is meted out according to the degree of one's religious fervor. Children and especially adolescents who have stronger interests than religion are chastised and rejected. They are made to feel not only like bad family members but like bad people.

Children who grow up in families like those mentioned feel that they have disappointed their parents and that their parents are ashamed of them. This, in turn, makes the children feel guilty for who they are. Many adults, even at ages fifty and sixty, feel like second-class citizens because they never met their family's expectations.

EFFECTIVE PARENTS TEACH THEIR CHILDREN HEALTHY SEXUALITY

Sex education is a hotly debated topic in some areas. Should sex be offered in the school and, if so, how and at what age? Should sex education be left to the parents and, if so, how do they best explain "the facts of life"?

The irony is that neither parents nor teachers choose whether or not to give sex education because they are always teaching it. The only question is whether or not the sex education is healthy.

It is important to distinguish between three types of sex education: reproductive, moral, and psychological. Reproductive sex education is simply telling a child how babies are conceived, carried, and born. This could take between five minutes and five hours depending upon how clinical one wished to be. This is what most parents refer to as "sex education."

A second type is moral sex education which teaches when sex is constructive or destructive, or, to put it in a religious context, when sex is sinful or when it is not. Moral education for most parents simply means telling their children that all sexual behavior is wrong until they are married. Then, all sexual behavior is all right—perhaps not beautiful, but all right. This moral education could take from five minutes to an hour depending on how philosophical and theological one wished to get.

The third type of sex education is psychological. This deals with how the child views his own sexuality, the opposite sex, and sex in general. Psychological sex education, as far as the home goes, begins at birth and continues until both parents die. Normally, a child has been privately tutored daily in sex education for from eight to fourteen years before he receives reproductive and moral sex education. It will be those many years of sex education that will influence the impact of the reproductive and moral education, not vice versa.

Psychological sex education is taught through four messages. The first is: "You're lovable," or "You're unlovable." How children are allowed to feel lovable was discussed in detail earlier in this chapter. When a child feels lovable, he accepts himself, which includes sexuality. Girls are happy to be girls, and boys are happy to be boys. As they grow through childhood and adolescence, these children accept their sexuality as an integral part of themselves.

Children who feel unlovable dislike themselves and consequently dislike their sexuality or at least feel uneasy about it. As they grow older, these children either deny or hide their sexuality, attempting to make themselves neuter, or they flaunt their sexuality, hoping that someone will say it's all right. In late adolescence and adulthood, these children may use their sexuality as a means of buying love from others to compensate for their lack of self-love.

The second message children are given about sex is: "Same-sexed people are lovable," or "Same-sexed people are unlovable." It is important for children to learn that people of the same sex are lovable. One reason for this is that a child will become confused by being taught that he is lovable, but others of the same sex are not. This subtle distinction is beyond the ability of most children to make. The child is more likely to assume that since he is a member of an unlovable sex, he must also be unlovable.

The second reason that it is important for children to view same-sexed people as lovable is that it doubles the number of potential need-fulfillers (emotional grocers) in his life. When the same sex is viewed as generally unlovable, it places a good deal of pressure to pursue and be successful in opposite-sexed relationships. When opposite-sexed relationships falter, these individuals are left with nothing.

Children are taught that the same sex is unlovable when the parent of the same sex as the child behaves in generally unloving ways. For example, if a father typically behaves in a distant, unreliable, or hurtful manner, his son learns that men are not people with whom he wants to relate more than is necessary.

Also, the opposite-sexed parent can teach children that people of the same sex as the child are unlovable. A father may ignore or ridicule his wife or women in general in the presence of his daughter. His behavior and his wife's acceptance of it cause the daughter to view women as inferior.

The third message taught by psychological sex education is "The opposite sex is good," or "The opposite sex is bad." This message is sent by parents in several ways.

The manner in which a child sees the opposite-sexed parent treated by the other parent tells the child a good deal. Children generalize in their perceptions, so that if a mother's message to her daughter is: "Your father's no good," the daughter easily generalizes it to "Men are no good." When a father treats his wife in a distant, subservient, or scornful way, the message to his son is "Women are no good." Divorced parents have to be especially careful because sometimes there is a temptation to blame and demean the spouse for the difficulties and hurts incurred in the marriage.

The manner in which a father speaks of women in the presence of his son is important. Fathers who view "typical women" as stupid, silly, disorganized, weak, manipulative, and cunning, are sending a very clear message: "Don't take women too seriously, and don't get too close to them."

The way in which a mother speaks of men is equally important to her daughter. Mothers who view "typical men" as cold, childlike, sex-crazed, selfish, arrogant, and domineering are giving a very clear message to their daughters: "Man are bad; don't get involved with them."

When *each* parent demeans the opposite sex of the child, the child often decides unconsciously to be neuter, thus avoiding the evils connected with each sex.

The way the opposite-sexed parent treats the child is also important. Sons who are rejected or emasculated by their mothers, and daughters who are ignored or treated cruelly by their fathers may develop negative attitudes toward the opposite sex. When parents treat the opposite-sexed children with warmth, tenderness, strength, and freedom, the children will find the opposite sex unfrightening and attractive.

The final message taught through psychological sex education is "Sex is good," or "Sex is bad." This message is also learned in early childhood and reinforced throughout middle childhood and adolescence. Children learn that sex is good when they see their parents are not ashamed of their bodies but treat their nakedness as natural and good. They learn that sex is good when they see their parents embracing and kissing each other openly and joyfully. They learn sex is good when their sexual curiosity and experimenting is met with understanding and kindness. They learn sex is good when both parents speak to the children about sex in open, unashamed ways and answer any questions that the children are mature enough to ask.

A child receives the message "Sex is bad," when parents are excessively modest and nakedness is a cause for shame or embarrassment; when genitals are never mentioned or are only referred to obliquely ("Did you wash between your legs?"). Children learn sex is bad when childhood sexual language and curiosities are punished and the child is made to feel dirty; when sexual topics are never mentioned or are discussed in cynical, contemptuous, or moralistic tones; when parents don't speak to the child about sex, or, if they do, it is done in a hurried, embarrassed way.

Children who grow into adulthood believing that sex is mostly bad either extinguish their sexuality in order to feel good about themselves or experience sexuality with feelings of shame and guilt. They either avoid sexual relations or participate in them with a sense of shame (even after marriage) or with a sense of duty. Children who grow into adulthood feeling that sex is mostly good allow themselves to experience their sexuality in an enjoyable, natural way.

Some adolescents arrive at adulthood feeling lovable, believing that the same sex, the opposite sex, and sex itself are mostly good. These people have a strong foundation for a fulfilling life. Others arrive at adulthood feeling unlovable, or feeling lovable but not appreciating the opposite sex, or loving the opposite sex but believing that sex is not good. Typically these attitudes have taken a definite shape by the time the child is ten years old.

This does not mean that children with negative sexual attitudes at ten years of age are doomed to a life of unhappiness. Factors such as a reversal of parental attitudes, or positive attitudes of teachers, clergy, friends, or psychotherapists, can intervene and reverse the process. But it's infinitely easier to teach positive attitudes from the start.

EFFECTIVE PARENTS TEACH PERSONAL RESPONSIBILITY

A mature person is marked by the ability to say: "It was my fault, and I'll have to accept the consequences and rectify the situation." Many people, however, are unable to accept the responsibility for their own behavior. This is a serious liability because it precludes rectifying one's mistakes. Personal responsibility is a trait that is best taught early in life, although it is never too late either to teach it or to learn it.

When personal responsibility is not learned early in life, the person who at three years of age says: "It's not my fault that I spilled my milk; my sister made me do it" is saying at thirty years of age: "It's not my fault that our marriage is unhappy; my wife is to blame." Several principles are helpful in learning and teaching personal responsibility.

It is not helpful (charitable, loving) to make excuses for a child's mistakes or misdeeds. Even when a mistake is legitimate, one is less inclined to analyze how he contributed to the mistake if he is excused from all responsibility for it. The following are some typical excuses we create for ourselves and our children, and the unintentional but destructive messages attached to them:

"He's just tired; that's why he did that."

"She's been under a lot of pressure; that's why. . . . "

"He's been so good until now; I'll let this mistake go."

"The other person behaved wrongly; he just acted in kind."

"She didn't mean to do it; it wasn't on purpose."

"He's not feeling well; that's why."

"It's just a part of growing up; she'll grow out of it."

"He just lost his temper; he didn't mean it."

"She's just absent-minded; that's why she forgot to. . . . "

"I've done the same thing myself; how can I punish him?"

Often parents are unaware of the real message that they are giving the child, especially if these excuses are used with any degree of frequency. We are teaching the child: "When you're tired, under pressure, trying hard, feeling ill, etc., you don't have to assume any real responsibility for your behavior." So, at forty years of age, the excused adult is saying with little remorse or sense of responsibility: "I cheated because I was under a lot of pressure." "I was unfaithful to my wife because she no longer loves me." "I've been so good recently, I deserve to go out on a good drunk." "I broke the law, but I didn't mean it." "I'm dishonest at work because other people are too." "I guess I'm not a very sensitive person, but then my father wasn't either."

It is not helpful to blame others for an individual's mistakes and misdeeds. With children, the favorite excuse is: "His friends got him into this." Each parent blames the other parents' kid, so, in actuality, it is no one's fault. But the questions one should ask are: "Why does my child choose to hang around friends who misbehave?" "Why does my child choose to participate in the behavior—what needs or fears are ruling him to the extent that he cannot withstand peer pressure?" So, one's friends are in no way a mitigating factor—they only raise more questions about the child.

The second favorite scapegoat is the teacher, as in "Everything was fine until he got Miss Smith in the seventh grade." It is not impossible for a personality conflict between a student and teacher to occur. But it is more likely that this easy-to-draw cause-and-effect relationship is not a valid one; that problems outside the school are reflecting themselves in school rather than vice versa. And, even if Miss Smith doesn't understand the child, this should not set a precedent, so that every time the child meets up with someone who is not understanding, he gets to misbehave.

Efforts to protect one's children are often heavily loaded with a need to protect oneself from assuming responsibility as parents. If it's not my son's fault, I, as his parent, need not analyze my part in the situation. It is sadly ironic that the same parents who have typically displaced the responsibility for their children's behavior onto others, are surprised and confused when their sons and daughters blame *them* for the problems they face as adults.

A child should learn not to participate in an act unless he is ready to assume reasonable responsibility for the consequences. With the exception of physical coercion or severe emotional disturbance, there are no valid reasons for an individual to act with less than full accountability for his behavior.

Bogus mitigating circumstances are often used by children to explain away their responsibility. These children make statements such as the following:

—"I didn't do my homework because I didn't understand what the teacher wanted." However, the child's responsibility is to find out what the teacher wants before leaving school.

—"I'm late because my boyfriend had to pick up his mother at work." This daughter's responsibility was to find out that information first and make other arrangements so she would not be late.

—"What was I supposed to do—my friends just started opening the beer while we were driving to the dance." The options are clear: Ask them to get rid of the beer and, if they don't, get out of the car—or be willing to accept personal responsibility for whatever consequences occur.

Effective parents should see to it that their children experience the natural consequences that flow from mistakes and misdeeds. There are three barriers to the successful learning of this principle. The first is that a parent whose need to be loved by the child is stronger than the need to be a good parent will be reluctant to be instrumental in the child's suffering. What looks like parental love is actually parental selfishness because it is the parent protecting himself from the wrath of the child. Consequently, this parent goes through the motions of discipline, but invariably it is done with neither the parent nor the child enduring much pain. It is quite comfortable for all, but terribly destructive for the child.

Secondly, less effective parents may allow themselves to be "conned" out of facing a child with the consequences of his behavior. This is demonstrated in sentiments such as: "He's so darling [good-looking, bright, humorous, well-meaning] that I just *can't* get angry with him or see him hurt." Before long, the child learns to employ his charms to escape the normal consequences of his behavior. This leaves the child with no reason to change the caliber of the behavior.

Thirdly, parents may bail out the child from experiencing the consequences of the behavior. This is done by directly interceding for the child. For example, a child gets suspended from school for three days by the teacher. But the parents manipulate the principal, who suggests that the teacher rescind the suspension. In the short run, the child wins and the teacher loses, and the child notices this more than anybody. In the long run, the child ends up a loser because as he grows older, there are fewer and fewer people capable of rescuing him from difficult situations.

EFFECTIVE PARENTS TEACH SOUND VALUES

Sound values help a person behave in ways that increase feelings of goodness about himself and about others. All healthy values have justice as their foundation—justice to oneself and to others. The more a value can encompass both these elements, the healthier it is.

Parents who teach a healthy value system understand the following principles:

Values are learned; they are not inherited. There is no such thing as "bad blood" or "bad seed." If a child misbehaves it is because such conduct meets more needs than good behavior. Healthy values do not automatically appear with maturation. Children do not grow out of unhealthy values; they unlearn unhealthy values and learn healthy values in their place.

Society is not to blame for a child's misbehavior. In general, children who have learned healthy values do not significantly misbehave regardless of the unhealthy society in which they live, while children who have learned unhealthy values will misbehave regardless of the healthy society in which they live.

Verbally teaching values does not mean that they will be learned. Children pay little attention to what is said to them but learn primarily from watching and hearing. The child is always watching—learning indirectly about fairness and unfairness; concern or lack of concern for others; saying one thing and doing another; using people or relating with them; what is said to be important and what is actually important; what behaviors get rewarded and which are left unrewarded. The child sees and learns what makes his parents laugh and what makes them angry; how the parents act in company and what they say when the visitors leave; what dad says about the people at work and what mom says about the teachers and the neighbors; what place religion plays in the family—a ritual, an enforcer of parental laws, or a source of loving and sharing. All of these behaviors teach values, i.e., what is viewed as good or bad, more than all the lectures and admonitions that a child could ever receive.

Whether a value is learned or not depends upon who is teaching the value. The following are examples of the relationship between the person teaching the value, the type of value he is teaching, and the effect on the child learning the value:

Affectionate parents who teach healthy values. This is the only healthy combination. An affectionate adult is one who is consistently warm and caring. "Warm" means that the parent is approachable, understanding, and sensitive. "Caring" means that the adult is honest, strong, and freeing. Children willingly imitate parents who are viewed as attractive, effective, and loving. Consequently, the child internalizes (makes his own) the values of the adult, creating a benchmark for what is right and wrong behavior. Affection causes imitation which, coupled with healthy values, causes good behavior.

Affectionate parents who teach unhealthy values. Because the parents are affectionate, the children will imitate them. Since the parents' values are unreasonable or pragmatic, the children will behave in ways detrimental to themselves and/or to others. This will be a source of confusion to the parents because they correctly view themselves as loving parents so they cannot understand why their children are experiencing emotional and social problems.

Unaffectionate parents who teach healthy values. Unaffectionate parents have difficulty being warm and caring. This does not necessarily mean that the parents are antagonistic toward the children. Often these parents are nice and intelligent people, but because they did not have affectionate parents themselves, or because of personal or marital problems, their ability to share affection is short-circuited.

The problem with unaffectionate parents teaching healthy values is that the child does not feel strong attraction to the parent. The parent is viewed as a caretaker rather than as someone to love and admire. Consequently, the child feels little motivation to identify with the parent and internalize his values.

Understanding this combination makes it easier to understand how children from good homes become delinquent. The values in the home are sound, and the parents are good, hard-working people. But the child may find a group of peers who give him the attention, care, and affection that are not received at home. If the group's values are unhealthy, the child will likely imitate them even though they are contrary to the values in the home. This combination can also explain how one child in a family can behave well while another in the same family behaves poorly. The parents who are affectionate to the first child are for some reason unaffectionate toward the second child.

Unaffectionate parents who teach unhealthy values. The child in this family will be like "psychological mercury"; his psyche will roll all over the place, mostly for imperceptible reasons. When the child senses some affection, no matter how slight, he will gravitate toward the source of the affection. Whatever that individual's values, the child will imitate them temporarily. As this child approaches adulthood, he is a mélange of low-powered values: healthy, unreasonable, and pragmatic. A dramatic example of this type of individual is the person who drifts for a few years committing petty crimes, enters a monastery to reform and help others, leaves the monastery, and embezzles several thousand dollars from his next employer.

Parents are not completely affectionate or unaffectionate, and the values they teach are not totally healthy or unhealthy. Also, one parent may fall into one of the above categories, while the other is in a different one. This discussion is meant to elucidate some principles that parents may find helpful.

All parents teach values; there is no such thing as a home without them. The question is what kind of values do parents want to instill in their children, and are they going about it in an effective way.

EFFECTIVE PARENTS TEACH GOOD BEHAVIOR

Healthy discipline is the main method of teaching good behavior—that which is helpful to others or at least not harmful.

Healthy discipline has two purposes. The main one is to help a child behave well so that he can think well of himself. This is the cornerstone of self-love. A second purpose of healthy discipline is to help a child grow into an adult who is confident in his ability to behave well under any circumstances. This allays the anxiety caused by being at the mercy of one's impulses.

Unfortunately, the concepts of discipline and punishment are almost synonymous in our society. When we say that a child needs more discipline, we almost always mean that the child needs to be punished more. This misunderstanding is harmful because punishment alone is the least effective of the five ingredients of healthy discipline, the others being demonstrated affection, good example, reward, and consistency.

Showing affection is the best form of discipline. When children feel lovable, they tend to behave in lovable ways. Parents who openly demonstrate warmth, understanding, and fondness for their children on a reasonably consistent basis seldom need to punish.

"Openly demonstrate" is an important qualification. As adults, we can look back on our parents and *infer* from their behavior that they loved us, even though they may not have openly demonstrated it. But children are not good at inferring love. If they see it, feel it, and hear it, they know they are loved. If they don't, they're uncertain or feel unloved. When children do not feel affection, they seek attention as a substitute. If their good behavior doesn't win this attention, they will misbehave because negative attention is better than no attention. Parents who complain: "I've yelled at him about the same thing for a week now, and he continues to do it," don't understand this principle.

A second element of healthy discipline is good example. Children learn the vast majority of their behavior from their parents. Children who frequently misbehave have parents who frequently misbehave, although the parents would not recognize this connection. A father who sits in the yard with his radio blaring, disturbing the neighbors, is the same father who yells at his son to turn down the stereo because it is distracting *him*. The mother that yells: "Oh, shut up!" to her daughter is the same mother who punishes her daughter who yells "Shut up" at her. The father who criticizes his wife in front of company is furious when his daughter criticizes him in front of visitors. The mother who drinks too much "grounds" her seventeen-year-old son for a week for having a beer with his friends. For the most part, our children's behavior is a fairly accurate mirror of our own.

Effective parents generally behave well; consequently, they teach good behavior daily. When they do misbehave, they admit it in front of their children who can then make appropriate corrections in their imitating.

Rewarding good behavior is another ingredient of healthy discipline. Typically, middle class parents *expect* their children to behave well, even better than themselves. Because good behavior is expected, they feel it would be inappropriate to reward it, any more than a person is rewarded for breathing. It is only when children misbehave that parents feel called upon to act.

Normal children prefer to be rewarded rather than to be punished. Consequently, in a home where good behavior is rewarded, there will be much more good behavior than poor behavior. A reward could be anything from a smile, to a hug, to a compliment, to an ice-cream cone or a chance to use the family car.

A reward is not bribery. A reward follows when a child spontaneously behaves well, especially when he shows some real concern or sacrifice. Bribery occurs when a parent promises a reward if the child behaves well during an upcoming situation. For example, a mother promises: "If you're good at Grandma's, I'll buy you an ice cream." Bribery is never healthy because it teaches a child to behave well for purely pragmatic and selfish reasons. As soon as those reasons are not present, there is no longer a need to behave well.

Consistency is the fourth element in healthy discipline. Most families have good rules but poor enforcement. For example, parents may have a rule that the TV must be turned off by 9:00 P.M. on school nights. But, when the parents are in a good mood or when they are tired, the children are allowed to watch TV until 9:30 or 10 P.M. Some parents are manipulable because they continually need their children to like them. So when a child says: "Oh, please; it's a special show, and we have been good, and we'll never ask again—please!" the parent is likely to relent.

Inconsistency in discipline teaches children not to take people at face value and that if you're clever enough, you can get what you want despite the rules. Children who come from inconsistent homes have more problems than those who come from authoritarian or permissive homes.

Consistency in discipline also means that the parents are relatively consistent with each other; i.e., both parents share essentially the same values. If one parent encourages assertiveness and the other punishes it, the children will be placed in an impossible situation. Parents do not have to agree on all values, but should generally agree on basic values.

A generation ago children were better behaved but for the wrong reasons. They behaved out of fear. Modern parents understandably did not wish to bridle their children with the same fears. But some made a serious mistake. Instead of substituting positive and healthy reasons for behaving well, they removed fear but put nothing in its place to encourage good behavior. The result is seen in a child's reply to a teacher who told him it was wrong to steal money from a classmate: "Why?"

EFFECTIVE PARENTS ALLOW THEIR CHILDREN TO BE CHILDREN

A child is a child and should be treated as a child. However, some parents require their children to assume other roles. The following are some common roles that children are required to fill.

The Child as Spouse. A child may be cast in the role of a spouse, with all the conflicts, responsibilities, and privileges thereof. Though either a boy or a girl can be made a spouse of the opposite-sexed parent, it is more typical that it occurs with the boy being a husband-substitute to the mother. This happens when, for some reason, the husband no longer functions psychologically as a husband.

Though this spouse-making syndrome is essentially a marriage problem, the chief symptom carrier is the child. The boy becomes elevated to the position of husband. Much of the warmth, closeness, and feeling of being needed and appreciated, which were once felt from the husband, are received instead from the son. The child-husband can be six months old or sixty years old and can be married or unmarried.

The destructive effects of being a child-husband can be seen throughout life. The child is treated as special by his mother. The best of everything is saved for him. He is allowed the responsibilities and privileges that his siblings (and maybe even his father!) are not given. He is protected from most punishment, hurt, and failure. This makes it very difficult for him to grow normally with his peers.

As the child goes through adolescence, he often has trouble growing into manhood. The mother, in her deepest self, may anticipate losing her son to girls, so she neuterizes or feminizes him so that he will remain hers.

Making a child a spouse is very gradual and insidious. One of the problems in dealing with it is that everyone is content with the situation. The son is content because he has a free ride at home. The mother is content because she is getting some deep needs met at a bargain price, since there are few risks involved. And the father is content, because, by relinquishing his role to his son, he is free to do whatever it is he would rather do.

The Child as Ambassador. The child may be deputized as an official representative of the parents. The child-ambassador has the two duties of any ambassador: to reflect whomever he represents in the best light possible and to fulfill the needs of the represented party.

As an ambassador, the child is to reflect the high quality of the parents, whether it exists in reality or not. Ironically, it is more likely that the high quality is not present because parents who are truly good do not use the child as an ambassador.

Pressure, sometimes very subtle pressure, is placed on the child to carry the parents' banner. The banner might read: "We are great leaders"; or "We are quite religious"; or "We are very attractive physically"; or "We are very well-liked and respected"; or "We are very mentally healthy." Some parents give a child the rather unwieldly banner: "We are perfect."

The problem with being an ambassador is that there is inordinate pressure to excel in the specific banner area, whether or not the child's abilities, interests, or values happen to lie in this area. The child's sense of worth hinges on how well he carries his parents' banner—not on who he truly is.

The second duty of the child-ambassador is to see to it that the ongoing needs or the never-met needs of the parents are met through him. An example of ongoing needs is seen in parents who are fond of saying: "We have two expensive homes, three expensive cars, and a daughter at Stanford." The daughter is required to take her place dutifully on the shelf of family trophies, and she had better not quit school or she will become an "unmentionable" overnight.

An example of parents using the child to meet their own never-met needs would be the parent who always wanted to be "somebody" but never made it. The parent has slaved and planned throughout life to give the child the opportunity the parent never had. It could be a mandate to be a doctor, a nurse, or a lawyer. It may be pressure to be popular, admired, or sought after. The parents may wish the children to have power, prestige, fame, or wealth. It is the mandate for the child to have happiness, *but as defined by the parent.*

The Child as Scapegoat. Scapegoating is a process whereby a person subconsciously displaces onto an individual the anger, disappointment, or frustration that is actually directed toward someone else. In a family, parents can scapegoat their unpleasant feelings toward each other onto the children.

Scapegoating occurs in families where a parent is unwilling or unable to admit difficult feelings toward a spouse or to express them directly. Often one particular child is chosen more than the others. This child is selected because he embodies or symbolizes the sources of the family tension. For example, if the wife wishes her husband had more backbone, she is likely to displace her disappointment and frustration on the son who tends to be more passive and fearful. Moreover, the husband is likely to scapegoat his anger with himself for being weak onto the same child because the boy reflects the trait the father finds most unacceptable in himself.

The effects of scapegoating are destructive to both the child and the marriage. The child feels he is a burden to his parents. The child seldom does anything right, and when he does, it is ignored or met with faint praise. The child defines himself as responsible for whatever unhappiness there is in the family and feels guilty about it. This causes behavior that makes the child an even better candidate for scapegoating.

The effect of scapegoating on the marriage is that marriage problems are labelled "child problems" because it is more acceptable to have a "problem child" than a "problem marriage." Consequently, the focus and energy are directed away from the real problems onto an unconsciously constructed decoy. The result is a never-ending vicious circle because the real problem is never abated.

The Child as Weapon. There are two ways in which a

child can become a weapon in the family. The child can be used by one parent as a weapon against the other parent. This often occurs in a marriage when the parents are unable to communicate anger directly to each other, or when such attempts are met with indifference. It is then that the child becomes the medium through which the anger is communicated. This can be accomplished in several ways. For example:

—One parent can observe the child treating the other parent with disrespect or hostility and subtly condone or even encourage the behavior. It is as if the parent is saying to the child: "Go to it; I'd love to say the same things myself, but I don't dare."

—One parent may taint the perceptions of the child toward the other parent as a way of "winning" the child. Examples of comments that can achieve this are: "Your poor father; I don't know when he is ever going to grow up"; or "Don't pay attention to your mother; she's neurotic about things like this."

The child can also be used as a weapon against society. In this case, the child actualizes the parents' latent anger toward society or specific segments of society such as teachers, police officers, bureaucrats, elders, etc. Such parents are typically mild-mannered, peaceable, and sometimes religious. They may have several well-behaved children, but choose one as their weapon because of certain characteristics he may possess.

These parents typically harbor a good deal of hostility which is repressed or denied. They do not have sufficient courage to stand up to all the hurt and injustice (real or imagined) that they encounter in life. Hence, they send out their soldiers (children) to win back the psychological territory they feel they have lost. This is done with the unconscious message to the child: "Don't let people push you around the way I let them push *me* around."

When the child gets into trouble, his misbehavior is subtly rewarded. The reward may be the parents' underlying pride that the child stands up for himself. The threatened punishment may never be carried out, or it may be carried out only partially. The punishment may be inordinately light, or the parents may side with the child. All of these attitudes communicate the parents' approval of the child's misbehavior.

EFFECTIVE PARENTS TEACH INTERDEPENDENCE

Interdependent people have two complementary characteristics. They have an independence that is born of simple strength and reasonable assuredness. They can stand on their own two feet and are not unduly influenced by the opinions, attitudes, or values of others. They can cooperate with others without being swept away by them and can stand by their convictions without being stubborn.

A second characteristic of interdependent people is that they realize that they cannot be effective and happy alone; that it is good and necessary to depend upon some people in some ways for some things. But they are able to lean on others without losing their balance and without becoming stuck. Interdependence is a smooth blend of independence and dependence.

If parents wish their children to be interdependent at twenty years of age, they must begin the journey in infancy. And it helps if the parents who are sponsoring the trip are interdependent themselves. Mothers who are overly dependent on their husbands and children, and fathers who are very independent from their families will be poor models.

In healthy families interdependence begins in the crib when the totally dependent infant gradually realizes that he still exists even when the parents are not present. The child learns that he can explore the world and entertain himself without the aid of parents. As the infant matures, he prefers at times to be with a toy rather than with parents, and later would rather be with friends. And, as the child reaches eight and nine years of age, he may sometimes prefer to be alone. During adolescence the child often prefers to be with boyfriends and girlfriends. Each stage prepares the child to make the ultimate emotional break from home—to move away and possibly marry.

Effective parents encourage and reward each of these steps and view the process with more joy than sorrow. Less effective parents attempt, often unconsciously, to slow down the process and sometimes even to stop it— often at twelve, before the child "becomes sexual," or at eighteen, before the child can leave home. They view the final stages with more dread than joy.

Parents have difficulty allowing their children to become interdependent for two ,reasons. One is that some parents are not interdependent themselves; hence, they enter into dependency relationships with the children. A typical situation is a father whose immersion in work or hobbies places a distance between himself and his wife. The mother may gravitate toward the child to get her needs met. Her child becomes her chief grocer and to help him become interdependent represents losing her main source of emotional support. Thus she has a vested interest in keeping the child dependent. While overprotective mothers are often blamed for the problems of the child, it is as much the father's responsibility as it is the mother's.

Some parents are not good at teaching interdependence because they want "the best" for their child and feel they know what is best. Consequently, they function as managers rather than as parents. They decide for the child, or "help" the child decide everything from what the child should wear to what courses the child should choose in college to whom the child should marry.

Some parents act as managers because they are very satisfied with their lives and want to guide the children into the same level of satisfaction. Others are quite dissatisfied with their lives and want to help the child avoid the same pitfalls. The problem is that what constitutes a satisfactory life for the parent may be a life of misery for the child. The best way to help a child avoid a miserable life is not to make decisions for the child, but to give him the ingredients that go into making good decisions: love, freedom, and sound values. If a child has these, he does not need to be pushed into "good decisions." If the child doesn't, making decisions for him will be like building a house on sand.

Unfortunately, some parents feel that their children should remain children until they move out of the house. In effect, they are sending a twelve-year-old out into the world in a twenty-year-old body. They view the children's efforts to become more independent as ungrateful, disrespectful, and recalcitrant.

In families in which the growth toward interdependence is squelched, normally there will be no conflict because there are no opposing forces. Parents in these families often brag to their friends that they never have any problems with their children. But one of two situations will eventually occur. The child, usually during late adolescence, may suddenly rebel with the force of eighteen years of repressed energy. This causes shock waves throughout the family, great confusion, and sometimes panic. The parents protest: "But he was such a good child until now. I can't understand it!" At the other extreme, the child may never reach interdependence and be a passive, dependent person forever or until he actively attempts to change.

In families in which the growth toward interdependence is gradual but continuous, there will be many low-key conflicts and psychological tugs-of-war between the parents and the child. When the tugs-of-war are participated in fairly, both sides will become stronger. Since dependency makes true love impossible, it is only interdependent children who can genuinely love their parents.

The main point to remember is that our children were created *by* us and not *for* us. As Kahlil Gibran writes in *The Prophet* in a section "On Children" (Knopf, New York, 1972):

> You may give them your love but not your
>   thoughts
>   For they have their own thoughts.
> You may house their bodies but not their souls,
>   For their souls dwell in the house of
>   tomorrow
>   which you cannot visit, not even in your
>   dreams.
> You may strive to be like them, but seek not to
>   make
>   them like you.
> For life goes not backward nor tarries with
>   yesterday.

Reflection Questions

1. What is the biggest obstacle to my spending quality time with people? What can I do about it?

2. What is the main excuse I give myself for not being as effective a parent as I could be? Is it a good excuse?

3. Of the four messages adults send to children regarding sex (You're lovable or unlovable; the same sex is lovable or unlovable; the opposite sex is good or bad; sex is good or bad), which one could I do a better job with?

4. What is one trait that I have that I hope my children don't learn from me? How will they *not* learn it?

5. Why is it easier for me to scold the children when they make a mistake than to show affection solely because the children are lovable?

Thoughts to Contemplate

1. The most precious gift parents can bestow upon a child is a sense of self-appreciation and love. From this sense flows all that is good in human behavior.

2. Even small children realize that we spend time with people we like and avoid people we don't like. When a parent's message is: "You're really lovable, but I don't have much time for you," it is unacceptable even to a three-year-old.

3. The irony is that neither parents nor teachers choose whether or not to give sex education because they are always teaching it. The only question is whether or not the sex education is healthy.

4. Showing affection is the best form of discipline. When children feel lovable, they tend to behave in lovable ways. Parents who openly demonstrate warmth, understanding, and fondness for their children on a reasonably consistent basis seldom need to punish.

5. Some parents feel that their children should remain children until they move out of the house. In effect, they are sending a twelve-year-old out into the world in a twenty-year-old body.

EPILOGUE

One must do more than read a book to make tomorrow better. The principles discussed in this book offer insights as to how to make tomorrow better, but the insights must be cashed in to bring about change.

As I complete this book, I have some hopes that I would like to think are realistic.

For the readers of this book I hope you deeply understand and believe that your tomorrow can be better. Some people accomplish a great deal in life, but don't enjoy it very much. Others seem to enjoy life immensely, but life is not much better off for having been visited by them. But you can have both: accomplishment and joy.

For some of you this book was an affirming experience. You learned that you're doing a pretty good job with life. That's good. Remember, though, that doing well now is not a life-time guarantee. I work with people in therapy who had a reasonably good life until they reached thirty, forty, fifty, or sixty years of age. Then things "turned sour" because they let down a little in one or two important areas, and things caught up with them.

Some of you feel that you have a way to go yet before you can consistently make your tomorrows better. I do, too. But, believe me, we can do it. It will take some work. It may call for some letting go. It definitely will entail some risks. It may cause some pain in ourselves and others. It definitely will necessitate some changes in our behavior. It could mean disappointing some people who are important to us. We are going to make some mistakes. But we *can* do it. And let's face it: There's not a soul in the world who is going to do it for us.

Some of you feel besieged by this book. You feel that

there is so much to change that it seems impossible. You feel that things are such a mess that the only way tomorrow is going to get better is if there is no tomorrow. Your reaction to the book is: "I already knew I was in bad shape. All I got out of the book was *how* bad!" I've felt that way on more than one occasion. Remember the suicide note of the young woman in the section on Hope. That's about as low as a person can feel. She now has a master's degree, is married, and writes to me yearly, sharing her accomplishments and joy. Start by taking one point from the book that you feel you need to work on. It may take a few weeks or a few months before you start seeing results. Then pick a second point and do the same thing. You can, if you really want to, gradually make your tomorrows better.

And I have a hope for me. No one recognizes better than I the difference between *knowing* something and *living* it. I hope that by writing this book and teaching it, I can make myself and my tomorrow better.

RECOMMENDED READINGS

Alberti, Robert E., and Michael L. Emmons, YOUR PER-
FECT RIGHT, San Luis.Obispo, Calif., Impact Pub-
lishers, 1978.

Allport, Gordon W., THE INDIVIDUAL AND HIS RELI-
GION, New York, The Macmillan Co., 1968.

Bach, George R., and Peter Wyden, THE INTIMATE EN-
EMY: HOW TO FIGHT FAIR IN LOVE AND MAR-
RIAGE, New York, Avon, 1970.

Bach, George R., and Herb Goldbert, CREATIVE AG-
GRESSION, New York, Avon, 1975.

Bry, Adelaide, HOW TO GET ANGRY WITHOUT FEEL-
ING GUILTY, New York, Signet, 1976.

Frankl, Viktor E., MAN'S SEARCH FOR MEANING, New
York, Washington Square Press, 1963.

Fromm, Erich, THE ART OF LOVING, New York, Ban-
tam Books, 1970.

Fromme, Allan, THE ABILITY TO LOVE, No. Hollywood,
Ca., Wilshire Book Co., 1972.

Gagnon, John H., HUMAN SEXUALITIES, Glenview, Ill.,
Scott, Foresman and Co., 1977.

Hodge, Marshall Bryant, YOUR FEAR OF LOVE, New
York, Dolphin Books, 1967.

Horney, Karen, OUR INNER CONFLICTS, New York, W.
W. Norton, 1966.

Jourard, Sidney, THE TRANSPARENT SELF, New York,
Van Nostrand, 1964.

Madow, Leo, ANGER, HOW TO RECOGNIZE AND COPE
WITH IT, New York, Charles Scribner's Sons, 1972.

May, Rollo, MAN'S SEARCH FOR HIMSELF, New York,
Signet Books, 1967.

May, Rollo, LOVE AND WILL, New York, W. W. Norton,
1969.

Powell, John, THE SECRET OF STAYING IN LOVE,
    Niles, Ill., Argus Press, 1974.
Powell, John, WHY AM I AFRAID TO TELL YOU WHO I
    AM? Chicago, Peacock Books, Argus Communica-
    tions, 1969.
Rubin, Theodore Isaac, THE ANGRY BOOK, New York,
    Collier Books, 1977.
Viscott, David, HOW TO LIVE WITH ANOTHER PER-
    SON, New York, Pocket Books, 1976.
Viscott, David, THE LANGUAGE OF FEELINGS, New
    York, Pocket Books, 1977.